THE RHETORIC OF EMPIRE

Post-Contemporary Interventions

Series Editors: Stanley Fish

and Fredric Jameson

THE RHETORIC OF EMPIRE

Colonial Discourse in Journalism,

Travel Writing,

and

Imperial Administration

DAVID SPURR

Duke University Press   *Durham & London 1993*

Third printing, 1996

© 1993 Duke University Press   All rights reserved

Printed in the United States of America on acid-free paper ∞

Typeset in Galliard by Tseng Information Systems

Parts of the Introduction and Chapter 2 appeared in

"Colonialist Journalism: Stanley to Didion," *Raritan: A
Quarterly Review* 5, no. 2 (Fall 1985). Grateful acknowledg-

ment is made for permission to reprint this material.

Library of Congress Cataloging-in-Publication Data appear

on the last printed page of this book.

for Laurie Gottlieb Spurr

CONTENTS

ACKNOWLEDGMENTS

THE IDEA FOR A BOOK LIKE THIS BEGAN IN THE EARLY
1980s, when Massud Farzan and I used to meet for breakfast in the campus
grill at Dickinson College. He would go over the coverage of the Iranian
Revolution in the morning papers, expressing alternate amusement and
indignation at the printed misconceptions concerning the culture and society of his native country. I pursued the idea in an NEH summer seminar
splendidly directed by Giles Gunn at the University of North Carolina,
and later as a fellow of the Institute for the Humanities at the University
of Illinois at Chicago.

My colleagues at the University of Illinois and elsewhere have contributed knowledge, criticism, encouragement, and practical help. They include Jonathan Arac, Ross Chambers, James Dee, Clark Hulse, John Hun
tington, Lansiné Kaba, Maryline Lukacher, Gene Ruoff, Gerald Sorensen,
and Linda Williams. The students in my seminar on Criticism and Colonial
Discourse have been more helpful than they may know. Reynolds Smith
of Duke University Press has displayed a rare combination of enthusiasm,
wisdom, and patience. And, finally, I am grateful to Ned Lukacher for his
genuine intellect and his genial spirit.

Chaque homme porte en lui un monde
composé de tout ce qu'il a vu et aimé, et où
il rentre sans cesse, alors même qu'il parcourt
et semble habiter un monde étranger.
—*Chateaubriand,* VOYAGES EN ITALIE

INTRODUCTION

THE FORMAL END OF EUROPEAN COLONIALISM DUR-
ing the latter half of the twentieth century has in more recent years given
rise to a new range of studies devoted to reexamining the history, politics,
psychology, and language of colonization. Within the field of literary study
alone, scholars have experienced a major paradigm shift in which literary
works once studied primarily as expressions of traditionally Western ideals
are now also read as evidence of the manner in which such ideals have served
in the historical process of colonization. The particular languages which
belong to this process, enabling it while simultaneously being generated
by it, are known collectively as colonial discourse.

In the following chapters I propose to identify the basic rhetorical features of this discourse and to study the way in which it has been deployed,
both in the modern period of European colonialism (roughly 1870–1960),
as well as in the more recent period of decolonization. My study, which
draws its examples primarily from British, French, and American writing
of the nineteenth and twentieth centuries, offers a general introduction
to modern European colonial discourse, rather than focusing on a more
narrowly defined historical moment or geographical area; it emphasizes
rhetorical analysis rather than historical narrative; and while borrowing
from the language of contemporary literary theory, it carries this analysis
beyond the boundaries of literature into other forms of writing.

In the course of this study, it will become clear that what we call colonial
discourse is neither a monolithic system nor a finite set of texts; it may more
accurately be described as the name for a series of colonizing discourses,
each adapted to a specific historical situation, yet having in common cer-

tain elements with the others. This series is marked by internal repetition, but not by all-encompassing totality; it is a series that continues, in some forms, through what we call the postcolonial world of today. In speaking of colonial discourse, one necessarily treads on unstable ground; one seeks to identify the colonizing gestures in language while recognizing the impossibility of containing them within a bounded textual field. My discussion, then, will take place on a kind of border terrain, within an area of tension between definition and powerlessness to define, between containment of my subject and recognition of its uncontained plurality.

The problematic nature of this subject has required imaginative and often nontraditional critical approaches. In the English-speaking world alone, a number of studies in recent years have begun to create new knowledge about colonial discourse and its variations, such as Orientalist, Africanist, and primitivist discourse. Edward Said, Christopher Miller, and Patrick Brantlinger have examined the discourses of colonialism primarily in canonical works of English and French literature, and in popular adventure novels. James Clifford and Marianna Torgovnick have written provocatively on the connections between twentieth-century literature, art, and ethnography. Mary Louise Pratt has written a comprehensive study of travel writing as part of the history of European imperialism since the Renaissance. Sara Suleri has studied the rhetoric of the British in India. Ashis Nandy has given new life to the study of the psychology of colonization. Gayatri Spivak and Homi Bhabha have helped to formulate theoretical models for what promises to be an ever-renewing intellectual project.

My own work, which is indebted to all of these writers, seeks both a return to basic principles of rhetorical study and an expansion of the field of inquiry into certain new areas. I have found most of my examples in literary and popular journalism and in related genres such as exploration narratives, travel writing, and the memoirs of colonial officials. My focus on nonfiction writing is motivated by a desire to examine the discourse in a form unmediated by the consciously aesthetic requirements of imaginative literature. Journalism is distinguished from fiction by the conventional expectation of its grounding in an historical actuality; its relation to this actuality is understood to be primarily metonymic and historically referential rather than metaphoric and self-referential. Nonfiction writing in general often combines this metonymic quality with an absence of formal closure, so that it opens directly onto the fractures and contradictions of colonialist epistemology.

However, I also try to show how journalism and other forms of nonfiction, despite conventional expectation, depend on the use of myth, symbol, metaphor, and other rhetorical procedures more often associated with fiction and poetry. Thus I present nonfiction writing, and literary journalism in particular, as the means for staging an introductory analysis of colonial discourse. The questions to which I continually return are the following: How does the Western writer construct a coherent representation out of the strange and (to the writer) often incomprehensible realities confronted in the non-Western world? What are the cultural, ideological, or literary presuppositions upon which such a construct is based?

My exploration of these questions involves two basic procedures: (a) a *mapping* of the discourse, which identifies a series of basic tropes which emerge from the Western colonial experience, and (b) an informal *genealogy*, in which the repetitions and variations of these tropes are seen to operate across a range of nineteenth- and twentieth-century contexts. These basic procedures are accompanied throughout by a reflection on the nature of writing itself, not only as an epistemic violence and a colonizing order, but also, to cite Michel Foucault, as that which opens up "a whole field of responses, reactions, results, and possible inventions" (1983:220), including the subversion of its own order.

I have devoted a chapter to each of twelve rhetorical modes, or ways of writing about non-Western peoples. Taken together, these constitute a kind of repertoire for colonial discourse, a range of tropes, conceptual categories, and logical operations available for purposes of representation. Since these rhetorical modes are not confined to journalism, I also have occasion to cite their occurrence in such genres as essays in political and moral philosophy and documents in colonial administration. In doing so, I wish to suggest that journalism follows on more systematic orders of discourse, adapting them to particular events and translating them into a language of popular appeal. Journalistic language is a kind of palimpsest, underneath which the texts of Rousseau, Diderot, or Carlyle lie just barely effaced. These rhetorical modes, however, must be understood as more than merely literary or philosophical; they are the tropes that come into play with the establishment and maintenance of colonial authority, or, as sometimes happens, those that register the loss of such authority. There is nothing especially conscious or intentional in their use; they are part of the landscape in which relations of power manifest themselves. As in any organizing taxonomy, this project involves a certain degree of abstraction, not to say reduction: it subordinates the complexity and discreteness of any moment to the need for understanding it within a larger context. If I find that the language of the French in Algeria conforms in certain ways to that of the British in India or the Americans in the Philippines, it is not that I choose to ignore the substantial differences—political, cultural, ideological, geographical—which distinguish these encounters from one another. Rather, given the obvious differences, I have instead tried to identify the unexpected parallels and the common genealogies that unite these apparently disparate occasions of discourse. Taking historical difference as a matter of course, I have looked for lines of convergence, correspondence, and analogy.

By the same token, the list of rhetorical modes which provide titles for the following chapters should not be considered definitive; there may be other modes or other ways of defining the ones I have designated. Nor should they be understood as entirely discrete from one another; on the contrary, they overlap continually, and certain tropes might be classified as subcategories of others. What I have called the rhetorical strategies of *debasement,* for example, is a form of *negation* in the sense that it negates the value of the other. Likewise, the trope of *idealization* in practice often merges with *aestheticization,* just as the figure of the noble savage represents both a philosophical and an aesthetic ideal. This slippage between categories is probably inevitable to any rhetorical taxonomy, including classical treatises on rhetorical figures. It is to be hoped that the imprecisions of this procedure may be tolerated, however, in the interests of describing the nature of a discourse whose forms are related, as in all writing, by both repetition and difference. Having sketched a general outline of my project, I would now like to consider more closely some of its critical assumptions.

In writing about Claude Lévi-Strauss's studies of the Indians of western Brazil, Jacques Derrida has identified what he calls the *anthropological war*— "the essential confrontation that opens communication between peoples and cultures, even when that communication is not practiced under the banner of colonial or military oppression" (1976:107). Derrida argues that the writing produced by this confrontation always involves a "violence of the letter" imposed by one culture upon the other, a violence, in other words, "of difference, of classification, and of the system of appellations." The very process by which one culture subordinates another begins in the act of naming and leaving unnamed, of marking on an unknown territory the lines of division and uniformity, of boundary and continuity.

One already sees that this notion of the anthropological war extends beyond anthropology as a discipline and beyond the initial confrontation of cultures. In its broader sense, it includes the entire system by which one culture comes to interpret, to represent, and finally to dominate another. It includes, in other words, the discourses of colonialism as produced in such forms as imaginative literature, journalism, travel writing, ethnographic description, historiography, political speeches, administrative documents, and statutes of law.

Culture and colonization are etymologically as well as historically related; both derive from the Latin *colere:* to cultivate, to inhabit, to take care of a place. The Latin *colonus* designated both a farmer or husbandman and a member of a settlement of Roman citizens, or *colonia,* in a hostile or newly conquered country (*OED*), while *cultura* referred both to tilling the soil and to refinement in education and civilization.

Modern uses of *colony* and *colonialism* are no less ambiguous and multivalent than their Latin roots. The British divided their colonies into three classes—crown colonies, colonies with "representative" governments, and those with "responsible" governments—designating increasingly indirect forms of crown rule. Colonies with "responsible" governments were eligible for elevation to "dominion" status. An equally diverse range applied to the French Empire under the Third Republic (1871–1940), where the Ministry of Colonies ruled most territories, but Algeria, considered part of France itself, came under the Ministry of the Interior and Tunisia and Morocco under the Ministry of Foreign Affairs. European colonies in general were unofficially divided between those established for the *control* of resources and populations (French Indochina, the Belgian Congo, Dutch Indonesia, the United States Philippines), and those designed for the *settlement* of Europeans (Algeria, South Africa, Australia and New Zealand).

Just as the Romans saw the establishment of overseas colonies as part of the larger designs of their empire, it is still possible to distinguish colonialism from imperialism as part from whole. Benita Parry thus writes of colonialism as "a specific, and the most spectacular, mode of imperialism's many and mutable states, one which preceded the rule of international finance capitalism and whose formal ending imperialism has survived" (34). In speaking of the *discourse* of colonialism, however, the distinction tends to collapse, since the basic principles of this discourse, rooted in the very foundations of Western culture, also constitute the discourse of imperialism. Imperialism has survived the formal ending of colonial rule, but so has colonial discourse.

Theories of colonialism and colonial discourse begin by combining the various historical instances of colonization under the rubric of the "colonial situation," a notion for which the French anthropologist Georges Balandier provided a classic definition in 1963. According to Balandier, the colonial situation is characterized by "the domination imposed by a foreign minority, 'racially' and culturally different, over a materially weaker indige-

nous majority in the name of a racial (or ethnic) and cultural superiority."
A set of relations is put into place between two different cultures: one fast-
moving, technologically advanced, and economically powerful; the other
slow-moving and without advanced technology or a complex economy.
These relations are antagonized by the "instrumental role" which the colonized society is forced to play, so that in order to maintain its authority the
colonizing society resorts not only to force, but also to a series of "pseudo-
justifications and stereotyped behaviors" (34–35). Balandier thus sees the
colonial situation as one of "latent crisis," an order maintained precariously
by ideology and representation as well as by formal administration.

Contemporary critics would question some of Balandier's assumptions:
the notion of technological and economic "advancement," for example, or
the insistence on a simple binary division between one culture and the
other. Most would agree, however, in the value of a theoretical model
for the colonial situation as something that exists in the real world and
that linguistic representation belongs to it either as an instrument of colonial rule or, more fundamentally, as the set of signs in which the colonial
situation can be read. In pointing out that the essential confrontation of
cultures marking the colonial situation extends beyond the "banner" of
colonial rule itself, Derrida recalls Antonio Gramsci's notion of hegemony
and the power of ruling ideas which continue to hold sway outside the historical and institutional limits of direct domination. My own study treats
colonial discourse as belonging both to the classic colonial situation and
to the more elusive, more powerful forces of cultural hegemony in the
postcolonial world.

"Postcolonial" is a word that engenders even more debate than "colonial," in part because of the ambiguous relation between these two. In
the pages that follow I shall refer to the postcolonial in two ways: as an
historical situation marked by the dismantling of traditional institutions
of colonial power, and as a search for alternatives to the discourses of the
colonial era. The first is an object of empirical knowledge—new flags fly,
new political formations come into being. The second is both an intellectual project and a transcultural condition that includes, along with new
possibilities, certain crises of identity and representation. Gayatri Spivak,
for example, an Indian-born American academic, speaks movingly of her
estrangement both from "Western liberalism" and from the indigenous
peoples of her native country (70–72). But in neither the historical nor the
cultural sense does the postcolonial mark a clean break with the colonial:
the relations of colonizer to colonized have neither remained the same nor

have they disappeared. The instability of the colonial/postcolonial divide belongs to discourse as well.

With this instability always in mind, my concentration is on writing itself rather than on other manifestations of colonial rule. Returning for a moment to that classic situation, one can see a metaphorical relation between the writer and the colonizer. The problem of the colonizer is in some sense the problem of the writer: in the face of what may appear as a vast cultural and geographical blankness, colonization is a form of self-inscription onto the lives of a people who are conceived of as an extension of the landscape. For the colonizer as for the writer, it becomes a question of establishing authority through the demarcation of identity and difference. Members of a colonizing class will insist on their radical difference from the colonized as a way of legitimizing their own position in the colonial community. But at the same time they will insist, paradoxically, on the colonized people's essential identity with them—both as preparation for the domestication of the colonized and as a moral and philosophical precondition for the civilizing mission.

The colonizer's traditional insistence on difference from the colonized establishes a notion of the savage as *other,* the antithesis of civilized value. And yet the tendency of modern literature and science has been to locate the savage within us, in our historical origins and in our psychic structure. As modern, civilized human beings, we assert authority over the savage both within us and abroad, but the very energy devoted to such an assertion acknowledges its own incompleteness *as* authority. When we obey or are obeyed, how much of that obedience is mere mimicry? Colonial discourse bears this constant uncertainty, leading to an inherent confusion of identity and difference, a simultaneous avowal and disavowal of its own authority. This fundamental instability makes for a rich profusion of rhetorical forms which often clash with one another, and yet which all enter equally into the matrix of relations of power that characterizes the colonial situation. The crisis-ridden, unstable context of colonial power makes for a shattering of its discourse, not unlike the profusion of different voices in a paranoid schizophrenic or in *The Waste Land.* Colonial discourse, despite its rather constant function in serving the forces of order, actually assumes a number of widely divergent rhetorical forms, like a series of fragments made by stress fractures under the burden of colonial authority.

It will be apparent by now that I use the phrase "colonial discourse" to designate a space within language that exists both as a series of historical instances and as a series of rhetorical functions. Historically speaking, the phrase refers to the language employed by representatives of the great colonial powers in establishing authority over vast regions of Africa, Asia, the South Pacific, and Latin America during the period of imperial expansion that reached its height at the end of the nineteenth century. But I have written a rhetorical study rather than a history and thus have attempted to describe the aspects of this language which survive beyond the classic colonial era and which continue to color perceptions of the non-Western world. Here I follow Paul de Man's notion of rhetoric as being not just the study of tropes and figures, but also as a procedure that suspends the internal logic of a given trope in order to place it within a larger narrative framework which includes the history of literature and of philosophical thinking. Any given trope can thus be read as part of a pattern of repetition. De Man's theory of the "grammatization of rhetoric" implies that the trope will implicitly claim its own subjective and independent status, while a critical deconstruction shows its syntagmatic position within a narrative pattern, as well as its declension from a set of historically determined concepts and categories. Thus "a vast thematic and semiotic network is revealed that structures the entire narrative and that remained invisible to a reader caught in naive metaphorical mystification" (16). Although de Man refers specifically to literary narratives, the critical procedure he defines is applicable to nonliterary texts as well and to the hybrid known as literary journalism.

Given my reliance on literary journalism for examples of colonial discourse, it may be useful to say something about the discursive specificity of this kind of writing. My initial attraction to literary journalism is better explained autobiographically than theoretically. Having worked as a journalist in more than one European country before moving into the study of literature and critical theory, I began with a personal as well as intellectual interest in the interpretation of cultures. These interests combined with a sense of living in a moment of historical urgency—interpretation had real consequences for living people who had little control over how they were represented to more powerful nations and cultures. The study of fiction, while obviously relevant to questions of cultural interpretation, seemed at a formal and aesthetic remove from the historical reality of the postcolonial situation. The material of the daily news media, on the other hand, was, in Walter Benjamin's phrase, so "shot through with explanation" (89), so transparently the expression of ideology as to obviate the need for critical intervention. The news media's reliance on institutional sources, their place in a market economy, and their standardized discourse produce an ideology that is fairly easily explained (e.g., in Said's *Covering Islam*) in terms of national policy and public opinion.

Literary journalism, however, combines an immediate historical interest with the complex layering of figurative language that conventionally belongs to imaginative literature. It often has a symbolic character that, in comparison with journalism as information, tends to multiply its possible levels of meaning. The presence of the writer as part of the narrative scene, moreover, conceals the most obvious effects of ideology and suppresses the historical dimension of the interpretive categories that are brought into play. The writer implicitly claims a "subjective and independent status" free from larger patterns of interpretation and deriving authority from the direct encounter with real events.

This authority, of course, is as problematic as the claim to a subjective and independent status in interpretation. At the risk of betraying an ontological naïveté, one may say that this writing is about things that really happen (no matter how they are interpreted) and that on another level it is about the struggle with events not entirely within the writer's control. There is in journalism an element of subordination to the aleatory nature of the event not present in the relative mastery of the fiction writer over the invention and ordering of narrative events. The journalist also relies on narrative as a resistance to the aleatory, but this is a defensive position in comparison to the novelist's more creative and even capricious power.

Essentially this point is made by T. S. Eliot in an essay which demonstrates the impossibility of distinguishing journalism from imaginative literature on a scale of literary value. Swift's *Drapier's Letters* and Newman's *Apologia Pro Vita Sua* (both literary journalism to Eliot) are infinitely superior on such a scale to a second-rate novel. For Eliot, then, the distinction is futile on grounds of textual form and can only be made by referring to the circumstances of composition; the journalist writes "under the pressure of an immediate occasion" (*Selected Essays*, 440). Eliot's move has the effect of displacing questions of form with those of practice when making critical distinctions; it evokes an image of the literary journalist as caught within the play of more powerful forces, yet laying claim to a space of interpretive authority within that field. The task of criticism, then, would be to demystify the grounds of that authority by defining its conditions and its place within a larger, unacknowledged discursive framework.

A final distinction between literary journalism and fiction seems to be made possible by the existence, in the former case, of alternate frames of historical reference. Graham Greene's *The Lawless Roads* (1939) is a nonfiction account of his journey through the tropical Mexican states of Chiapas and Tabasco, where, under the socialist regime of Lazaro Cardenas, Catholic churches had been destroyed and priests driven out or shot. This text provides the setting and theme for Greene's novel, *The Power and the Glory* (1940). One difference between these two texts is the lack, in the former, of any implied distance between the author and the first-person narrator; like most literary journalism it is avowedly autobiographical. More important, however, is the fact that the reader of *The Lawless Roads* can compare it to other historical accounts of southern Mexico under the Cardenas regime. Without doubting the truth of Greene's personal account, we can nonetheless question his interpretation in the light of rival accounts and can connect it to Greene's extraliterary affiliations (in this case, the work was commissioned by the Catholic church). Of course, we can do the same with *The Power and the Glory*, and we do it all the time, but only by violating the terms of the novelistic convention which would protect it from being read as historical representation. We have to read the novel, in other words, as if it were *The Lawless Roads*. One could also argue, however, that the convention of fictional ahistoricity is violated by Greene himself in writing a novel with a historical setting. The distinction between the novel and literary journalism on grounds of historical referentiality turns out not to be so clear, after all.

Conrad's *Heart of Darkness* (1910), a work which serves as a continual point of reference in the succeeding chapters, offers another case study in the problem of historical referentiality. Conrad's suppression of any direct reference to Africa or the Congo has the effect of universalizing his narrative, making it possible to read it as a "statement of the human condition" rather than as simply an account of conditions in the Belgian Congo in the early twentieth century. Fictional conventions thus enable a universalizing metaphor that we do not ordinarily grant to literary journalism, which is read as localized in time and place. Criticism, however, has the power both of historically localizing fictional narrative and, conversely, of expanding the frame of reference belonging to nonfiction. Thus *Heart of Darkness* has been read as incorporating the racism of men, like Conrad, who took part in the work of colonizing the Congo, while journalistic narratives like Henry Morton Stanley's *In Darkest Africa* (1891) can be read metonymically as part of a long history of representations of the Congo. The irony of this particular case is that *Heart of Darkness* tells us more about what the Belgian Congo was really like than any journalistic or historical account.

The study of discourse, however, explodes these categories of genre in the effort to seize hold of a more global system of representation. The question that matters for this study is, finally, not how one literary form differs from another, but how writing works, in whatever form, to produce knowledge about other cultures. That is why, at the risk of failing to show the proper respect for literary distinctions, I have freely drawn together examples from so many different kinds of text, treating them as moments in the production of a larger discursive phenomenon.

In addition to transgressing boundaries of literary form, the study of discourse also recognizes an inherent ambiguity in the relation between author and text. The text speaks ambiguously. Is it the voice of an individual writer, the voice of institutional authority, of cultural ideology? It is all of these things, often at the same time. In the colonial situation as well as in its aftermath, this ambiguity in writing itself joins with the logical incoherence of colonial discourse to produce a rhetoric characterized by constant crisis, just as colonial rule itself continually creates its own crisis of authority. The anxiety of colonial discourse comes from the fact that the colonizer's power depends on the presence, not to say consent, of the colonized. What is power without its object? Authority is in some sense conferred by those who obey it. That they do so under extreme forms of constraint does not change their place in the balance, their indispensable role in granting authority its proper value. Hence the uneasiness, the instability, the frequent hysteria of colonial discourse.

There is no real center to this discourse, apart from the historically central motive that authority must be maintained. But even the nature of this authority changes from one era to the next. The intense and localized colonial administration of fifty years ago, for example, has shifted to a more indirect and global supervision of Third World political and economic development. Colonial discourse thus does not simply reproduce an ideology or a set of ideas that must constantly be repeated. It is rather a way of creating and responding to reality that is infinitely adaptable in its function of preserving the basic structures of power. Foucault makes a similar point:

> There is not, on the one side, a discourse of power, and opposite it, another discourse that runs counter to it. Discourses are tactical elements or blocks operating in the field of force relations; there can exist different and even contradictory discourses within the same strategy. (1980:100)

Discourse may be understood here as a series of discontinuous segments that combine in various ways in the service of power. But power should no more be conceived as a monolithic structure than discourse. Foucault asks us to think of power not as simply the privilege of law, prohibition, and sovereignty, but as "a multiple and mobile field of force relations, wherein far-reaching, but never completely stable, effects of domination are produced" (102).

Would it be possible to create a discourse that avoids the violence of the letter and thus the imposition of power? This question, the occasion of my final chapter, has also been asked by James Clifford of ethnography. Clifford finds that the "textual embodiment of authority" is a recurring problem, even for contemporary experiments that replace traditional models of ethnographic description and interpretation. Any coherent presentation in itself "presupposes a controlling mode of authority" (1988:54). The same question applies to other forms of writing. In the description and interpretation of the non-Western world, it is not only the non-Western point of view that must be entertained; it is rather an alternate symbolic universe that must be imagined or whose existence must at least be recognized. Here the writer must allow for a certain self-inflicted sabotage, a disruption of the categories that govern conventional interpretation. Even so, it may be impossible to break free from these categories and still produce a meaningful text. However, if, as Pierre Bourdieu remarks, "there is no way out of the game of culture" (1984:12), there are still lessons to be learned from criticism. Criticism, and the interpretation of cultures *as* criticism, will not free us from the relations of power inherent in all discourse, but at least they may help us to know the consequences of that power.

1 SURVEILLANCE

Under Western Eyes

REPORTING BEGINS WITH LOOKING. VISUAL OBSERVA-
tion is the essence of the reporter's function as witness. But the gaze upon
which the journalist so faithfully relies for knowledge marks an exclusion
as well as a privilege: the privilege of inspecting, of examining, of looking
at, by its nature excludes the journalist from the human reality constituted
as the object of observation.

A passage from James Agee's writing on conditions in the American
South during the 1930s is remarkable for its self-conscious awareness of
the power implied by the gaze. Agee describes the gathering of black
farmworkers near the house of their white foreman:

> They all approached softly and strangely until they stood within the
> shade of the grove, then stayed their ground as if floated, their eyes
> shifting upon us sidelong and to the ground and to the distance, speak-
> ing together very little, in quieted voices: it was as if they had been
> under some magnetic obligation to approach just this closely and to
> show themselves. (27)

They are obligated to show themselves *to view* for the white men, but they
themselves lack the privilege of the gaze; though looked at, they are forbidden from looking back. The foreman calls for the black men to sing, and
they begin the song "now that they were looked at and the order given."
When the song is ended, Agee hands some money to one of the men: "He
thanked me for them in a dead voice, not looking me in the eye, and they
went away." The gratuity offered to the singers in effect acknowledges the
unevenness of the exchange. Gazed upon, they are denied the power of the
gaze; spoken to, they are denied the power to speak freely.

The scene, however, is more than a simple demonstration of power where it reveals signs of resistance on the part of the black farmworkers. The man receiving the gratuity thanks Agee "in a dead voice, not looking me in the eye," withholding his thanks even in the act of giving it. Here the avoidance of eye contact constitutes a refusal rather than a sign of submission: it says in effect, "Forbidden from looking on you freely, I refuse to meet your eye when called on to do so."

With an eye for these complexities, Agee demonstrates how looking and speaking enter into the economy of an essentially colonial situation, in which one race holds, however provisionally and uneasily, authority over another. To look at and speak to not only implies a position of authority; it also constitutes the commanding act itself: "now that they were looked at and the order given." By entering into this economy of uneven exchange, Agee becomes an accomplice to the very system of authority, of control, and of surveillance that causes him so much anguish and that removes him from those people whose lives he would attempt to understand. For all his awareness of its ironies, Agee's position is nonetheless analogous to the classic position of the Western writer in the colonial situation: the conditions of access to colonized peoples also mark an exclusion from the lived human reality of the colonized.

In 1982 Joanne Omang, a reporter for the *Washington Post*, shared a ride in a van with a group of other North American and Western European reporters to a tiny, remote village in El Salvador. Here she tries to imagine the effect of their arrival on the handful of peasants who witnessed the scene:

> The van emptied—men in sunglasses with headphones wielding shiny microphones on long stalks pouring out behind other burly men carrying huge TV cameras and photographers drenched in Nikons— men and women alike wielding tape recorders and notebooks. We were clearly invaders from another planet. (47)

These remarks are printed not in the *Post* itself, but in the *Washington Journalism Review*, a trade journal. As a commentary on how her work is actually done, it would be out of place in a news report. Although reporters tend to know better than anyone else the limitations inherent in their methods of work, the standard journalistic forms do not easily permit reflection on the conditions—technological, economic, historical—that make reporting possible.

These conditions give the reporter a privileged point of view over what is surveyed, yet the nature of this privilege and the distance that it imposes between the seer and the seen rarely enters into the explicit content of journalistic writing. In those cases where the particular advantage inherent in the reporter's position is openly acknowledged, we suddenly see the dynamics of power that underlie even the most ordinary journalistic modes of surveillance.

In a series of articles on the Vietnam war written originally for the *New York Review of Books* in 1967, Mary McCarthy describes being taken up in a helicopter outside Saigon for "a ringside view of American bombing"— a routine part of the war correspondent's work. Her eyes wander over the great patches of earth scorched by the defoliation program and watch as a small plane below hits a bombing target. A typical day in the war includes 460 such bombing sorties "in support of ground forces." She comments:

> The Saigonese themselves are unaware of the magnitude of what is happening to their country, since they are unable to use military transport to get an aerial view of it; they only note the refugees sleeping in the streets and hearing the B-52s pounding a few miles away. . . . The Air Force seems inescapable, like the Eye of God, and soon, you imagine . . . all will be razed, charred, defoliated by that terrible searching gaze. (32–33)

McCarthy's account shows, first of all, that her logistical, if not her ideological, point of view is identical to that of the U.S. Air Force; her own airborne eye commands the same position as that terrible Eye of God. More importantly, her commentary implies that because of that position, the war for her takes on a different order of reality from that experienced by the Vietnamese. By looking down at the bombing targets rather than being on them, she literally sees another war.

In their disparate ways, Agee, Omang, and McCarthy are all concerned with the overpowering and potentially destructive effect of the gaze. But as any visual artist knows, the gaze is also the active instrument of construction, order, and arrangement. What one might call the ideology of the gaze takes on one of its clearest forms in the convention of the commanding view. One knows the importance of the commanding view—the panoramic vista—to architecture, landscape painting, and sites of tourism, as well as to scientific research, military intelligence, and police surveillance: it offers aesthetic pleasure on one hand, information and authority on the other. This combination of pleasure and power gives the commanding view a special role in journalistic writing, especially in the colonial situation, for it conveys a sense of mastery over the unknown and over what is often perceived by the Western writer as strange and bizarre. At the same time the commanding view is an originating gesture of colonization itself, making possible the exploration and mapping of territory which serves as the preliminary to a colonial order.

In his discussion of the intimate relation between power and visual surveillance, Michel Foucault recalls the Panopticon, Jeremy Bentham's eighteenth-century design for a circular prison divided into individual cells, all of which could be observed from the single vantage point of an enclosed central tower (1977:200–228). This architectural design has served as the model for modern prisons such as Stateville in Joliet, Illinois, as well as for other institutions where discipline and productivity are most economically monitored by an arrangement where the eye can survey an entire operation at a glance, while remaining free to focus on the minutest detail. Hence the widespread use of the panoptic principle in schools, libraries, hospitals, and factories.

In analyzing this principle, Foucault notes that what guarantees control in the Panopticon is the analytical arrangement of space: the circular structure of the building is divided into cells of uniform size, each of which can be seen from the same angle and at the same distance from the central point. The power exercised over those who dwell in this field of vision is therefore noncorporal: it depends on spatial configuration rather than on the use of force. This means that the position of visual authority is equally accessible to anyone who occupies the center of the structure: the eye of a worker or a schoolboy commands the same view as that of a prison warden. Furthermore, a series of partitions and blinds ensures that the observer remains invisible to those who are the objects of surveillance, making the Panopticon what Foucault calls a machinery of dissymmetry, disequilibrium, and difference. For the observer, sight confers power; for the observed, visibility is a trap.

I have borrowed the image of the Panopticon in order to suggest that its principle has bearing on any occasion where the superior and invulnerable position of the observer coincides with the role of affirming the political order that makes that position possible. The device of the commanding view in colonialist writing constitutes one such occasion. Like the supervisor in the Panopticon, the writer who engages this view relies for authority on the analytic arrangement of space from a position of visual advantage. The writer is placed either above or at the center of things, yet apart from them, so that the organization and classification of things takes place according to the writer's own system of value. Interpretation of the scene reflects the circumspective force of the gaze, while suppressing the answering gaze of the other. In this disproportionate economy of sight the writer preserves, on a material and human level, the relations of power inherent in the larger system of order.

LANDSCAPES

The rhetorical convention based on the sweeping visual mastery of a scene is an important feature of nineteenth-century poetry and fiction, as well as of the narratives of explorers such as Mungo Park and Sir Richard Burton. Mary Louise Pratt calls this rhetorical gesture the "monarch of all I survey" scene and notes its use by these Victorian explorers to convey moments of important geographical discovery (201). The convention is also essential to the writing of Henry Morton Stanley, one of the most daring and brilliant journalists in the history of the British and American press. Stanley's characteristic rhetorical method is to place himself on some "noble coign of vantage" and to survey the scene below in such a way as to combine spatial arrangement with strategic, aesthetic, or economic valorization of the landscape.

In September 1871, the third month of his journey to the African interior in search of David Livingstone, Stanley describes the land known as Unyamwezi. The rocky hill on which he stands is a "natural fortress," from which,

> if you look west, you will see Unyamwezi recede into the far, blue, mysterious distance in a succession of blue waves of noble forest, rising and subsiding like the blue waves of an ocean. . . . Hills of syenite are seen dotting the vast prospect, like islands in a sea, presenting in their external appearance, to an imaginative eye, rude imitations of castellated fortresses and embattled towers. Around these rocky hills the cultivated fields of the Wanyamwezi—fields of tall maize, of holcus sorghum, of millet, of vetches, etc.—among which you may discern the patches devoted to the cultivation of sweet potatoes and manioc, and pasture lands where browse the hump shouldered cattle of Africa, flocks of goats and sheep. (1970:36)

Stanley's eye moves systematically out to the horizon, then returns to the ground which can be inspected in its minute particulars. It ranges freely over the scene, providing general outline and points of focus, bringing about spatial order from a fixed point of view. The rhetorical trope known as parataxis—placing things side by side—by the mid-nineteenth century had become a standard adaptation of language to the scientific method, in which the process of knowing the world became largely a matter of establishing natural objects as visually accessible (Stafford 34).

But the "imaginative eye" of the journalist-explorer goes beyond the mere arrangement of visual data. Pratt, in her analysis of a passage in Burton's *The Lake Regions of Central Africa* (1860), identifies three parts of this rhetorical convention: the landscape is first aestheticized, then it is invested with a density of meaning intended to convey its material and symbolic richness, and finally it is described so as to subordinate it to the power of the speaker (204). Returning to our passage in Stanley, we find that it conforms to Pratt's model: The "far, blue, mysterious" distances of the forest become, metaphorically, those of a blue ocean inviting voyage and adventure, investing the scene with aesthetic value. The metaphorical transformation of the syenite hills into fortresses and embattled towers confers a strategic value on the landscape, showing that it could be held, safeguarded, protected. The rich detail devoted to farm and pasture land points to the natural abundance of the land, while at the same time domesticating the scene, referring it both backward and forward to a mythic time and place—where sheep may safely graze.

In our own largely postcolonial world, the commanding view still reflects the writer's authority over the scene surveyed, but the perceptual appetite is more likely to find itself unsatisfied, and the writer's tone to be one of disappointment or disillusionment. For a 1984 *New Yorker* article on the Ivory Coast, V. S. Naipaul visited the president's ancestral village of Yamoussoukro, now being newly constructed as a modern city. Naipaul looks down from the sealed glass window of his hotel room to an enormous swimming pool surrounded by lounge chairs. Beyond that, he sees the golf course created out of the bush: "a foreign eye had drawn out the possibilities of what to an African would have been only bush." His gaze lingers:

> It was a great creation, the golf course—perfection, in a way. It represented prodigious labor. Yet it was only a view; one look took it all in. And soon it wasn't enough. Splendor on this scale, in this setting, and after a hundred-and-fifty-mile drive, only created an appetite for more: the visitor began to enter the ambition and fantasy of the creator. There was a main street, very wide; there was a market; there were workers' settlements. Something like a real town was attaching itself to the presidential creation. But the visitor, always quickly taking for granted what had been created, continued to be distracted by the

gaps, the scarred earth, the dusty vacancies. And if you didn't want to play golf, there was nothing to do. (May 14, 1984)

Naipaul—born in Trinidad of Hindu parentage, educated at Oxford and resident in London—is an extraordinarily complex writer whose novels, essays, and travel accounts have confronted with stark vision the despair of a postcolonial world cast spiritually adrift. But even so gifted a writer shares certain conventions of representation with his less complicated literary and journalistic antecedents. Here, for example, Naipaul's description has an order comparable to Stanley's: beginning from a fixed point of reference, his eye travels steadily outward in a progressively expansive movement, arranging and dividing the field of vision. This visual survey carries with it an assessment of aesthetic and economic value: the golf course is beautiful, thanks to the skill of a "foreign eye." The city itself is ambitious but empty and incomplete, marked by gaps, vacancy, absence. In the judgment passed within Naipaul's gaze, the African town has made progress, but has yet to achieve the status of a "real town," has yet to achieve, that is, the reality of modernity and westernization. In both descriptive passages, the precolonial and the postcolonial, the rhetorical construct based on visual authority acts as a concrete sign of the writer's privileged point of view in the larger political sphere. The writer literally sees the landscape of the non-Western world in terms either of the promise for westernized development or of the disappointment of that promise. Stanley gazes out at Africa as it might become under colonial rule. Naipaul gazes at an Africa which, left to itself, can only parody the splendors of the West.

INTERIORS

When it descends from the heights of mountain ranges and hotel rooms, the gaze of the Western writer penetrates the interiors of human habitation, and it explores the bodies and faces of people with the same freedom that it brings to the survey of a landscape. The eye of the writer and its technological extension, the camera, take us inside the dwelling places of the primitive and exotic: a night club in Saigon, sacred caves in India, a terrorist enclave in Beirut, the winding alleys of the Algerian casbah, a prison in Uganda, a peasant hut in El Salvador. An entire tradition in Western literature, from colonial American captivity narratives to the novels of Forster and Malraux, has built itself around this trial of penetration into the interior spaces of non-European peoples. In these interiors the confrontation of cultures takes place face to face, or rather eye to eye, and it is here, at close range, that the gaze of the writer can have its most powerful effect.

Rudyard Kipling, accompanying the Calcutta police on their rounds, descends into the brothels and opium dens of "The City of Dreadful Night" (1888). As a journalist, Kipling penetrates a dark underside of the city ordinarily off limits to Europeans. A policeman explains, "If an Englishman messed about here, he'd get into trouble. Men don't come here unless they're drunk or have lost their way." Together, Kipling and the police enter a shadowy establishment:

> Two or three men with uneasy consciences have quietly slipped out of the coffee-shop into the mazes of the huts. The police laugh, and those nearest in the crowd laugh applausively, as in duty bound. Thus do the rabbits grin uneasily when the ferret lands at the bottom of the burrow and begins to clear the warren. (1970, 18:209)

Kipling's gaze identifies itself closely with the force and contempt of colonial authority, exposing the corruption of native Calcutta life when left to its own devices and finding a spatial metaphor for that life in the image of the deceptive, entrapping mazes. The searching, controlling gaze of the police is Kipling's as well. The metaphor of predatory violence underwrites the power of that gaze, while it reveals the duplicity of those who are its object: they do not return the searching look, but "laugh applausively, as in duty bound."

Of course, the journalistic eye is not always so clearly or consciously the instrument of colonial authority: it can be used to resist such authority or to regard, ironically, the privileges of the colonizer and the disadvantages of the colonized. But even where the Western writer declares sympathy with the colonized, the conditions which make the writer's work possible require a commanding, controlling gaze. The sympathetic humanitarian eye is no less a product of deeply held colonialist values, and no less authoritative in the mastery of its object, than the surveying and policing eye.

In a 1984 article on China, also in the *New Yorker*, Orville Schell writes about the Great Wall Hotel in Beijing, a new, first-class Western hotel based on the design of the Dallas Hyatt Regency. Here is an interior space that is actually exterior to the culture surrounding it, so that Chinese crossing its threshold are effectively taking leave of their own world and entering the vertiginous space of Western capital. One of Schell's pastimes is to sit on one of the French sofas in the lobby and watch the comings and goings of the American, European, and Japanese businessmen. From this vantage point, Schell witnesses an unusual event: the arrival of two "unchaperoned" Chinese, elderly men dressed in the gray tunics and caps of the Revolution:

> Once inside the door, they paused, doffed their caps, and gazed around in wonder. All eyes immediately fixed on their entrance. Their presence transformed the atmosphere of the lobby, which suddenly became not an isolated Western preserve but a confluence of two cultures, one living within the hotel and the other living outside. . . . After several moments of gazing around like wild animals on the edge of a clearing, one whispered to the other and gave him an encouraging tug on the cuff. (November 19, 1984)

Schell watches the two men sit down tentatively on a sofa opposite him and surmises from their conversation in a cultivated Beijing dialect that they have an appointment with a Frenchman visiting China on business. He hears one of them ask, "Has it been long since you ate with a knife and fork?" The other responds, "Paris, 1948."

Once they enter the hotel, the Chinese become in a sense subjects of a foreign power again, subject to the temptation and order of the West, and subject above all to the penetrating inspection of the Western eye. In this case the reporter is sympathetic to the predicament of these bewildered Chinese, but it is not entirely coincidental that, like Kipling, Schell should draw upon a metaphor of animal fear to describe their reaction, for the figure acknowledges the elements of territoriality and predation that enter into the colonizing gaze. What he describes as the confluence of two cultures seems more like a staring-down, with one side clearly dominating. Despite the reporter's sympathy, he nonetheless enjoys a commanding view which unsettles the Chinese and accounts for the difference between his position of assurance and theirs of disorientation.

The Western journalist's essential position does not change even beyond the confines of a Western preserve in Asia. The eye remains mobile and selective, constantly filtering the visible for the *sign*, for those gestures and objects that, when transformed into the verbal or photographic image, can alone have meaning for a Western audience by entering a familiar web of signification. The journalist is literally on the lookout for scenes that carry an already established *interest* for a Western audience, thus investing perception itself with the mediating power of cultural difference.

BODIES

The final field of visual penetration for the journalist is that of the human body. In classic colonial discourse, the body of the primitive becomes as much the object of examination, commentary, and valorization as the landscape of the primitive. Under Western eyes, the body is that which is most proper to the primitive, the sign by which the primitive is represented. The body, rather than speech, law, or history, is the essential defining characteristic of primitive peoples. They live, according to this view, in their bodies and in natural space, but not in a body politic worthy of the name nor in meaningful historical time. The bodies, not only of so-called primitive peoples but of all the colonized, have been a focal point of colonialist interest which, as in the case of landscape description, proceeds from the visual to various kinds of valorization: the material value of the body as labor supply, its aesthetic value as object of artistic representation, its ethical value as a mark of innocence or degradation, its scientific value as evidence of racial difference or inferiority, its humanitarian value as the sign of suffering, its erotic value as the object of desire. Reading the private diaries of Bronislaw Malinowski, Torgovnick notes the ethnologist's obsession with the bodies of the Trobriand islanders and finds that by contrast his published ethnographies serve to sublimate his erotic desire by "converting feelings into magisterial observation guided by pure, untainted theory" (231). Surveillance thus enables both visual possession of the body and an interposition of technique which safely conceals the body of the observer.

Stanley, among others, comments continually on the bodies of the Africans he encounters, often subjecting them to anthropometric examination—the measurement of body parts commonly practiced by nineteenth-century researchers. In his writings on the Emin Pasha Relief Expedition (1888), Stanley cites sixteen separate measurements for the body of a pygmy male—height 4 feet, circumference of head 20¼ inches, circumference of chest 25½ inches, etc.—while he describes a female in slightly more subjective language:

> She is of a light brown complexion, with broad round face, large eyes, and small but full lips. She had a quiet modest demeanour, though her dress was but a narrow fork clout of bark cloth. . . . I notice when her arms are held against the light, a whitey-brown fell on them. Her skin has not that silky smoothness of touch common to the Zanzibaris, but altogether she is a very pleasing little creature. (1891, 1:368)

The eye treats the body as a landscape: it proceeds systematically from part to part, quantifying and spatializing, noting color and texture, and finally passing an aesthetic judgment which stressed the body's role as object to be viewed. However, the conditions which make this leisurely inspection possible are in this case those of forcible arrest and custody. Stanley's party has been skirmishing with the pygmies as he cuts his path through their territory, and these particular specimens are brought to him as prisoners of war. The situation serves as a reminder that the freedom of the gaze depends on the security of the position from which it is directed.

The counterpart to this detailed inspection of body parts is the sighting which takes in the entire body at once and removes it from its surroundings by means of a framing device. My example is from Hemingway, and in moving from Stanley to Hemingway we move not only a half century forward in time, and from the Ituri forest of the Congo Basin to the plains of East Africa. We also move from the era of geographic exploration to its leisurely imitation in the sport of the big game hunter. And we move, finally, from robust nineteenth-century ideals of progress and civilization to a modernist sensibility that defines itself in terms of impotence, anxiety, and loss.

In *The Green Hills of Africa* (1935), Hemingway's "absolutely true" account of a hunting expedition, there is a moment when the writer's eye narrows its focus from a landscape to a single human body:

> We glassed that valley until the sun came onto us, then hunted around the other side of the mountain where the other B'wana . . . had shot a fine bull kudu, but a Masai walked down the center of the valley while we were glassing it and when I pretended I was going to shoot him Garrick became very dramatic insisting it was a man, a man! (172)

Garrick is Hemingway's name for his theatrical Mbulu guide. When warned of the nature of his ostensible target, Hemingway turns to this man and asks, "Don't shoot men?" Taking the bait, the guide puts his hand to his head, saying, "No! No! No!" This little scene, perhaps harmless in intent, serves as a metaphor for certain aspects of the colonial presence in Africa: the Masai, representative of the tribe that proudly rejects assimilation to the colonial order, here is framed in the sights of a gun barrel. The act of drawing a bead on him is used to instill terror in the relatively colonized African guide, who may have reason to think that the white man could kill a Masai for sport, or out of ignorance.

Although Hemingway's irony is directed at his histrionic guide, the task of the critic of colonial discourse is to step back from the scene in order to ironize the ironizer. Thus we may say that Hemingway's practical joke works only at the expense of the joker: he mimics the terrible gaze which means death to those on whom it rests, but in doing so reveals his relative impotence in comparison with Stanley, who never took aim at an African but in deadly earnest. There may be, for a man of Hemingway's sensibility, arriving late on the colonial scene, a nostalgia for the moral certainty of a Stanley, as well as for Stanley's power to follow his aim with a true report.

Western journalism is filled with situations where the observer, from an exterior position, views the bodies of the captured, imprisoned, incapacitated, or dead. In the postcolonial era the dead or dying body has become in itself the visual sign of human reality in the Third World. Visiting the sacred banks of the Ganges at Varanasi, a writer for the Sunday travel section of the *Chicago Tribune* evokes a scene reminiscent of the river Acheron in the nether world. From the top of a *ghat* overlooking the Ganges, he surveys the scene: "Several large fires, tended to by scrawny ascetics clad in loin cloths, cast macabre shadows over the water." Corpses placed on ceremonial bamboo stretchers await the fire. Setting out from shore, the writer marvels at the riverborne bodies of the dead—Hindu faithful too poor to be cremated. "The boatmen, anxious to please their patrons, keep a sharp lookout for floating corpses, straining their eyes and posturing themselves in the bow of the boat like African safari guides" (June 26, 1983). The bodies are surveyed as an object of touristic interest, a fact that the writer records with an irony directed primarily at the Charonic boatmen rather than at himself and the other "patrons" of this ghoulish sight-seeing. The scene becomes an image of Eternal India, exotic land of spirituality, poverty, and death, its essence untouched by the modern world.

Images of the dead and dying of course ordinarily occur elsewhere than in the Sunday travel section. At a camp for Cambodian refugees, Gail Sheehy describes the new arrivals: "Wasted by malnutrition they kept coming. With bodies shedding life as nonchalantly as feather falling off a bird, they kept coming." The camp already holds "twenty thousand people with fixed looks, their faces void of animation, their minds frozen"— another image seemingly inspired by Dante's *Inferno*. Sheehy's article (*Chicago Tribune*, August 1, 1982) contains a just and urgent humanitarian appeal which relies, perhaps necessarily, on scenes so familiar to the Western imagination as to constitute a stock set of images. Thus she writes of the refugees, "They were stacked upright like sticks, they had to be removed from the truck like rag dolls." In such scenes the writer's eye colonizes the victims of famine or disaster by reducing the victim's identity to a *sign* of suffering and, by extension, of the catastrophic Orient. On a similar scene in a documentary film about Malaysia, Roland Barthes remarks ironically, "They are eternal essences of refugees, which it is the *nature* of the East to produce" (1972:96). Such reduction in the name of humanitarian appeal involves a cost in human dignity: the human is effaced by the overpowering sign of the refugee.

The visual enframing and metaphorical transformations that characterize such images have a distancing effect: while calling attention to suffering, they also show it as *out there*: contained, defined, localized in a realm understood to be culturally apart. But the speed with which these images are brought to us do not bring us closer to that world or make it more real for us. On the contrary, the technology of the modern media alienates us from the reality of the foreign and remote by the very ease with which it produces images of that world; the images are produced at random and can be made to disappear by the turn of the page or the dial. Wayne Booth observes that television news, through its stereotyping and the structure of its presentation, creates "a sense that somebody out there, *in there,* is taking care of these issues in quick order" (48). Benjamin finds that newspapers achieve a similar distancing effect. The principles of journalistic style as well as the visual makeup of the pages, in which individual news items are not connected with one another, are designed "to isolate what happens from the realm in which it could affect the experience of the reader" (158–59). The reader is thus absolved of responsibility; the crime has been identified, the authorities notified. The skilled order of presentation compensates for the reader's inability to assimilate these mass-produced images into the structure of private experience.

When we speak of the role of the eye in establishing knowledge of the world and authority over space, we are referring to a fundamental characteristic of Western thinking. What I have called the gaze and the commanding view makes possible an understanding of the non-Western world as an object of study, an area for development, a field of action. The desire for a systematic visual knowledge of non-Western cultures has become the subject of analysis by critics of ethnology such as Johannes Fabian and Pierre Bourdieu. Fabian calls by the name of *visualism* ethnology's tendency to base its knowledge on visual observation and to define its object in the form of spatial images, maps, diagrams, trees, and tables. The problem inherent in this bias toward visualization is that "primitive" cultures are reduced to synchronic objects of aesthetic as well as visual perception, while more generally, non-Western cultures are constructed as the other "in terms of topoi implying distance, difference, and opposition"—that is, as an ordered space for Western thought to inhabit (111, 121).

Fabian's visualism is close to what Bourdieu has called *objectivism*:

> Objectivism constitutes the social world as a spectacle presented to an observer who takes up a "point of view" on the action, who stands back so as to observe it and, transferring into his object the principles of his relation to the object, conceives of it as a totality for cognition alone, in which all interactions are reduced to symbolic exchanges. (96)

Bourdieu notes that this point of view is generally available only to persons of privilege, from whose position the social world at large appears as a representation, both in the philosophical sense and in the sense offered by a painting or a theatrical performance. This authoritative and privileged, yet distanced, position is one held in common by the ethnologist and other Western writers in the colonial world.

Both Fabian and Bourdieu argue for a break with visualist and objectivist models of ethnology. For Fabian, this break involves the recognition that field work is a form of "communicative interaction" between the ethnologist and the group under study—an interaction that takes place within a shared time and space. Similarly, Bourdieu calls for an understanding of the social world as human practice rather than as an abstracted, conceptualized model. He includes within this practice the ethnologist as well, whose inquiry must consider the conditions (cultural, economic, political) that make ethnographic study possible.

If we were to transfer these principles beyond ethnography to other forms of writing, they would entail not only the writer's sense of how he or she must look to the group being observed, as Joanne Omang attempts when she arrives like an invader "from another planet" at a village in El Salvador, but also the writer's own perspective—including its motivations, its conditions of possibility, and its consequences—as a subject of awareness in the writer's own account. Such awareness is ideally combined with the recognition that writing not only follows the visual perception of space, but that writing itself, in its linear and syntactical structure, is a form of parataxis that spatializes and regularizes its object in time and space (Derrida 1976:201).

In *La Tentation de l'Occident* (1926), André Malraux's fictional correspondence between a young Frenchman and a young Chinese, the latter says of the Western mind:

It wants to draw up a plan of the universe, to make of it an intelligible image, i.e. to establish between the unknown and the known a
series of relations which would reveal that which has been hitherto
concealed. It wants to subordinate the world, and finds in its own
actions a pride that much greater for believing that it possesses the
world already. (155)

Malraux makes the point that the nomination of the visible is no idle metaphysic, no disinterested revealing of the world's wonders. It is, on the
contrary, a mode of thinking and writing wherein the world is radically
transformed into an object of possession. The gaze is never innocent or
pure, never free of mediation by motives which may be judged noble or
otherwise. The writer's eye is always in some sense colonizing the landscape, mastering and portioning, fixing zones and poles, arranging and
deepening the scene as the object of desire.

2 APPROPRIATION

Inheriting the Earth

COLONIAL DISCOURSE TAKES OVER AS IT TAKES cover. It implicitly claims the territory surveyed as the colonizer's own; the colonizer speaks as an inheritor whose very vision is charged with racial ambition. Simultaneously, however, this proprietary vision covers itself. It effaces its own mark of appropriation by transforming it into the response to a putative appeal on the part of the colonized land and people. This appeal may take the form of chaos that calls for restoration of order, of absence that calls for affirming presence, of natural abundance that awaits the creative hand of technology. Colonial discourse thus transfers the locus of desire onto the colonized object itself. It appropriates territory, while it also appropriates the means by which such acts of appropriation are to be understood.

The doctrine of this appropriation is put forth most explicitly in the writings of European colonial administrators who saw the natural resources of colonized lands as belonging rightfully to "civilization" and "mankind" rather than to the indigenous peoples who inhabited those lands. Frederick Lugard, the British governor general of Nigeria in 1907–1919, considered the European powers to be "custodians of the tropics" and "trustees of civilisation for the commerce of the world": "The tropics are the heritage of mankind, and neither . . . has the suzerain Power a right to their exclusive exploitation, nor have the races which inhabit them a right to deny their bounties to those who need them" (60–61). Lugard uses "heritage" in the sense of "inheritance," invoking the rhetorical figure which traditionally casts nature in the mythic roles of both bequeather and bequest. The right of inheritance belonging to "mankind"—one established by the history of this construct in European Enlightenment thought—naturally

supersedes the narrower political interests of the other two political enti-
ties present here, suzerain power and subject races. In the course of this
supersession, however, two other discursive events take place: the native
races are now subsumed under the title of "mankind"—appropriated by
this construct—while it is taken for granted that the rights of mankind can
only be served with the suzerain power in place. The preservation of colonial rule, as well as the exploitation of colonized territories, thus becomes
a moral imperative as well as a political and economic one.

A variation on this theme is offered by Albert Sarraut, governor general
of French Indochina in 1911–1914 and 1917–1919, later minister of colonies.
Here nature is again mythologized, not as wisely benevolent but rather
as the source of an unequal apportionment which humanity must amend.
Nature's "double abundance" of intellectual and material resources has
been unevenly distributed so that the one now finds itself cut off from
the other:

> While in a narrow corner of the world nature has concentrated in
> white Europe the powers of invention, the means of progress, and the
> dynamic of scientific advancement, the greatest accumulation of natu-
> ral wealth is locked up in territories occupied by backward races who,
> not knowing how to profit by it themselves, are even less capable of re-
> leasing it to the great circular current that nourishes the ever growing
> needs of humanity. (109)

Writing in 1931, at a time when André Gide's reports from Equatorial Africa
have stirred anticolonial sentiment in France, Sarraut concedes that colonial rule originates with "a primitive act of force," but argues that it has
developed into "an admirable act of law": colonization is now a gesture
of "human solidarity" which unites the intellectual and moral qualities of
Europe with the material wealth of the tropics.

This doctrine of the colonizer's natural inheritance often determines
the very manner of perceiving a landscape. As Stanley, in 1871, gazes out
over the country of Ukawendi near Lake Tanganyika, the wild, unpeopled
landscape is already being transformed by his imagination into familiar
terrain:

> What a settlement one could have in this valley! See, it is broad enough
> to support a large population! Fancy a church spire rising where that
> tamarind rears its dark crown of foliage, and think how well a score
> or so of pretty cottages would look instead of those thorn clumps and
> gum trees! Fancy this lovely valley teeming with herds of cattle and

fields of corn, spreading to the right and left of this stream! How much better would such a state become this valley, rather than its present wild and deserted aspect! (1970:75–76)

Stanley constructs out of the scene an English country village—pretty cottages, cattle by the stream—already a nostalgic image in the late nineteenth century. But the European experience in Africa allows for nostalgic pastoralism to be projected onto the future and made into the object of utopian desire. This utopian vision imposes an entire series of European institutions on the natural landscape. Stanley's language implies all of the structures of civil order, commerce, agriculture, family life, and religion, yet does so in such a way as to cover over the act of imposition. Under Stanley's gaze, the landscape has already prepared itself for the marriage with civilization. Everything is in order; it is a question of simple substitution and supplement rather than true transformation: the dark tamarind and the gum trees need only be replaced by the church spire and the pretty cottages. The stream already feeds pasture and farmland. In its deserted aspect, the valley calls for the colonizer to bring it into being.

John Buchan, who on the eve of his literary career served as private secretary to the South African High Commissioner in 1901–1903, indulges in a more personal vision as he gazes on a piece of land in the northern Transvaal and imagines his future country house, complete with flower gardens, fruit orchards, and imported Highland cattle grazing on the hillsides: "There will be wildfowl in my lake, and Lochleven trout in my waters." As in Stanley's view of East Africa, this utopian scene is created whole cloth out of nostalgic cultural memory, while the rhetorical act of appropriation is submerged in the process of regenerating a mythic past: South Africa is Zion to this Baron Tweedsmuir displaced by history from the Scotland of *Waverley*. Appropriation thus is not acknowledged as itself, but as a spiritual return, a *nostos,* summoned not only by historical vision but by the nature of the land itself:

> It is a land of contrasts—glimpses of desert and barbarism, memories of war, relics of old turmoil, and yet essentially a homeland. As the phrase goes, it is "white man's country"; by which I understand a country not only capable of sustaining life, but fit for the amenities of life and the nursery of a nation. (1903:91)

Buchan is selling South Africa to prospective European immigrants; the colony needs more white, and especially British, settlers to strengthen its government and economy. The power of this solicitation lies in the assumption that South Africa is already white, already home; the colonizers have only to accept what is their own.

The colonizing imagination takes for granted that the land and its resources belong to those who are best able to exploit them according to the values of a Western commercial and industrial system. This presupposition operates not only in cases of direct colonial rule, but also in the kind of indirect power exercised by the United States over the countries of Central America, where, by 1920, private U.S. interests owned most of the arable land, the railroads, and the communications systems. On a visit to Honduras in 1896—three years before the founding of the United Fruit Company—the American writer Richard Harding Davis registers wonder at the rich pasture lands, the abundant woods, the mineral treasures of silver, gold, and iron, and the soil rich enough to supply the world with coffee. He writes:

> There is no more interesting question of the present day than that of
> what is to be done with the world's land which is lying unimproved;
> whether it shall go to the great power that is willing to turn it to ac-
> count, or remain with its original owner, who fails to understand its
> value. The Central Americans are like a gang of semi-barbarians in a
> beautifully furnished house, of which they can understand neither its
> possibilities of comfort nor its use. (1896:147)

Davis's metaphor of the beautifully furnished house recalls the pretty cottages of Stanley's vision and the noble estate transported in Buchan's imagination from Scotland to the gently rolling hills of the Transvaal. Together, these images evoke a benevolent pastoralism, an ideal of domestic order and tranquillity which suppresses the underlying desire for a radical transformation of colonized territory. The discourse once again takes over by taking cover, revealing and concealing the appropriating impulse in the same rhetorical gesture.

In "African Grammar," an essay on France's official vocabulary for addressing its colonial affairs, Roland Barthes notes the predominance of substantives as a sign of "the huge consumption of concepts necessary to the cover-up of reality" (1979:107). This variant of colonial discourse destroys the verb and inflates the noun, so that the noun tends to identify not specific objects or actions, but more generalized notions (nature, mankind, humanity) which carry the moral weight of the discourse. Language is thus petrified and solidified around a series of concepts whose substance is presented as already known and therefore beyond contestation. The *heritage* of *mankind* and the benevolence of *nature* are like France's *mission* and

Algeria's *destiny* in that their substantive form presents them grammatically as postulates not open to dispute; it naturalizes them within the discourse and confers upon them the quality of hypostasis. The pervasive character of the nominative in colonial discourse reflects a desire to set forth as self-evident the substantive reality of a moral abstraction. As Barthes writes, "Nomination is the first procedure of distraction." Nomination and substantivization may also be seen as grammatical forms of appropriation: by naming things, we take possession of them. Employed as substantives in the web of syntax, these names acquire an ontological status—a substance—of their own, thus obscuring or concealing the original act of appropriation.

Once the land has been appropriated, there remains the problem of appropriating the hearts and minds of the colonized. In 1898 Queen Victoria wrote to Lord Salisbury concerning the choice of a new viceroy for India:

> He must be more independent, must *hear for himself* what the *feelings* of the Natives really are, and do what he thinks right and not be guided by the *snobbish* and vulgar, over-bearing and offensive behavior of our Civil and Political Agents, if we are to go on peacefully and happily in India, and to be liked and beloved by high and low—as well as respected as we ought to be—and not trying to trample on the people and continually reminding them and making them feel that they are a conquered people. They must of course *feel* that we are masters, but it should be done kindly and not offensively. (3:251)

The queen's letter to her prime minister points to another paradox of colonial discourse: the desire to emphasize racial and cultural difference as a means of establishing superiority takes place alongside the desire to efface difference and to gather the colonized into the fold of an all-embracing civilization. The European role in colonial territories depends on the clear demarcation of cultural and moral difference between the civilized and the noncivilized. But the ultimate aim of colonial discourse is not to establish a radical opposition between colonizer and colonized. It seeks to dominate by inclusion and domestication rather than by a confrontation which recognizes the independent identity of the Other. Hence the impulse, whether in administrative correspondence or journalistic writing, to see colonized peoples as ultimately sympathetic to the colonizing mission and to see that mission itself as bringing together the peoples of the world in the name of a common humanity.

This rhetorical appropriation of non-Western peoples insists on their identification with the basic values of Western civilization and tends to interpret their acquiescence to the colonial system as approval of Western ideals. But this equation of simple collaboration with a deeper moral identification, far from being regarded as a weakness in the logic of colonial discourse, instead provides one of its fundamental principles: a colonized people is morally improved and edified by virtue of its participation in the colonial system.

David Livingstone was among the first to establish the ideological link between commercial exploitation and moral improvement among the races that were later to become subject to European colonization. During the Zambesi expedition of 1858–1863, he sees "so much of this fair earth . . . unoccupied, and not put to the benevolent purpose for which it was intended by its Maker" (1865:264). Christianity was a necessary condition for the peaceful commerce among nations that would allow the exploitation of Africa's resources according to God's will. Christian conversion would therefore improve the social as well as the spiritual condition of the African. By encouraging trade, it would bring the African "into the body of corporate nations, no one of which can suffer without the others suffering with it" (1865:28).

Stanley, though hardly the humanitarian that Livingstone was, had a similar tendency to see African compliance in the colonial enterprise as affirming a spiritual and familial bond between colonizer and colonized. On one occasion he is deeply moved by an incident in which the natives are made to understand that he is willing to pay wages—an idea ostensibly foreign to them—for their labor in building a river station on the Congo. He sees this introduction of labor value as a transformation of the native's spiritual state: "It created a hope . . . in every man, that he possessed something that was saleable . . . that the force of those masses of muscle had become marketable and valuable" (1885, 1:171).

Apart from the principle of free labor, another essential part of Stanley's design for the exploitation of the Congo was the establishment of open marketplaces at the river stations where the natives could come to exchange their goods, instead of foraging the countryside every day in search of food. When the natives finally begin using such markets, the event takes on enormous significance for Stanley:

> When I saw the terrace plaza being employed as a common market-ground, I became conscious that the victory against aboriginal conservatism was won. . . . I felt, when I saw two scores of women and children squatted in the perfect enjoyment of unlimited confidence, that I had become endowed with the honour of paternity, and not for

untold wealth would I have permitted that confidence to be tarnished with the least exhibition of distrust or violence. (1885, 1:500–501)

This language not only appropriates native resources to European colonial ends; it also appropriates the native point of view, so that Stanley speaks *for* the African. Wage labor creates new hope in the African mind; the African women enjoy unlimited confidence within the confines of the terrace plaza, a European structure that by its very architectural configuration enforces the principles of inclusion and domestication inherent in the rhetoric of appropriation. The victory which Stanley celebrates is that which is won throughout the European empire when native peoples are gathered into the fold, and when they are seen as embracing the institutions of their conquerors.

It is a victory, however, already hedged with a rhetoric of protection, for the threat of distrust or violence remains inherent in this classic colonial situation. The notions of paternal honor, perfect enjoyment, and unlimited confidence, like those of mankind and human solidarity, are used to represent the imposition of colonial rule as the restoration of a harmonious order—not that of aboriginal conservatism, but of a more benign conservatism, at once natural and civilized, like the love between father and daughter. The language of this conservatism itself effects a rhetorical pacification of the colonial enterprise, while it also serves as an instrument of policing power: not the least exhibition of distrust or violence shall be permitted to tarnish the perfect confidence of the colonized.

Stanley's impression of the Africans' unlimited confidence in his design conforms to the convention which represents European intervention as the response to an *appeal* from less fortunate peoples, an appeal often combined with the theme of moral and political improvement. Sarraut sees the precolonial history of such peoples as a tragic story of war, massacre, and slavery: "The unceasing clamour of warfare issuing forth from this anarchy and from this heredity of violence over the centuries raised toward us a pathetic appeal [*un appel pathétique*] that was impossible to ignore" (125). Colonial intervention thus responds to a threefold calling: that of nature, which calls for the wise use of its resources; that of humanity, which calls for universal betterment; and that of the colonized, who call for protection from their own ignorance and violence.

With the end of the classic colonial era, it has become all the more important to find signs among non-Western peoples of their sympathy and identification with the West. The spread of Western influence in its various forms has been a preoccupation of the media, which finds the avid consumption of Western goods to be evidence of the approval of Western culture as a whole. Early explorers won the natives over with a display of the phonograph or the fork. More recently it has been Dior fashion and the hamburger. During the Salvadoran civil war of the early 1980s, a *Chicago Tribune* correspondent reported the following:

> McDonald's has been bombed twice in the last year by guerillas who view Big Macs as symbols of American imperialism. Nevertheless, Salvadorans continue to flock to the house of Ronald McDonald.
>
> "A war is a war," said Armando Carranza, a flower shop owner, as he bit into a quarter-pounder, "but a good hamburger is heaven." (September 6, 1981)

The example is extreme in its sheer silliness, yet it belongs to an entire class of reporting that seeks to minimize conflict and cultural difference by celebrating the unifying power of Western (or North American) commercial and cultural institutions. The nature of the discourse being produced here is such that this theme often exists alongside one which decries the loss of traditional ways of life to Western influence and which, occasionally, will even romanticize those who seek to resist such influence. The combination of these themes, sometimes called "balance" in journalism, in fact is symptomatic of a profound disequilibrium, for what it reflects is not the object as it really is, but rather the conflict and anxiety inherent in the representation of cultural difference.

In this particular instance, the appropriated point of view is that of the conveniently middle class shopowner, for whom Western-style consumption takes precedence over the realities of revolution. Even his idioms, borrowed from the language of advertising, are as thoroughly Americanized as they are improbable. In a gesture of seemingly desperate reassurance, the writer seems to say that this is the real voice of El Salvador, representing those thousands who risk guerilla attack in their eagerness to consume North American products.

The demand for such signs becomes most intense in those places where revolution, socialism, tribalism, or religious fundamentalism calls into question the power of Western influence. In a series of articles written in 1981 while traveling with Jonas Savimbi's UNITA forces in Angola, a *Washington Post* reporter stresses the Western virtues of his hosts, who are struggling to overthrow the country's Marxist government. When Savimbi's troops perform in parade formation, they are "not as elegant as Britain's Coldstream Guards, but they have a lot of elan." One of their commanders reminds the reporter of a Marine drill sergeant from his own past. The soldiers sing like the Mormon Tabernacle Choir. The native population in UNITA-controlled territory attend Protestant and Catholic services; they play soccer and organize Boy Scout troops. They even celebrate July 4 in honor of the visiting American journalist (July 19–25, 1981). Such attempts to manipulate *him* do not deter the *Post* correspondent from appropriating *them* as courageous champions of Western ideals in a hostile political and natural environment. Under the headline "UNITA's Shoestring Enterprise: Guerrillas' High Morale and Determination Inspire Respect," the *Post* series concludes with an implied plea for U.S. military assistance to Savimbi: "How these people have kept going for all these years with such high levels of morale is one of the many mysteries of this great continent" (July 25, 1981).

To see non-Western peoples as having themselves become the standard-bearers of Western culture is in some ways a more profound form of colonization than that which treats them merely as sources of labor or religious conversion. In such cases the object of appropriation is no longer the human body nor even the individual soul, but the very nature of reality in the Third World, now seen in its potential as an image of the West. This form of appropriation gives rise to a curious phenomenon: the West seeks its own identity in Third World attempts at imitating it; it finds its own image, idealized, in the imperfect copies fabricated by other cultures.

The American involvement in Vietnam was fought in the American press as a war of appropriation, a rhetorical war which centered around the problem of Vietnamese identification with American values. The journalistic combatants of this war sought continually an image of America in Vietnam, an image that would render Vietnam *appropriate* to American interest. The question was not so much whether, but rather which Vietnamese belonged to America, either in a strategic sense or in a moral and spiritual sense.

In the beginning, it was Ngo Dinh Diem, president of the Republic of South Vietnam, who was America's man. During the late 1950s, when the United States was spending about $400 million a year to support Diem's regime, he enjoyed a period of adulation in the American press. On a visit to the United State in 1957, Diem was introduced by the mayor of New York as "a man history may yet adjudge as one of the great figures of the twentieth century." President Lyndon Johnson later called him "the Winston Churchill of Asia," and to *Life* magazine he was the "tough miracle man of Vietnam" (FitzGerald 96).

Here is how *Newsweek* wrote about Diem in 1957:

South Vietnam today is proof of what an authentic patriot, resolute and shrewd, can accomplish with the full backing of the major instruments of American policy. . . . In two years South Vietnam has been transformed. The private armies and the main Communist pockets have been wiped out. Most of the countryside has been pacified and brought under control of the central government. Most of the refugees have been resettled. Diem has become the authentic symbol of Vietnamese nationalism. . . . The credit belongs primarily to Diem, but, as he unhesitatingly proclaims, he could not have succeeded without largescale American support. (May 20, 1957)

The elements of wishful thinking in this passage should not distract us from the subtleties of its rhetorical strategy, which alternates between self-congratulation on the power of American influence and an attempt to represent the ostensible transformation of South Vietnam as an indigenous phenomenon. While Vietnam has been rhetorically appropriated as an American satellite, there is still the need to locate the source of its radical transformation in Vietnam itself. Hence the repeated insistence on Diem's authenticity—authentic patriot, authentic symbol—as if to deny by mere repetition Diem's status as an American *fantoche*. The adjective here, Barthes would point out, betrays an anxiety that the substantives it modifies (patriot, symbol) have suffered a wear and tear that make it necessary to reinvigorate them. The *authentic* patriot or symbol must be distinguished from those that are already too familiar or overused, hence inauthentic. The adverb plays this same rejuvenating role with respect to the tired verb. We are accustomed to hearing the proclamations of petty dictators with a degree of cynicism. The assurance that Diem proclaims his debt to America *unhesitatingly* reflects an anxious effort to restore some of the verb's tarnished dignity.

The association of Diem with Vietnamese nationalism, which sounds strange in view of the later history of the war, amounts to a double co-optation: it claims the nationalist movement as belonging within the range of American interests, while it also represents the instrument of American intervention, Diem, as subordinate to Vietnamese nationalism, as an authentic *symbol* of nationalism. The source of appropriation is thus shifted to Vietnam itself: Vietnam has appropriated American aid for its own independent purposes. In this confusion of the relations of power, one finds yet again the principles of "African Grammar" at work in the American press. Barthes notes that the emphasis in French colonial discourse on the morally inflated noun is accompanied by a corresponding subversion of the verb.

The verb, which can otherwise act so powerfully to signify action, means, and agency, is either reduced to a simple copula ("Monsieur Pinay to the UN: 'There *would be* an illusory detente'") or removed to a future or conditional mode ("A Moroccan government *will be constituted*") (1979:108). The *Newsweek* article on Diem neutralizes its verbs in a similar manner by the use of passive construction and a vocabulary which obscures the nature of concrete action: the countryside "has been pacified" and "brought under control." This leaves unnamed the agents and means of pacification and control, while it also suggests that the transformation of Vietnam is really a conservative return to traditional ideals.

The rhetoric of appropriation carries within it the transference and displacement of its own colonizing motives. This displacement can take the form of euphoric idealization as well as fantasy. We may compare the *Newsweek* article on Diem to the following piece in the *New Republic*, which also appeared in 1957:

> The Republic that came into being in the South has managed in three years to eliminate the last of the French military, economic, and bureaucratic influences; to set up its own national army, school system, and monetary system; to establish political administration in every part of the country, and to come close to eradicating traditional graft and organized vice.
>
> It has not only adopted a constitution guaranteeing basic human rights, created a multi-party political system and held a national election, but it has moved forward with constructive economic reform.
>
> In brief, the Republic of Vietnam, having got out from the colonialism of the French and the neo-colonialism of the Communists, has proved that freedom is a mighty force when it is made to serve the general welfare. (May 6, 1957)

"Innocence," writes Graham Greene in *The Quiet American*, "is like a dumb leper who has lost his bell, wandering the world, meaning no harm." The *New Republic*'s discourse offers a study in such innocence. It rings with the language of Western democratic enlightenment: constitutional guarantees, basic human rights, the strength of freedom. The effect is to create an infectious image of South Vietnam as the miraculous regeneration of Western values; Vietnam becomes a nostalgic version of the early American republic, creating a new political order out of the ideals of Locke and Rousseau. In this way Vietnam is colonized by the very language of the American political imagination.

This colonizing movement, however, is rhetorically deflected by the language of anti-colonialism: South Vietnam has eliminated the last vestiges of official French influence; it has cast off the successive colonialisms, presented here as rhetorically equivalent, of both the French and the Communists. According to the spirit of this self-deceptive innocence, the substitution of American influence for these earlier colonial orders is not colonialism at all, but the strongest form of anti-colonialism, for "freedom is a mighty force." Once again, a paradox is born: the more deeply Vietnam is drawn into the American sphere, the more perfectly it realizes its own independent identity. Like the village that had to be destroyed in order to be saved, Vietnam must be colonized to make it free.

In the waning stages of the war, when Diem was long since dead and discredited and the miracle of South Vietnam had turned into a nightmare, an ideological space opened up in the American press for a rival appropriation. For an important group of journalists, it was Ho Chi Minh of the North who was "the George Washington of his country." In an evolving mythology of the war continually reproduced and revised in the press, the Communists began to assume the roles of liberators and martyrs. For an influential faction of the American press, the Vietnamese object of appropriation had shifted from one side of the conflict to the other, but the rhetorical strategies of this appropriation were essentially unchanged. Colonial discourse is not a matter of a given ideological position, but rather of a series of rhetorical principles that remain constant in their application to the colonial situation regardless of the particular ideology which the writer espouses.

During the Vietnam war few were more eloquent in their opposition to American neocolonialist policies than Susan Sontag, whose *Trip to Hanoi* (1968) recounted the struggle of the Vietnamese to defend themselves against United States bombardment, as well as the writer's "interior journey" toward an understanding of the Vietnamese way of life. In her effort to divest herself of Western cultural prejudices and to enter a revolutionary Oriental world, Vietnam is miraculously transformed from an alien and mysterious other to a familiar and, above all, American ideal.

Early in her narrative Sontag struggles with "the test of being able to identify myself with the Vietnamese" while comparing them unfavorably to the Cubans, who come out better "by the standard of what's useful, instructive, imitable, relevant to American radicalism" (28–31). Already one may recognize in this stance a gesture of appropriation which represents itself as the desire to be appropriated; the struggle to identify with the Vietnamese will mean, in this case, the task of creating an identity for the Vietnamese within the context of Western political and moral value.

Midway through her account, Sontag recovers from a "psychic cramp" that had prevented her from understanding the Vietnamese. She suddenly awakens to their virtues. One is that, despite the bombs falling around them from American warplanes, the North Vietnamese maintain a keen interest in American culture. They read Whitman and Poe; they inquire after Arthur Miller and Norman Mailer. "We are very interested in American literature," someone at the Hanoi Writers' Union tells her. North Vietnam is, moreover, the only Communist country Sontag claims to know "in which people regularly praise the United States for being, after all and despite everything, 'a great democracy.'" The foreign minister mentions respectfully the American Declaration of Independence. A Hanoi newspaper editor speaks of his love for the United States and its "tradition of freedom" (75–81). Far from being the enemy, North Vietnam represents, in other words, one of the great successes in the spread of American influence. Sontag's presentation escapes the jingoism of the reporting on Diem in 1957; its patriotism is indirect, using the Vietnamese in an evocation of the *real,* which is to say ideal, America. This ideal is both mythic and essentially literary: the America of the enlightened Jefferson, the democratic Whitman, the earnest Miller, the florid and passionate Mailer.

Like early Americans, Sontag's Vietnamese nourish themselves on disaster, tirelessly rebuilding a country continually reduced to rubble by the fire from above. Their errand in this particular wilderness is the creation of a "new man," a people morally improved by the effort to overcome adversity. And, also like the early Americans, their moral courage combines with astonishing ingenuity: college students build their own campuses and grow their own food; bomb craters are converted into fish-breeding ponds; even the tires from downed American bombers are cut up and made into rubber sandals. This technical resourcefulness is joined with the virtues of sexual fidelity and a strong family life:

> Sexual self-discipline, I imagine, must be taken for granted in Vietnam. It's only a single aspect of the general demand made on the individual to maintain his dignity and to put himself at the disposal of others for the common good. In contrast to Laos and Cambodia, with their "Indian" or "Southern" atmosphere that derives from an eclectic blend of Hindu and Buddhist influences, Vietnam presents the paradox of a country sharing the same severely tropical climate but living by the classical values—hard work, discipline, seriousness—of a country with a temperate or cold climate. (52–53)

Sontag finds the Vietnamese to be an anomaly precisely by falling back on a standard practice of colonial discourse, which is to establish a connection between the moral standing of a people and its climatic environment. The heat of the tropics, according to this logic, produces races characterized by indolence and easy sexuality, while the harsher conditions of northern climates have created a race devoted to diligence and self-control. Sir Samuel Baker, the nineteenth-century discoverer of the Albert Nyanza, complained of the "lack of industry" in Africans and noted the absence of progress more generally among natives of tropical countries who, "enervated by intense heat . . . incline rather to repose and amusement than to labor" (xxiii). Stanley claimed a "visible improvement," in both character and physical type, of the native African races as one moved steadily northward from the Equator (1891, 2:386).

The point is not to make a Stanley out of Susan Sontag, but to show that her discourse incorporates the classic colonial standards of Western civility—hard work, discipline, sexual continence—in passing judgment on the darker races. Sontag's imagination colonizes Vietnam as an outpost of classical *American* values, free from the Southern or Indian influences of the sensuous, exotic East. Vietnam, redeemed from that Oriental otherness, is placed at the center of American mythic consciousness—it is, finally, the America of Jonathan Edwards and Cotton Mather. Sontag's report offers an example of what Derrida calls in Lévi-Strauss "ethnocentrism *thinking itself* as anti-ethnocentrism" (1976:120). Even as she would have herself transcend the narrow Western view of Asia, she nonetheless holds to the distinctions between hard work and indolence, discipline and indulgence, as the criteria for cultural value. The familiar standards remain at the heart of her judgment.

The image of Vietnam as an earlier, more pure America connects Sontag unexpectedly with the euphoria surrounding Diem in the 1950s, as well as with earlier rhetorical practices that treat colonized territory as both the embodied potential for the realization of Western ideals and the site of a return to a simpler, nobler way of life. Sontag's nostalgia for the lost innocence and harmony of Western life focuses on the people of Vietnam themselves, while in the case of Stanley or Buchan, it fixes on the natural abundance of the land. Distanced from one another by ideology and by history, these writers yet have in common the desire to appropriate the non-Western world to their visions of the West. "The Vietnamese," writes Sontag, "are 'whole' human beings, not 'split' as we are." The temptations of the colonizer are both narcissistic and therapeutic. They betray a desire to recreate, in these unconquered territories or in these unsubdued hearts and minds, one's own image, and to reunite the pieces of a cultural identity divided from itself.

3 AESTHETICIZATION

Savage Beauties

THE PRESS HAS ITS OWN AESTHETIC, PLAYED OUT along the dual axes of time and space. Consider the spatial aspect of this aesthetic in the visual presentation made by a newspaper, with its rich display of typefaces, columns, boxes, and pictures and its breezy arrangement of the most diverse subjects in juxtaposition: the photo of a South African protest demonstrator under the whip encroaches on an interview with the new Miss America. Both items compete with a story about a boy, a dog, and a drowning. This exposure of so many different items together, Marshall McLuhan observes, gives the press its own complex dimension of human interest and makes the newspaper an art form in its own right. McLuhan looks at the ordinary newspaper page as a work of surrealism and argues that historically the newspaper has served as an inspiration to symbolist and surrealist art: "Approached as newspaper form, any part of Joyce's *Ulysses* or any poem of T. S. Eliot's before the *Quartets* is more readily enjoyed" (193).

Even without subscribing to McLuhan's theories on Eliot, Joyce, and surrealism, one can see how the analogy helps to define the particular aesthetic of the newspaper. What makes the press unique as an art form is that its mosaic quality is shaped anew every day by communal design and by the independent, aleatory nature of the *event*. No other art form has this intimate, constructive engagement with the unpredictable forces of circumstance, or opens itself so readily to the clash of the trivial with the consequential, of cheap sentiment with impending apocalypse.

The temporal dimension of the journalistic aesthetic lies in its narrative approach to reality. The press treats events in a primarily episodic manner which follows a characteristic narrative form: an episode or "story" typically begins with a revelation, introducing a dramatic situation and a series of characters. The second stage is devoted to development: the expansion or explication of elements in the original discovery, the chronicling of changes that advance the action, the heightening of tension and pathos. The final stage brings about a resolution, as the action plays itself out and stabilizes, while an appropriate response to the action is produced. If the story concerns social crisis or disorder, more frequently than not this response will come from sources of official authority: the police quell the rioting, labor and management leaders reach an agreement, the State Department approves or condemns the latest coup d'état in South America. The press in this way establishes a subtle relation between narrative order and the perception or representation of political order.

Todd Gitlin makes a similar point in commenting on the "orderliness" of television news. The orderly format of such programs promotes social stability, he argues, by providing a sense that whatever goes wrong in the world, it can be put right by official agencies and authoritative expertise: "Even if the story is about disorder, it likely turns to the restoration of order under benign official aegis" (266). Thus the press presents a dynamic image of the world that is curiously both volatile and stable, in which periodic explosions into disorder are always brought somehow back under control. This restoration of order, however, is not simply the subject of journalistic observation and approval; it is also a structural element of narrative representation: the story imposes its own order quite apart from, if supplementary to, the order restored by official action.

The aesthetic qualities of media form allow for an interest on the part of the media audience which depends on a certain detachment from the real conditions that constitute the object of representation. This detachment is related to the traditional disinterestedness of aesthetic judgment; we must observe the separation between stage and audience if we are to appreciate the drama. The mosaic form of the newspaper, like the rapid succession of images in television news, helps to maintain this aesthetic distance. A story on Vietnamese boat people is made spatially and rhetorically equivalent to a story on the lottery and another on a corporate takeover. All are recounted in the same tone, and all compete to displace one another in the visual field. The journalistic treatment in itself gives us no reason for devoting our attention to one particular subject at the expense of the others.

The episodic form, like melodrama, releases us from active engagement at the moment of its inception. The revelation of a scandal, a massacre, or a putsch carries the implied promise of its dramatic arc: the story will unfold and eventually come to rest with some appropriate resolution. In the case of social disorder, disaster, or injustice, the narrative constructs imposed by the press constitute a narrative and symbolic response that tends to obviate the demand for concrete, practical action on the part of its audience. Faced with this display of the "march of events," the audience's role is largely passive and consuming, though appreciative of what it perceives as the satisfaction of its desire for information and amusement.

The very ritualization of news production and consumption becomes part of the mechanism by which journalism creates a distance between audience and reality. More than any other writer of our century, Marcel Proust was obsessed by the problem of the aesthetic transformation of social reality; he sees this transformation at work even in the act of reading the morning paper:

> I wanted to glance at *Le Figaro*, to enter into that abominable and voluptuous experience called *reading the newspaper,* by virtue of which all the sorrows and upheavals of the universe during the last twenty-four hours, the battles that have cost the lives of fifty thousand men, the crimes, strikes, bankruptcies, fires, poisonings, suicides, divorces, the wrath of statesmen and performers—conveyed for our personal use, to us who are not affected—in a morning feast—all this goes excellently, in a particularly stimulating and tonic manner, with the recommended ingestion of several mouthfuls of *café au lait.* (217)

By associating it with sensory stimulation, Proust characterizes the act of reading the newspaper as a decadent aesthetic. The pure pleasure to be derived from the abominable and voluptuous qualities of this act makes it inferior to the more noble and disinterested contemplation of beauty, according to traditional Kantian aesthetic value. Yet Proust insists on his own disinterested relation to the subject matter of the newspaper. The pleasure to be derived from this experience depends on the reader's power to remain, in the realm of the concrete and practical, unaffected by the sorrows and upheavals recounted in the press. More than that, there is a sense in which one actually enjoys reading about suffering in the world, because the form in which it is presented is so easily consumed. It is the presentation of the news, served up like morning toast, that keeps the reader at a safe remove from reality while stimulating in the reader the pleasure of the text. The disinterested nature of this pleasure relates it to aesthetic experience, though it might be called a corrupt aesthetic, an aesthetic of consumption.

Up to now I have been discussing the aesthetic value of the news media in general, considering the structure of news production as creating an art form of its own. To make this point, however, is different from examining the way in which the news or another form of journalism can engage in the aesthetic treatment of a certain subject. The aestheticization of human reality in a given context is to be distinguished from the aesthetic value of what McLuhan calls the communal mosaic of the press.

The tendency to treat certain subjects as having inherently aesthetic value has special consequences for representations of the Third World in the Western press. Above all, the cultural and geographic distance of Third World reality makes it more susceptible to a kind of aesthetic treatment, however imperfect or corrupt, than is the case with subjects closer to home. The Third World continually provides what writers call "material" of a special nature: the exotic, the grotesque, the bizarre, the elemental. Commenting on a story in *Paris Match* which looks at Africa through the eyes of a European child, Barthes writes, "Ultimately the Black has no complete and autonomous life: he is a bizarre object, reduced to a parasitical function, that of diverting the white man by his vaguely threatening *baroque*: Africa is a more or less a dangerous *guignol*" (1979:37). The intensive media attention given to the cruel regime of Idi Amin in the 1970s allowed for perfectly justified expressions of outrage, while it also provided a macabre diversion. Amin satisfied the traditional demand for someone to play the role of the savage African buffoon. Would it have been possible to report honestly on Amin without representing him in this way? Probably not, since the image of the *guignol* was precisely what he chose to project, as if contemptuous of the humanity required of a national leader. The point is not that Amin was misrepresented, but that his actions, to the horror of other Africans, lent renewed vigor to an old stereotype.

The images purveyed by the Western media often make the people of the Third World appear unprotected by the restraining constructs of advanced civilization. Their suffering is interpreted as giving expression to elemental passions which law and reason are supposed to have suppressed in the West; hence the fascination with religious fanaticism, bloodthirsty dictators, and tribal atrocities. The atavism of the Third World becomes the object of interest and attraction, as if it offered an image of our own more primitive being. Madness, revolution, barbarism, natural disaster—all seem closer to the surface there, offering a constant source of pathos.

But, like Proust at his breakfast table, one can experience this pathos safely by virtue of an aesthetic mediation whose transforming power increases with cultural distance.

It is precisely this transforming power in journalism that disturbs Agee in his assignment from *Fortune* magazine to write about the tenant farmers of the South. He considers that he is being asked "to pry intimately into the lives of an undefended and appallingly damaged group of human beings for the purpose of parading the nakedness, disadvantage, and humiliation of these lives," and in such a way that *Fortune* will profit from this representation both in prestige and in financial gain. The terms of his assignment, as he understands it, demand a revisive "digestion into art," a commodification of suffering that betrays the great "weight, mystery, and dignity" of real human lives. "However that may be, this is a book about 'sharecroppers,' and is written for all those who have a soft place in their hearts for the laughter and tears inherent in poverty viewed at a distance, and especially for those who can afford the retail price" (11–14).

The aestheticization of Third World reality (in Agee's case a Third World inside America) is made possible by this cultural and geographic distance, while it also marks the ratio of power that holds between one class of people and another. As suggested by the connection in journalism between the resolution of narrative order and the imposition of political order, the aesthetic stance itself is taken from within a position of power and privilege: the power to perceive poverty as aesthetic value is a privilege not granted to the poor.

In 1981 and 1982 the major organs of the American press were gripped by the plight of Cuban and Haitian refugees making the perilous voyage to Florida's shores in flimsy, overcrowded vessels. The story had a number of attractions: adventure on the high seas, the theme of the American dream, a subject for humanitarian concern, an occasion for xenophobic alarm. Prominent among these was the clearly dramatic interest in the desperation of the refugees. The *Washington Post* recounts the harrowing tale of a Haitian named Joseph (no surname given), a man with "no money, no crops, no future," whose only hope is "to educate his young son":

> So Joseph caught a dinghy . . . for La Tortue, the legendary island hideout for pirates and smugglers across the bay. He began knocking on doors. He had another $200, borrowed from friends, and the name of a middleman. The name led him to an open sailboat dangerously overloaded with 58 Haitians. The captain ordered some off. When no one moved, a dozen passengers were beaten and tossed over the side.

Stormy seas tossed the flimsy craft and waves washed over a shiver-
ing Joseph. One passenger threw himself into the deep. At night, some
chanted voodoo prayers to "make the boat go." They ran out of water.
On the fourth day the boat landed at Nassau. (December 24, 1981)

Suddenly, amid the sober pages of the *Washington Post*, we are plunged
into the world of *Kidnapped* and *Treasure Island*. Here is all the melodrama
of the boy's adventure story, with its evil captain, its island hideout, and
its hapless voyagers who meet their fate in Davey Jones's Locker. For all its
vividness and human interest, the *Post* story establishes a realm of perception in which reality is interpreted according to a minor literary aesthetic.
The struggle for simple human survival, the terrified refugees, the atavistic prayers are all standard Third World material. The emphasis is on the
picturesque such that, as Agee would say, the suffering of the refugees is
offered to all those who have a soft place in their hearts for poverty viewed
at a distance. Proust remarks on a sentimental article in *Le Figaro*, "This is
what wrings a tear from us, a tear we would not shed for suffering closer
to us."

When the picturesque and the melodramatic are given prominence, they
displace the historical dimension, isolating the story *as* story from the relations of political and economic power that provide a more meaningful
context for understanding poverty. Here, however, poverty exists simply
as a given condition of the melodrama, created *ex machina* and unrelated,
except for purposes of dramatic contrast, to the prosperity that thrives
on other shores—unrelated, that is, to colonial history, including its postcolonial form as the history of American support for a repressive Haitian
regime. Barthes finds a similar tendency to accept the notion of history's
nonresponsibility in colonial French rhetoric concerning the "agony" of
African nations in their struggle for independence: "Colonization evapo-
rates, engulfed in the halo of an impotent lament which *recognizes* the
misfortune in order to establish it only the more successfully" (1979:104).

If the news establishes a consumer's relation to events, then travel writing may be said to establish a consumer's relation to entire cultures. But
travel writing in the popular press involves another style of representation,
in which violence and atavism are both evoked and tamed for the would-
be tourist. An article in the Sunday *Chicago Tribune* entices the reader with
the headline "Papua New Guinea: One of the Last Places on Earth to
Catch the Color and Beauty of Primitive Tribes." Written by a travel editor
of the *Toronto Star*, the story concerns a place called Konmei in the Sepik
River valley where the inhabitants celebrate the capture of a boy from a

neighboring, presumably hostile village. The ceremony involves a mock decapitation in which a clay head is substituted for the prisoner's own. The writer is nonetheless at pains to establish the authenticity of the scene:

> They may be doing the ceremony because there is a visitor present, but they mean it. This is no empty sham show run off routinely as entertainment. It's part of the culture of the region and but for the government ban there would be real blood to coat the ground and a real skull to adorn the *haus tambaran* or spirit house. (August 1, 1982)

Despite the signs of danger, the tourist can expect a friendly welcome from the natives:

> It is here . . . that my friend with the boar's tusks and his fellows dance round the severed clay head. It is here you see the skin cutting ritual. It is here, too, that you see and hear the dance of the flutes and are invited into the spirit houses.

The discourse of the travel writer may trivialize the spectacle through its gestures of touristic consumption, but it also raises questions concerning the nature of authenticity, art, and artifact.

James Clifford writes that Western institutions have developed a taxonomic "machine for making authenticity" which assigns cultural and economic value to objects collected from non-Western cultures. This system distinguishes "authentic" artifacts of folklore, craft, and material culture from "inauthentic" tourist art, curios, and commodities. On another axis, artifacts themselves are distinguished from true art, which belongs in art museums rather than in museums of ethnology or "natural history." Any object (or performance, presumably) may be classified according to its position within these four coordinates: art object, artifact; authentic, inauthentic (1988:223–225).

The travel writer's account of the New Guinea ceremony serves as an example of this machine in operation, as well as of the limitations inherent in the system of value it applies. The writer's claim for authenticity depends on its antithesis in an "empty sham show run off routinely as entertainment," an opposition closely related to that which, in Clifford's formulation, separates art from not-art and culture from not-culture. The writer clings to these distinctions even when the notion of authenticity in the classical ethnographic sense is undermined by the evidence before him: the substitution of the clay head in obedience to the law of the postcolonial government and the distinct possibility that the real occasion for this ceremony may be the writer's own presence. These elements of "inauthenticity," however, suggest a performance that genuinely reflects the moment as one of cultural intersection: the crossings of tribal tradition, postcolonial law, and the traffic of tourism create a ceremony authentic to the fluid cultural situation that actually exists, rather than to a nostalgic ideal of pure primitivism.

Dedicated to this ideal as to an aesthetic principle, the travel writer is prevented from recognizing the true authenticity of the moment. This "postcolonial" authenticity can be appreciated only by an aesthetic which accepts the interpenetration of cultures as creating a new kind of beauty. Thus Clifford comments on a scene in an ethnographic film about the game of cricket played according to unorthodox rules by Trobriand islanders:

> On a chair sits the umpire, calmly influencing the game with magical spells. He is chewing betel nut, which he shares out from a stash held on his lap. It is a bright blue plastic Adidas bag. It is beautiful. (148)

The conventional travel writer would either suppress this brilliant detail or treat it ironically for its failure to conform to a traditional ideal. The Sunday Travel Section, as it embodies the consumer's relation to non-Western cultures, values the pure exoticism of those cultures while it also demands free access to them, as if the latter did nothing to alter the former. The headhunters of New Guinea are thus represented as friendly to Western visitors, yet as remaining headhunters in essence: only a government ban prevents real blood from coating the ground. The journalistic appreciation of their ceremony both cultivates and neutralizes the bizarre, transforming it into a middle-class diversion, a primitive *guignol*.

The spirit of the Sunday Travel Section reaches its most exalted form in the sumptuous pages of magazines like the *National Geographic*, *GEO*, and *Réalités*, where social reality is submerged beneath the technical mastery of the camera and the soothing effect of a uniformly bland prose style. This genre of publication has its origins in the geographical societies of the nineteenth century—essentially gentlemen's clubs where men of science, travel writers, government officials, and wealthy amateurs met to share their impressions of distant lands. By 1890 such societies flourished in every major European capital and in many provincial cities, as well as in the American cities of New York, Washington, Philadelphia, and Chicago. Each of them published a monthly or quarterly bulletin, often richly illustrated and filled with travel narratives, memoirs, anecdotes, and speeches by prominent men, including colonial administrators. The 1888 *Bulletin* of the Société normande de Géographie (Rouen), for example, includes an address by Félix Faure, then a former undersecretary of state for colonies, on "French Interests in the Far East," alongside a memoir by the adventurer Camille Douls, who disguised himself as a Moslem in order to travel with the nomads of the Western Sahara.

Begun in 1899, the magazine of the National Geographic Society of Washington pursued a vigorously populist editorial policy whose commercial success coincided with the expansion of American interests abroad. One of its early exclusives was the printing, in 1905, of thirty-two full-page photographic plates from the U.S. War Department's illustrated census of the new colony of the Philippine Islands. The spectacular issue brought in a flood of new member-subscribers (Abramson 62). Gilbert H. Grosvenor, editor of the *National Geographic* from 1899 to 1954, championed a set of "principles" which included the following:

–Abundance of beautiful, instructive, and artistic illustrations.
–Nothing of a partisan or controversial nature is printed.
–Only what is of a kindly nature is printed about any country or people, everything unpleasant or unduly critical being avoided. (Grosvenor 4–5)

This policy has produced a publication more uniform and predictable than its nineteenth-century prototypes. Indeed, in reading the *National Geographic* today, one begins to have the impression that in this magazine every article about the Third World is essentially the same article about the same country. This country is inhabited by cheerful people with quaint and colorful customs. They smile alluringly for the camera, and their attitude toward the writer is invariably genial.

The people of this all-purpose Third World country proudly assert their independence from colonial rule, but they are forever doing charming things that are "typically French," like admiring Parisian *haute couture,* or "typically British," like playing cricket and having afternoon tea. Chinese women bobbing their hair, Africans eating ice cream—they are "catching up" with Western lifestyles, though they cherish their traditions, and continue to engage in fascinating rites of voodoo worship and self-flagellation. This generic *Geographic* story nods briefly at social problems—illiteracy, famine, revolution, what have you—but invariably concludes on an upbeat note about progress and modernization. The overall effect is to homogenize the Western experience of the Third World, to neutralize the disturbing aspects of social reality, and to minimize the importance of relations of power in creating the conditions under which people live. This is the buried ideology that makes possible the popular aesthetic of consumption in travel journalism.

The photography of the *National Geographic* produces this same effect of distancing the reader from social reality through sheer force of technique, which establishes its own precedence over the ostensible subject matter, so that the encounter with a foreign reality becomes a pretext for the display of the photographer's art. In an address delivered in Paris in 1934 at the Institute for the Study of Fascism, Walter Benjamin commented on the way photographs alienate us from reality in their very attempt to capture it. The camera, he said,

> is now incapable of photographing a tenement or a rubbish heap without transforming it. Not to mention a river dam or an electric cable factory: in front of these, photographs can only say, "How beautiful." . . . It has succeeded in turning abject poverty itself, by handling it in a modish, technically perfect way, into an object of enjoyment. (Sontag 1973:107)

This is precisely the case with the *National Geographic*, where an article on drought in Somalia, "fabled land of frankincense and myrrh," is dominated by stunning photographs of desert landscapes, of gleaming white cities rising from the dunes along an azure coastline. The beauty of these images—the sharpness of focus, the richness of color, the impeccable compositional arrangement—ends by overpowering the reality of the drought and its consequences for the people of Somalia (June 1981). A mother holding her starving infant is photographed in the manner of the *Pietà*, evoking not so much pity as the acknowledgment of the aesthetic representation of pity. The photograph is not the sign of starvation, but the sign of a sign, removing itself from the reality of starvation as it strives toward iconicity.

What really is the role of journalistic representation in making people aware of the suffering of others? There is clearly a sense in which the media can declare an emergency, can make an appeal on behalf of refugees or victims of famine, and elicit a practical response. Yet the very artfulness of this appeal, the images and techniques on which it relies, allows for a certain nonidentification on the part of the audience, and perhaps even allows that audience to take some satisfaction in the image of suffering as it belongs to the other.

In his discussion of ethics in Rousseau, Derrida defines an "economy of pity" in which the sensible presence of suffering is exceeded by its image, so that pity is awakened only by imagination and reflection. We can imagine and judge that others suffer, but this is to experience their suffering precisely as *theirs,* and not as our own. To identify totally with the agony of others would be dangerous and destructive:

That is why the imagination, the reflection, and the judgment that arouse pity also limit its power and hold the suffering of the other at a certain distance. One knows this suffering for what it is, one pities others, but one protects oneself, and holds the evil at arm's length. (1976:190)

Imagination and reflection both connect us to and protect us from pain. One could relate this doctrine to a theory of dramatic representation, as Derrida suggests, or even to a theory of psychoanalysis. The point is that all representation, as the elaboration of a symbolic structure that displaces its object, has this mediating and limiting effect on our experience.

If the economy of pity engages imagination and reflection in such a way as to make the suffering of others both real and removed from us, then what happens when suffering is presented in a purely formulaic way, with little chance for reflection, and with imagination reduced to relying on a series of clichés? The consequence of this reduction is the alienation produced by ordinary journalistic representation.

The crudeness of journalistic aestheticization upsets the delicate balance of the economy of pity, so that suffering evokes not pathos but an easily commodified sentimentality. Recognizing this danger in journalism, Agee was led to mistrust the value of his own writing: "If I could do it, I'd do no writing at all here. It would be photographs; the rest would be fragments of cloth, bits of cotton, lumps of earth, records of speech, pieces of wood and iron, phials of odors, plates of food and excrement" (13). Agee valorizes the purely metonymic, finding a betrayal of reality in the metaphorical character of writing. This ideal journalism—in fact an antijournalism—seeks to avoid conventional representation in order to provide *evidence*, not of poverty as an abstract concept, but of life as lived under the conditions we call poverty. In its rejection of a facile aesthetic formulation, Agee's work approaches the level of a higher art by attempting to draw the reader into an unmediated encounter with the lives of the poor. It may be that journalism alienates us from reality not when it reaches the level of art, but when it reaches only the level of bad art.

For Agee, the photograph has primacy over the written word as a more immediate sign, because the making of a photographic image requires the actual presence of its object. Yet photography has a language of its own that relies as much on convention as writing does, and photojournalism has a tendency to aestheticize its object equal to that of print journalism. Barthes finds at an exhibition of journalistic "shock photos" that the deliberately cultivated aesthetic of horror paradoxically diminishes the power of the photograph to evoke horror in the viewer. These images—of a crowd of soldiers beside a field of skulls, of a soldier looking at a skeleton—fail to move the viewer in their obvious intention to create horror as a construct: "as we look at them, we are in each case dispossessed of our judgment: someone has shuddered for us; the photographer has left us nothing— except a simple right of intellectual acquiescence" (1979:71). It is precisely this crudely aesthetic formulation that defeats imagination and reflection, a formulation so overdetermined that it fails to disorganize or disturb the viewer. Susan Sontag makes a similar remark about the studied composition and elegant perspective of Lewis Hine's photographs of child workers in American mills at the turn of the century: "The aestheticizing tendency of photography is such that the medium which conveys distress ends by neutralizing it" (1973:109).

For Barthes, the only photographs which have true shock value are the news agency photos shot in an instantaneous reflex action, without thought as to angle, focus, and composition: a group of Guatemalan Communists being executed, a policeman raising his truncheon over a rioter. Like Agee's bits of cloth and wood and iron, these artless photographs have the concrete and metonymic value of evidence, compelling the viewer to imagine and reflect not only upon the terrible reality which produces them, but also upon the viewer's own relation to that reality. Their fortuitous origin, capturing an image as if on the run, preserves the naked actuality of the event, an actuality obscured and compromised by conventional journalistic formulation.

Apart from the practice of treating the Third World as material for sentimental human interest or melodramatic entertainment, another movement in journalism has made more explicit reference to traditional aesthetic value. In some cases, the journalist refers metaphorically to established art forms in order to provide a context for the understanding of foreign reality. In others, the journalist openly acknowledges an imaginative power and assumes a role identical with that of the artist. In both instances, aesthetic judgment intervenes as a mediating and transforming power in the interpretation of cultures.

I shall begin with the simplest use of art as metaphor, moving from there to more complex instances of the trope. On a trip to Africa in 1907, Richard Harding Davis describes Zanzibar as a "comic-opera capital." The architecture and decoration of the city are that of the stage designer, and Davis feels sure that "the chorus of boatmen who hail you will reappear immediately as the Sultan's bodyguard, that the women bearing water-jars will come on in the next scene as slaves of the harem, and the national anthem will prove to be Sousa's Typical Tune of Zanzibar" (1907:211). Zanzibar is, in short, "a most difficult city to take seriously." This is the same Davis who, as a practical joke, once led a charge on horseback through the streets of the Honduran capital, shouting "Viva Guiteris!" to create the popular belief that a new revolution had begun in favor of his host in that country.

The ability to view African cities and Latin American revolutions as operatic material was a natural part of Davis's blithe persona, while it was to become a standard device in reporting on the Third World. It takes a slightly sinister turn in Joan Didion's reports from El Salvador in 1982. Didion finds herself and her North American journalistic companions waiting in the garrison town of San Francisco Gotera, near the scene of heavy fighting between government troops and guerrillas. In the midst of this war, which often seems dreamlike and unreal in Didion's portrayal of it, the town is transformed by her imagination into the stage set for *Carmen* or *Tosca*. Any event, such as the arrival of a troop transport or a funeral procession by the church, "tended to metamorphose instantly into an opera, with all players onstage: the Soldiers of the Garrison, the Young Ladies of the Town, the Vendors, the Priests, the Mourners" (44).

Didion's operatic vision differs from Davis's partly in the force of its irony considered in the context of the random carnage taking place around it. Where Davis's irony directs itself mainly at the Africans, leaving his critical position secure, Didion includes her own presence in the object of ironic commentary. She puts herself and the other *gringo* journalists onstage as well, "a dissonant and provocative element" in North American costume: khaki shorts, tennis shoes, a cap advertising American beer. In 1982 the dissonance and provocation in general of the North American presence in El Salvador had become highly problematic for many journalists. But here Didion finds a way to resolve, at least for the moment, the political ambiguity of that presence: the North Americans simply assume their own roles in the grand opera of Latin revolution. The journalist likewise resolves the question of her own interpretive authority by giving herself, as well, a part to play. In ways that differ markedly as to their relative degree of complexity, Davis and Didion both resort to the theatrical metaphor in order to come to terms with an unfamiliar and potentially absurd reality.

The self-consciousness concerning her own position as a North American observer in Latin America is unique neither to Didion nor to the historical moment at which she writes. Stephen Crane, on assignment in Mexico for a syndicate of American newspapers in 1895, finds himself painfully aware of the compromises inherent in his position and states that "the most worthless literature of the world has been that which has been written by the men of one nation concerning the men of another." It is useless for the writer to make attempts at "psychological perception" or to sit in "literary judgment" on the manners of a foreign people. Instead, "he can be sure of two things, form and color" (74). Lacking a more meaningful basis on which to approach the reality of Mexico, Crane resorts to the purely visual. Yet even visual perception carries the burden of aesthetic and ideological value.

From a train passing through the Mexican countryside, Crane looks out upon a village, while at the same time observing the effect of the scene on two fellow passengers whom he identifies as an archaeologist from Boston and a capitalist from Chicago:

> Enough light remained to bring clearly into view some square yellow huts from whose rectangular doors there poured masses of crimson rays from the household fires. In these shimmering glows, dark and sinister shadows moved. The archaeologist and the capitalist were quite alone at this time in the sleeping-car and there was room for their enthusiasm, their ejaculations. Once they saw a black outline of a man upon one of those red canvasses. His legs were crossed, his arms were folded in his serape, his hat resembled a charlotte russe. He leaned negligently against a door post. This figure justified to them all their preconceptions. He was more than a painting. He was the proving of certain romances, songs, narratives. He renewed their faith. (74)

In this brief passage one finds all the complexity and ambiguity of the journalist's role in the colonial situation, as the attempt to create an interpretive context for a foreign reality collides with the calling into question of one's own authority to do so. Consciously avoiding judgment on the psychology and manners of the Mexicans, Crane relies on the vocabulary of the visual artist: form and color, light and shadow, outline and geometric shape. The light from household fires and a man are transformed, respectively, into a background of rich colors and a human figure outlined on a canvas. Crane, like Didion, acknowledges the irony of this two-dimensional aestheticization. But rather than, as she might do, paint his own figure onto the canvas, he attempts to distance himself from his own vision through the interposition of his fellow travelers: his observations, with their burden of a colonizing aesthetic, are suddenly made *theirs,* thus opening a space for his ironic commentary on American "preconceptions" of Mexico as romantic and picturesque.

Crane's vignette articulates the problem of the Western journalist in the Third World, who travels in a kind of no man's land between an unfathomable reality on the one hand and the already too familiar interests of power on the other. The capitalist and the archaeologist may be largely creatures of Crane's imagination, but they represent the traditional audience for the foreign correspondent: the powerful interests of Western scientific and economic mastery over the world. The archaeologist and the capitalist are both colonizers in their own right: each desires to appropriate and overturn the ground, to expose the hidden wealth of knowledge or material resources beneath the surface of the earth. In the face of this transformative energy, the peasant remains a figure of sheer passivity, his legs crossed, his arms folded, leaning negligently against a door post. In their power to consume the world, the Americans will have him for dessert, like a charlotte russe. They have, in fact, already dismissed the reality of the peasant by assigning him in their imaginations to the romance of Old Mexico.

Crane writes as if, recognizing the dilemma of the colonial writer, he could escape from the obligations of power by cultivating a purely aesthetic view, by reducing everything to "form and color." Yet ultimately he cannot avoid his identity with North American interests: his treatment of Mexico as a painter's canvas produces only a more refined version of the aesthetic which sees the essence of Mexico in song and romance. This aesthetic functions as a form of colonization in itself, relegating Mexico to the status of an object to be appreciated for its beauty, pathos, and passion. Simultaneously, however, this cultivation of an aesthetic ideal opens up a space for domination in the realm of concrete practice. When Mexico is removed by interpretation from the actual consequences of political and economic power, the capitalist and the archaeologist can more readily go about their business. Didion and Crane both resort to metaphors of art in the face of uncertainty concerning their own right to judge the real. Motivated by a primarily creative impulse, they nonetheless see this impulse as limiting their experience of social reality, as if the apprehension of this particular truth lay somewhere beyond the vision of the artist. Artists cast as reporters, they are unsure of their ground.

John le Carré, another novelist playing the role of journalist, avoids this dilemma by simply treating his reportorial experience as an episode from one of his own novels. It is as if, recognizing from the start that any journalistic account is essentially a fictional representation in the sense of *fictio*—a making—le Carré were to take this principle as license to interpret political reality according to novelistic formulas. The result is not, as in Crane and Didion, the invocation of art forms merely as metaphors for the real, but rather the complete reformulation of the real within the limits of a particular artistic genre.

Le Carré's 1982 interview of Yassir Arafat, written for the *Boston Globe*, distributed by the *Los Angeles Times* syndicate, and printed in the *Chicago Tribune* among other papers, is remarkable for the degree to which it reproduces the conventions of his own novels of espionage. Writing in the familiar British tone of urbane bemusement, le Carré presents himself in the first person as a slightly shabby figure mired in a world of absurd logistical detail: his efforts to make contact with Arafat entail a series of cryptic telephone calls, missed appointments, and nervous encounters with mysterious Arabs. An abortive visit to the residence of the PLO representative in London results only in the surveillance of the author by a closed-circuit television camera: "I imagined . . . yet another muddy photograph of myself entered in some far-off Whitehall file." Le Carré casts himself as one of Smiley's people, contemptuous of bureaucratic authority, yet resigned in the face of its power to brutalize human feeling.

Finally, in Beirut, after another round of frustrated connections, le Carré is suddenly whisked away to meet the PLO leader:

> Getting there is still a blur. Dead of night. A succession of brown Volvos with aerials, hurried changes in little courtyards, the wet rattle of machine guns as the guards hopped in and out beside me. . . . Enter a building, climb a staircase lined with fighting men, everyone smoking, and the windows are heavily curtained. Now we are in a ruin, now in a Hilton-style L-shaped drawing room with orange nylon carpets crackling with static. (June 20, 1982)

Arafat sits at a desk at the end of this room. He does not look up as the guards enter with the British interviewer, but continues signing letters. Conscious of his host's theatrical timing, le Carré incorporates this staginess into the theatricality of his own narrative, with its hurried body searches and swift passages, at gunpoint, through checkpoints in the bombed-out city. His narrative has a dual mimetic function, simultaneously imitating the lived experience of being there in Beirut and the literary world of the novels to which he implicitly refers. Le Carré's article is about both Arafat and *The Little Drummer Girl*, taking art and life together as its undifferentiated subject.

Le Carré's modernism lies partly in this conflation of realism and self-parody, partly in the opposition he establishes between the atavistic heroism of the Palestinians and the banality of contemporary life in the West.

Passing a Palestinian checkpoint, he observes the guerrillas, some of whom "looked old enough to remember T. E. Lawrence," sitting around a brazier as if it were a campfire "to keep away the animals." It is not by coincidence that le Carré invokes the name of Lawrence, for his Arabs, like Lawrence's, possess a courage and authenticity that are made to seem anachronistic in an age of television, Hilton hotels, and Whitehall files. These Palestinians speak with biblical simplicity. "We are exiles," one of them tells le Carré, "therefore we have only our country to love." Arafat himself declares, "Sir, I am a man of history. . . . I believe in the justice of our cause." Le Carré recalls that in an earlier interview, a "bold lady journalist" had asked Arafat whether he was homosexual. He had replied, with dignity, that he was married to Palestine. Taken in the context of le Carré's romantic characterization of Arafat, this reply does more than simply evade an indiscreet question. It implicitly reproves a contemporary world that has lost its sense of destiny and therefore its capacity for heroism. In le Carré's case, the experience of the Western journalist in the postcolonial setting provides not only new material for his novelistic conventions, but also the occasion for a new formulation of the modernist aesthetic. Treated in this way, the passionate intensity of Third World revolutionary movements offers a momentary escape from the ennui of everyday life in the West.

I have spoken of aestheticization in journalism as distantiation, transformation, privilege, displacement, consumption, and alienation. Taken together, these terms imply a certain possession of social reality which holds it at arm's length and makes it into the object of beauty, horror, pleasure, and pity. When this act of possession becomes a mode of representation by which a powerful culture *takes* possession of a less powerful one, it can be understood quite literally as colonization. In this sense, aestheticization does not so much falsify as it takes hold of and commodifies reality, securing it for the expansion of the observer's sensibility.

This expansion of sensibility made possible in aesthetic interpretation urges a final qualification of what I have said concerning the limiting and alienating power of that interpretation and recalls Derrida's argument concerning the space for imagination and reflection opened up by dramatic representation. At the risk of sabotaging my own argument, I shall cite one more passage to suggest that this mode can be liberating as well as distancing.

Writing for the *New Yorker* in 1984, Alex Shoumatoff visits the Ituri rain forest of the upper Congo region, the scene of Stanley's *In Darkest Africa*, of Conrad's *Heart of Darkness*, and of V. S. Naipaul's *A Bend in the River*. Where Stanley's expedition in 1891 had consisted of five European officers commanding 170 African soldiers and carriers, the journalist for the *New Yorker* has as his only companion a man named Gamaembi, a member of the local BaLese tribe. At one point, as the two men are walking along a jungle path, Gamaembi asks Shoumatoff, in French, if America's forest is like the Ituri:

> "No, not exactly," I said. "It isn't as thick with shrubs and vines. There aren't so many kinds of trees, and it isn't so green."
>
> Gamaembi's response was to turn over a leaf with a silver underside.
> "This is another leaf," he said. (February 6, 1981)

"This is another leaf." The BaLese's response creates a radical dislocation in the governing logic of the dialogue which has the liberating effect of imaginative play. The American journalist has spoken the language of empirical mastery over nature, commenting on the relative density of forestation and on the variety of species that distinguishes one part of the world from another. Gamaembi's response is both "out of it" in respect to this view of the world and profoundly "with it" in the sense that his speech seems to emerge from a complete absorption in the presence of the natural object. The discontinuity of the dialogue has an effect similar to the image of the blue Adidas bag among the Trobriand islanders: both mark a rupture in the discourse and become the occasion for an inventive reevaluation of the relation between cultures.

To characterize the African as a kind of mystical poet of his surroundings is no doubt an aestheticization in itself which removes him from a concrete historical reality. But this aestheticization also opens the way for a certain freedom in imagination and reflection. The African Gamaembi has allowed the observer, for a moment, to stand outside himself and to consider the limits of his own view of nature. This is indeed another leaf, another page in the book of the real as it reveals itself to us: the tribesman in darkest Africa suggests to us a different way of being alive.

4   CLASSIFICATION

The Order of Nations

IN A 1984 COVER STORY ON AFRICA, *TIME* PROVIDES A classic example of the survival of colonial discourse in the postcolonial era. The story reports on "the pattern of failure that has gripped the continent" since its independence from European colonial powers in the 1960s and measures this failure by both political and economic standards. In the political arena, nascent democracies have given way to assassinations, purges, and coups. African nations have fared no better economically and technologically, having allowed their "colonial inheritance"—the roads, railways, and cities built by Europeans—to deteriorate. Only a handful of these nations have achieved political stability, which requires "a mixed economy, a strong, pragmatic central government, and evolving democratic institutions, however imperfect." *Time* concludes this analysis with a call for civic responsibility among Africans, as well as its own prescription for Africa's troubles:

> A quarter-century after *Uhuru!*, African leaders must recognize that anti-colonial rhetoric may win votes, but it will not solve problems. . . . The positive legacies of the past must be emphasized, while new ideas are tested to deal with the problems of the present and future. . . . Africans must accept the essential requirement of political stability. Without that resolve, nationhood in Africa will too often be, as it has been in the past, a sad parody of itself. (January 16, 1984)

Africa's problems are indeed grave, and one might assume that Africans themselves do not need *Time* to tell them so. My concern, however, is not to analyze Africa, but to analyze analysis, that is, to examine the rhetorical position from which Africa is analyzed, judged, and admonished.

Time's presentation relies on a number of rhetorical features characteristic of much Western writing on the Third World: first, the condescending tone, which lectures Africans on how they should govern themselves. The failures of Africa are attributed, by implication, to the African character rather than to historical causes, as if Africans were somehow incapable of comprehending the value of political stability. Second, *Time* sets forth a single standard of economic and political organization to which all nations must aspire; there is no sense that different cultures may require different institutions of social order. Finally, there is the classification of nations according to their relative failure or success in meeting this standard, providing a hierarchy of political configurations while plotting these "evolving" institutions in the temporal dimension along a single line of development: African societies are more or less distant from the desired model according to how far they have advanced along this line. In his study of the temporal paradigm in anthropology, Johannes Fabian shows that the evolutionary sequences assigned to different cultures in the nineteenth century were closely linked to European policies of European colonialism and imperialism (16–17). *Time*'s analysis suggests the survival of the paradigm in the postcolonial world: the essentially political relation between Western nations and Africa is recast and naturalized as a temporal relation which has its roots in the social evolutionism of the Victorian era.

In this chapter I examine the nature of classification itself as a rhetorical procedure by which Western writing generates an ideologically charged meaning from its perceptions of non-Western cultures. In doing so, I shall trace a certain genealogy of classification which draws together disparate strands from the history of science, the language of colonial administration, and the postcolonial ideology of modernization.

We must not imagine, writes Foucault in *L'Ordre du Discours*, that the world offers to us a readable face that we have only to decipher. The world is not an accomplice to our knowledge. We must think of discourse as a violence that we do to things or as a practice that we impose on the world (1971:55). Every discourse orders itself both externally and internally: it marks itself off against the kind of language it excludes, while it establishes within its own limits a system of classification, arrangement, and distribution. The rational discourse of Western knowledge opposes reason to madness and truth to falsehood, placing its enterprise on one side of each such antithesis. Internally, the same discourse organizes the universe into disciplines, each with its own teratology which refuses the eccentric, the abnormal, and the monstrous in favor of those propositions that inscribe themselves within the theoretical horizons recognized by the discipline. A statement can lay claim to truth, Foucault says, only by obeying a discursive police. Within the realm of discourse, classification performs this policing function, assigning positions, regulating groups, and enforcing boundaries.

While this regulatory function of classification is always present, the nature of classification itself changes with the evolution of discourse. In *The Order of Things*, Foucault cites the example of natural history as it evolves from the Renaissance to the end of the classical age in the eighteenth century. In the Renaissance, to write the natural history of a plant or an animal was not merely to describe its elements or organs, but also to discuss "the virtues it was thought to possess, the legends and stories with which it had been involved, its place in heraldry," and so forth (1970:129). By the time of the naturalists Linnaeus, Lamarck, and Buffon, such *litteraria* had been excluded from scientific discourse, which now limited itself to a classificatory system devoted to the arrangement of things in a "table." This is what Foucault calls the "squared and spatialized" development of natural history.

At the end of the classical period, classification had moved beyond the mere nomination of the visible to the establishment, for each natural being, of a *character* based on the internal principle of organic structure. This principle gave rise to a system of ordering that allowed for a hierarchy of characters depending on their relative complexity of organic structure and for classification according to certain key functions: how a species reproduces or what it eats. To classify therefore meant no longer simply to arrange the visible, but to perform a circular analysis that related the visible to the invisible, its "deeper cause," then rose again toward the surface of bodies to identify the signs that confirmed the hidden cause. Such a system of understanding—one that orders natural beings according to function and establishes a hierarchy based on internal character—has consequences for the classification of human races in the Western mind and ultimately for the analysis of Third World societies in Western writing.

Charles Darwin's *Journal of Researches* (1839), written during the voyage of the H.M.S. Beagle to South America, belongs to an era in which travel writing, scientific observation, and natural philosophy could still be combined in the same work. It shows how completely the principles of observation and classification in natural history were adaptable to the study of human races. Describing a group of Indians at Tierra del Fuego, Darwin finds them "stunted in their growth, their hideous faces bedaubed with white paint, their skins filthy and greasy, their voices discordant, their gestures violent and without dignity" (1839:235). These Fuegans apparently have no homes, but sleep on the wet ground, and subsist on a miserable diet of shellfish, berries, and fungi. They seem to have no government or head.

In the manner of any naturalist of his age, Darwin moves from these visible signs and functions to the invisible character of his object. He doubts that the Fuegans have feelings of domestic affection and wonders whether they experience any pleasure in life at all: "How little can the higher powers of the mind be brought into play? What is there for imagination to picture, for reason to compare, for judgement to decide upon?" (235). This baseness of character, deduced from the relation of the visible to the invisible, is then projected back onto the concrete and observable: Darwin suggests that the technical skill of the Fuegans can be compared only to the instinct of animals, for the poor design of their canoes has remained the same for two hundred and fifty years. The analysis of character finally permits Darwin to classify the Fuegans among other human societies. He finds that here "man exists in a lower state of improvement than in any other part of the world." Even the South Sea Islander is more civilized, as is the Eskimo, who at least enjoys some of the comforts of life and shows skill in the design of canoes. Only the Australian aborigine comes nearest the Fuegan "in the simplicity of the arts of life." For Darwin, the hierarchy of human societies is thus established principally by technology, and by the nature of social and political organization: "If the state in which the Fuegans live should be fixed at zero in the scale of government . . . New Zealand would rank but a few degrees higher, while Tahiti, even when first discovered, would have occupied a respectable position" (502).

Both here and in his later, more advanced work, the contour of Darwin's thought reflects the "squared and spatialized" development of natural history, in which the objects of nature are arranged in spatial configuration—a scale or a table—which is then projected onto the temporal dimension. For Darwin, the map of the world is a great table which places the various peoples side by side, while his investigation of their functions and characters shows them to exist at different stages in a process of improvement whose end or highest point is represented by modern European civilization. The principle in natural history of internal organic structure is thus transferred to the classification of humanity in two ways, referring to moral or intellectual character in the human mind as well as to the social and political character of human society. These two subjects of valuation, moreover, remain intimately connected insofar as the higher orders of technology and government reflect a greater capacity for reason and human feeling.

The dual axes of time and space in Darwin's thought create a tension which sees humanity as historically capable of improvement, but which also reifies the existing hierarchy of human societies. The notion that societies can be classified according to their degree of advancement along the same path works, paradoxically, to support the notion of inherent ethical differences among races, that is, differences in *character*. The nineteenth-century debate over human race and evolution reflects this tension between an essentialist and an historical view, yet the two views tend to reinforce one another when it comes to a system of classification for the actual state of peoples.

One way to explore the dimensions of this debate is to compare Darwin's ideas with those of Joseph-Arthur, Comte de Gobineau, the diplomat, novelist, and historian for whom European interest in non-Western peoples provided the occasion for ethnic propaganda. In his *Essai sur l'Inégalité des Races Humaines* (1854), Gobineau divides humanity into three races which, for as long as they remain genetically distinct, will always be marked by basic differences in character indicated by bodily signs. For the black, "the animal character imprinted in the shape of the hip-girdle marks his destiny from the moment of birth. He will never develop beyond the narrowest range of mental powers." His voracious appetite, indiscriminate sensuality, and unstable emotions make him a "human machine" that is both dangerous and cowardly. The yellow race is superior to the black, but characterized by feeble desire, lassitude, and passivity. As a people, the members of this race form a malleable raw material that "any civilizer might willingly choose for the base of his society, although they would not suffice for the actual creation of such a society, nor lend it the qualities of energy, beauty, and action." Superior to the black and the yellow, the white race is characterized by energetic intelligence, perseverance, physical strength, an instinct for order, and a pronounced taste for liberty which despises on one hand, "the rigid social forms under which the Chinese willingly sleep, as well as the severe despotism which alone can restrain the blacks" (1:215–216).

Where Darwin sees the social and moral inequalities among races as produced by differences in the evolving human relation to natural environment, Gobineau sees them as "native, original, sharply defined, and permanent" (1:35). For Gobineau, one cannot identify the European race with the other two even in an evolutionary past, for the white race has never existed in the purely primitive state: "From the very beginning, it appears as relatively cultivated and in possession of the principle elements of a superior state which, developed later in its multiple branches, would become the diverse forms of civilization" (1:231). The European race, in other words, has *always already* been superior and innately civilized. Although Gobineau's ideas conflict with Darwin's on the question of social evolution, both positions were appropriated by the ideology of colonialism, which insisted on the essential superiority of the European colonizer as well as on the ideals of a civilizing mission bent on improving the moral condition of the colonized.

In another version of the nineteenth-century debate, the exchange between Thomas Carlyle and John Stuart Mill over the problem of black labor in the British West Indies shows how both authoritarian and humanitarian ideas can contribute to a fundamentally colonialist position. Published in the December 1849 issue of *Fraser's Magazine*, Carlyle's "Occasional Discourse on the Nigger Question" argues that the blacks, both for their own good and for that of the empire, must be compelled to work for whatever wages the white plantation owners are able to pay, and that the natural superiority of the British colonists ought to be sufficient justification for their mastery over the darker race. He thus presents a position at once racist, essentialist, and Platonic: "If precisely the Wisest Man were at the top of society, and the next-wisest next, and so on until we reached the Demerara Nigger (from whom downwards, through the horse, etc., there is no question hitherto), then were this a perfect world, the extreme *maximum* of wisdom produced in it" (15). In other words, nature has already determined a hierarchy of humanity which government, in the case of the West Indies, would be wise to act upon. In this ideal view of things, power follows reason, and history follows nature.

Mill's reply (January 1850) argues for the natural rights of the black race, but takes for granted their actual backwardness and lack of civilization. Mill acknowledges the great gulf that separates the African from the European, but does not attribute it to an *original* difference. Rather it is a matter of the European having advanced further in "the history of human improvement" and "the progress of science" (39). In the tradition of natural history, Mill proposes that the same methods of analysis used to discover "the laws of external nature" be applied to investigate "the laws of the formation of human character." Such an investigation would show, he argues, that differences in human character are as much the result of historical accident and external influence as of original nature: what makes the European civilized where the African is not can be attributed to an extraordinary and fortunate combination of circumstances. Thus insofar as it defines human character, nature follows history. However, while rejecting the essentialist and authoritarian doctrines of Carlyle, Mill nonetheless accepts the notion of racial hierarchy implicit in Carlyle's position. Mill's own argument is that black Africans can be improved not by being forced to work against their will, but by sharing in the benefits of European civilization.

The fundamental principle of relative degrees of *complexity* governs not only the rhetorical opposition between civilized and savage states, but also the hierarchical classification of humanity along a series of gradations ranged between the two poles of civilization and savagery. Though they differ on the question of where to locate the origin of differences in complexity, both Mill and Carlyle assume that human character and society are to be classified according to this measure. Again, it is an assumption they inherit from the natural history of the classical age. Foucault cites the theories of the eighteenth-century naturalist Jean-Baptiste Robinet, who posits a continuity of natural species ranging between an extremely simple, archaic prototype and the ultimate complication of this model in the form of the human being: "Between these two extremes there lie all the possible degrees of complexity and combination—like an immense series of experiments, of which some have persisted in the form of continuing species and some have sunk into oblivion" (1970:155).

Given the expansion in the knowledge of nature that accompanied the exploration and colonization of new territories in the nineteenth century, the principles of natural history inevitably provide paradigms for the rhetoric of colonial rule. We find, for example, that the principle of relative human complexity acquires a very practical value in the writing produced by colonial administrators. The British administration of South Africa in 1903 faced the immediate problem of governing a Boer population whose armies had just been defeated in war. For John Buchan, a member of that administration, the solution to this problem lay in an understanding of the Boer character which placed it only just above the level of the native black African. "In the case of a savage or a backward nation," Buchan writes of the Boers, "the history is simple, the ingredients in racial character few and intelligible." In such cases the nature of the society as a whole can be read in the individual, the entire race being "little more than the individual writ large." In complex societies such as the British, by contrast, "the composition is a chemical process, the result is a new product, not to be linked with any ingredient; the soul and mind of the populace is something different in kind from the average soul and mind of its units" (60).

In Buchan's mind, the simplicity of the Boer makes him ideal for the complex designs of British colonialism. Governing the Boers is "a simple problem" to the administration that understands them properly, while if the Boers are won over to the British side, "we shall have secured one of the greatest colonising forces in the world." Buchan's idea is that this simple, stubborn Boer could be settled on the colonial frontiers, thus insuring that the plateaus of Britain's Central and East African possessions would "be permanently held by the white man." The Boer, in other words, is a kind of white Kaffir who, though existing nearly at the level of the black native, can be used as an instrument of subjection for the benefit of a more highly civilized white society. The logic of this plan, of course, depends on a natural hierarchy that places the black African, the Boer, and the British colonist at successively higher stages on the scale of individual and social complexity.

The classification of indigenous peoples according to their relative complexity of social organization becomes more systematic and articulated as it directly serves the interests of colonial administration. Frederick Lugard divides the natives of British Tropical Africa into three classes: primitive tribes, advanced communities, and Europeanized Africans. The primitive tribes range in social status from those who still live in the patriarchal stage, recognizing no communal authority, to those with well-defined tribal institutions. The former, Lugard writes, are subject to cruel superstition and degrading practices such as cannibalism and human sacrifice. Those who have reached the tribal stage have more highly developed systems of authority, but lack a written language or "any approach to culture." Their political organization often takes the form of a despotism marked by "a ruthless disregard for human life" (75).

The more advanced communities have benefited from the political and social influences of Islam brought by Arab conquest. The Africans who comprise such communities have been improved by the admixture of Hamitic or Aryan blood and "may therefore claim to be of a superior race-type" than the aboriginal blacks of the primitive tribes. Here Lugard echoes both the letter and the spirit of Gobineau, who considered the mixture of Hamitic and Aryan blood with black Africans as fatal to the ancient Egyptian and Assyrian civilizations, but as beneficial to the blacks of northern Africa (1:350–351). These advanced African communities, according to Lugard, have a written language, a recognizable culture, and a relatively complex government, including systems of taxation and courts of justice.

The Europeanized African typically has been educated in England and returns to Africa to practice one of the professions, such as law—a choice which, Lugard writes, "affords opportunity for the African's gift of oratory"—and journalism. He imitates European dress and customs and has little in common with the indigenous tribes. "He must be treated—and seems to desire to be treated—as though he were of a different race."

This system of classification is indispensable to the ideology of colonization as well as to the actual practice of colonial rule. On the level of ideology, it serves to demonstrate the fundamental justice of the colonial enterprise by ranking native peoples according to their relative degree of technical and political sophistication as seen from the European point of view. On a practical level, these distinctions are made in order to show that each category of native requires its own administrative tactic.

In a view considered progressive for its time, Lugard acknowledges the need for direct British administration over the most primitive peoples, but he proposes a policy that would encourage tribal cohesion and the "education of the tribal heads in the duties of rulers," so that the colonial administration of these tribes would become gradually more indirect, more efficient, and thus more powerful. In the case of the advanced communities, Lugard recognizes the strategic value of the internal authority exercised by native rulers; he urges that this authority be turned to the advantage of colonial power by a process of co-optation in which the native chiefs would constitute "an integral part of the machinery of the administration." He holds up as a model the French colonization of Morocco, where General Louis Lyautey introduced the principle of collaboration with the native chiefs, and "by this means he everywhere conciliated the populations he subdued" (228).

Finally, for the Europeanized African, Lugard proposes the formation of a Cadet Service that would prepare natives for positions in the colonial Civil Service. Here the model is the Anglicized Indian who, however separated from the native masses in education and habits of thought, yet speaks their language and knows their country. Lugard's procedures of classification may be seen as emblematic of colonial discourse as a whole, which everywhere imposes a system of nomination, of identity and difference. This classificatory system by its very structure serves to make colonial power more universal and more internally thorough: it is a colonization that administers the order of thought itself.

The views of colonial administrators like Buchan and Lugard reflect an early form of the ideology of modernization that still governs the classification of Third World nations in the postcolonial era. Although the ideology of the modern has replaced an earlier ideology of the civilized, this newer system of value performs essentially the same function of classifying human societies according to Western standards of technological and political advancement. Political analysts such as Zbigniew Brzezinski and Samuel P. Huntington have defined modernization as the process which transforms a traditional, "pretechnological" society into one marked by the technology and economy of the machine, rational and secular concepts of authority, and a high degree of differentiation within the social structure.

As with the theory of natural evolution, the stages of advancement in the direction of modernization are seen as having the inevitability and irreversibility of history itself. Such is the understanding of Huntington, who has identified a number of key components of the modernization paradigm. In a summary of Huntington's theory provided by Jeane Kirkpatrick, modernization is described as a continual process: complex in its extension into all aspects of human life; systemic in the necessary and predictable interaction of its elements; global in that it eventually transforms all societies; lengthy in the time it requires; phased in that every modernizing society must pass through the same stages; homogenizing in that modernizing societies tend toward convergence and interdependence; irreversible in that the elements of the process determine a given direction of change; and finally, progressive in its ultimate benefit to humanity (Kirkpatrick 39).

It may be that the end of the classical colonial period has made the ideology of modernization both more central and more finely articulated in Western administrative policies and in the language of the press, for in the absence of direct colonial rule, it is the legitimacy of this ideology that justifies the pursuit of Western interests in the affairs of the Third World. In any case, modernization in the late twentieth century has become the standard of measure for an evolutionary continuum in which nations are classified as more or less developed forms of a single species that reaches its highest degree of refinement in the Western postindustrial state, or what Brzezinski calls the "technetronic" society.

Writing for the *Atlantic Monthly* in September 1982, the journalist Xan Smiley classifies African nations according to slightly different criteria. He divides the fifty member nations of the Organization of African Unity into a handful that have "marginally progressed," a few more that are only "marking time," and the vast majority that "have actually gone backward" since independence. Progress here means that "the average citizen of these countries enjoys a better all-round living now than before the colonial shackles were shed; more people are educated; health services have expanded." The fact that only a few African nations can claim even such modest gains is the fault of the Africans themselves: "The overwhelming reason for Africa's grim failure is that the continent is very badly governed by the Africans."

This argument follows a logical structure curiously analogous to the method revealed by Foucault in the classifications of natural history. In this case, certain measurable qualities of the object—type of government, economic production, the literacy rate—lead to the definition of its less observable organic *character,* a character whose identity is then reasserted in a movement back to the visible phenomena which tend to confirm it. Thus Smiley's analysis moves from citing the obvious failures of Africa to identifying inherent weaknesses in an abstracted African people and society: "Material glitter is cherished, but the boring, methodical rigor with which nations are built, and the dreary civic obligations that give cement to political decisions, are somehow to be dispensed with." If you want proof of this feeble character, Smiley says in effect, you have only to look at Africa as it is: the deterioration of infrastructure, the inefficiency of bureaucracy, the persistence of tribalism, the spread of disease and famine. The undeniability of these afflictions is offered as demonstration of the African's moral and social inferiority.

This weakness of African character is not something discovered or revealed to a pure, unfettered eye, but rather is determined by the logical order followed by Western observation and by the system of classification that governs the procedures of observation. In other words, the order that classifies non-Western peoples according to the paradigm of modernization contains within it, already and as a given, the judgment of their character. Yet the emphasis on observable phenomena obscures the way in which such observation is ordered in advance, a misrecognition that allows interpretation to pass for objective truth. Classification is a form of what Heidegger calls "enframing"—the process by which the mind transforms the world into an object. Yet "enframing disguises even this, its disguising" (46).

The material I have cited here suggests that classification as a form of knowledge is never free of critical valuation, and that, at least in forms of writing such as journalism and administrative documents, this value-positing activity always takes place within a sphere of relations marked by the presence of power. What motivates the classification of Third World peoples is the need to define a coherent stance that ultimately will determine the nature of Western policies toward the Third World: investment or disinvestment, increased credit or higher interest rates, military intervention or diplomatic negotiation, aggressive aid or benign neglect.

My final journalistic example comes from a writer who appears to question the paradigm of modernization, but who does so from a position that ends by reaffirming the normative values implied by this paradigm. Writing in the *New Republic* (December 17, 1984), Elie Kedourie divides the nations of Africa and Asia into two political traditions: black Africa has inherited a tradition of tribal rule, while China, India, and the Islamic Middle East descend from a tradition of Oriental despotism. Neither tradition produces conditions favorable for modernization.

Tribal rule, according to Kedourie, can be described as "primitive government" in that it is "not intricate in its arrangement and . . . does not possess any great powers of resistance when faced with more sophisticated kinds of political and military organizations." Where such organizations have been imposed upon the tribal order, the result is not modern democracy but "despotisms more or less ruthless, more or less arbitrary, haunted by insecurity and suspicion." Tribal society, in this view, is marked not only by simplicity but by innate weakness; when faced with the demand of modernization for a sophisticated system of law and political representation, it merely collapses into tyranny.

Oriental despotism has a simplicity equal to that of tribal rule. "Where Oriental despotism exists, political sociology is extremely simple: there are two social groups, those who are ruled and those who rule." This binary division has produced such fear of government that the only possible political stance for those who are ruled is passivity. "But development is not compatible with passivity. Development requires that the passive subject be mobilized into activity." Kedourie finally sees little hope for these societies, because of their inherent lack of initiative and enterprise. The fundamental passivity of Oriental peoples makes it impossible to "energize" them.

Raymond Schwab has shown that the idea of Oriental despotism has its origins in eighteenth-century European thought, and that, despite efforts at refutation, it was actually strengthened by the renaissance in Orientalist studies of the nineteenth century. As an ethical and historical category, the idea gained in intellectual authority with G. W. F. Hegel's *Lectures on the Philosophy of History*, based on material presented in 1830 and 1831. For Hegel, despotism is the inherent and distinctive principle of the Oriental world, ruled by a supremacy of laws whose origin is external to the subjective consciousness of the individual. In the absence of internal sanctions arising from individual conscience, morality exists only by virtue of legislation and authoritarian rule. The moral order of China and India, for example, rules "not as the moral disposition of the *Subject*, but as the despotism of the *Sovereign*" (111–116). Although Hegel's concept of history is infinitely more refined than Gobineau's, his notion of the absence of subjectivity in the Oriental world may be compared to Gobineau's image of the yellow race as passive and lacking in desire. More interesting than this comparison, however, is Hegel's conclusion that, being destitute of subjective thought, the Oriental state of things is "imperishable, but it is in its very nature destined to be mixed with other races—to be conquered and subjugated" (115).

Kedourie's analysis shows how eighteenth- and nineteenth-century ideas of Africa and the Orient are revived in contemporary Western discourse concerning the Third World. The argument that development—meaning economic and political modernization—is not compatible with Oriental passivity simply reformulates the Hegelian notion of the imperishability of the Oriental world, which can be conquered and subjugated, but never energized from within.

Kedourie calls into question one tenet of the ideology of modernization, namely that this process necessarily must transform all societies; apparently some societies are simply frozen in their current state of evolution or may even be regressing toward more primitive states. But he nonetheless holds to the basic assumption of the modernist paradigm which posits a single standard of value according to which all societies may be measured. Their failure to meet this standard is inevitably traced to a characteristic lack: lack of complexity, lack of activity, etc., while notions such as complexity and activity are understood in a sense limited by the conventions of discourse. In his discussion of the distinction between simplicity and complexity in political order, Huntington writes, "Complexity may involve both multiplication of organizational subunits, hierarchically and functionally, and differentiation of separate types of organizational subunits" (18). But is an order in which different functions are assigned to different classes of individuals necessarily more complex than one in which various functions are combined in a single subject? How in truth does one measure complexity, activity, or knowledge in a manner not determined by the strategies of a given discourse?

The systems of classification commonly employed by the Western press have a simplicity of their own: they tend to equate social complexity only with modernization, to ignore the human costs of such modernization, and to exclude the possibility of any standard that could find positive value in a non-Western model. While the press still clings to a normative view of civilization essentially formed during the colonial era of the nineteenth century, anthropology and cultural criticism have attempted to point out the consequences of such a view for the quality of life in traditional Third World societies.

The price of modernization is alienation. The anthropologist Stanley Diamond sees in the modernizing process a breakdown in the "cultural integration" of what we call primitive societies, where traditionally an entire series of values—religious, economic, social, and magical—combine in the meaning of any single activity. To the extent that the individual in such a society serves several functions simultaneously—warrior, artisan, village elder, etc.—modernization limits the range of this participation through its inevitable division of labor. It also undermines such aspects of primitive or traditional society as the tolerance of deviance in culturally institutionalized forms, the celebration of the sacred and the natural in ritual, the respect for and direct engagement with the natural environment, and the right to socioeconomic support as a natural inheritance rather than as a privilege subject to the individual's value in terms of labor.

Like Diamond, Michael R. Real has written on the differences between modern and traditional societies in a way which suggests the great sacrifices involved in modernization. Real focuses on the problem of communication as a primary index to cultural difference. In cultural systems organized around agricultural or hunting-and-gathering activities, communication takes place aurally or face-to-face, while individual consciousness defines itself in terms of participation in natural life cycles. In industrial and post-industrial capitalist democracies, communication takes the special form of print and electronic mass media, while the individual becomes a consumer or producer of machine-made commodities. This fundamental economic difference brings into play an entire series of differences in value, where traditional societies in a given context may favor the aesthetic over the technological, the sensual over the rational, preservation over consumption, and mosaic over linear modes of thought (209–212). Modernization thus does not simply build upon a lack or an absence; its influence may be seen as disruptive or reductive, as well as constructive, for it seeks to transform ways of life that have a coherence and complexity of their own.

In the examples of Diamond and Real, we see that anthropology, like journalism, employs its own classifications in the interpretation of non-Western cultures; we have also seen that anthropology is open to the criticism that it distorts human activity by formulating it as an object to be studied. But at least the classifications of anthropology do not take for granted the otherwise pervasive assumption that modernization is always and everywhere to be desired, that it inevitably serves the well-being of humanity, and that nations of the Third World can be meaningfully understood according to a Procrustean set of Western categories. Some anthropologists have tried to show the enormous difficulty (and complexity) of transformations brought about by the introduction of modernization to these nations. A single sentence in Clifford Geertz's *The Interpretation of Cultures* suggests the scope of these transformations:

The attainment of independence, the overthrow of established ruling classes, the popularization of legitimacy, the rationalization of public administration, the spread of literacy and mass communications, and the propulsion willy-nilly of inexperienced governments into the midst of a precarious international order that even its older participants do not very well understand, all make for a pervasive sense of disorientation, a disorientation in whose face received images of authority, responsibility, and civic purpose seem radically inadequate. (220–221)

When one considers this truly awesome complexity, the facile division of nations into "types of government" or "stages of advancement" makes sense only as the crudest application of the ideology of modernization.

At the beginning of this chapter I set out to show a certain relation between the structures of scientific thought and ideology or, to use another set of terms, between knowledge and mythology. Yet despite this relation, it seems in the end that the two forms of discourse remain distinct, that the production of scientific knowledge moves along a line that only occasionally intersects with the production of popular mythology. In his essay on *Paris Match* in Africa, Barthes remarks that the rigorous efforts by ethnologists such as Claude Lévi-Strauss, Marcel Mauss, and André Leroi-Gourhan to break free from such ambiguous notions as "primitive" or "archaic societies" have been lost on the popular imagination, resulting in a seemingly irreconcilable divorce of science and mythology: "Science proceeds rapidly on its way, but the collective representations do not follow, they are centuries behind, kept stagnant in their errors by power, the press, and the values of order" (38–39).

5   DEBASEMENT

Filth and Defilement

IN COLONIAL DISCOURSE EVERY INDIVIDUAL WEAK-
ness has its political counterpart—uncivilized society, according to this
logic, being little more than the uncivilized mind and body writ large.
Hence a certain parallelism in the themes of debasement employed by the
discourse: the qualities assigned to the individual savage—dishonesty, suspicion, superstition, lack of self-discipline—are reflected more generally in
societies characterized by corruption, xenophobia, tribalism, and the inability to govern themselves. In the same way, social problems in health and
sanitation, unemployment, or population growth come to be associated
with individual filth, indolence, and sexual promiscuity. The belligerence
of Arab nations, we are told, can be traced to the violence and fanaticism
of the Arab character. Here synecdoche and metaphor combine, marking
the individual as both cause and emblem of a more general degradation.

What are the motives of this rhetorical debasement of the cultural Other?
In *Tropics of Discourse*, Hayden White connects it to the need for positive
self-definition in times of sociocultural stress. When notions such as "civilization" and "reason" are in danger of being called into question, their
definition, as well as their identification with a particular people, is established by pointing to their supposed opposites, to what can be designated
as "savagery" or "madness." White observes that for the ancient Hebrews
what we call wildness, insanity, or savagery were all part of the same evil
condition, which took the form of *species corruption,* a pollution of the natural order that God had established at the Creation. In their savage pride,
men like Cain, Ham, and Ishmael had violated this order and so became
progenitors to entire races known for their pollution. The marks of these
accursed races were the homeless life of the hunter, linguistic confusion,

and physical aberration in both color and size (162). The Old Testament example suggests that the accursedness of the Other, like the jeremiads of the prophets, has its origin in anxiety over the preservation of cultural order and in the need to designate the unknown by a set of signs which affirm, by contrast, the value of culturally established norms.

With the expansion of knowledge into those parts of the world which traditionally had served as places of savagery and wildness for the European imagination, White sees a progressive despatialization of the concept of wildness, with a compensatory process of psychic interiorization. The Freudian model locates savagery within us and implies a continual psychic colonization and propitiation of the dark forces of the unconscious.

Here I would argue that modern colonial discourse has produced a re-spatialization of the savage, or that it at least maintains, on the level of ideology, a projection of anxiety onto the racial and cultural Other that has always been part of the human imagination. The contributions of psycho-analytic theory, moreover, suggest that the interiorization of savagery does not simply replace a concept of the savage as *out there,* but rather takes place simultaneously with a process of symbolic elaboration that objectifies savagery, wildness, and animality in other human beings.

What I am calling debasement in colonial discourse is not entirely dis-tinct from the strategies of classification discussed in the preceding chapter, in that the object of debasement supplies the negative end of a system of value. In isolating this trope, however, I wish to concentrate on the active production of images inspired by the fear and loathing that lie at the heart of classificatory systems presented as the products of rational thought. This discursive production typically centers around a notion of *abjection,* as in the following formulation by the French colonial administrator Albert Sarraut:

> Without us, without our intervention . . . these indigenous popula-tions would still be abandoned to misery and abjection; epidemics, massive endemic diseases, and famine would continue to decimate them; infant mortality would still wipe out half their offspring; petty kings and corrupt chiefs would still sacrifice them to vicious caprice; their minds would still be degraded by the practice of base supersti-tion and barbarous custom; and they would perish from misery in the midst of unexploited wealth. (117)

In this constellation of images, misery and abjection are presented as two faces of the same condition, each serving as the sign of the other, so that the physical suffering of indigenous peoples can be associated with their

moral and intellectual degradation: disease, famine, superstition, and bar-
barous custom all have their origin in the dark precolonial chaos. Colonial
discourse requires the constant reproduction of these images in various
forms—a recurring nomination of the abject—both as a justification for
European intervention and as the necessary iteration of a fundamental
difference between colonizer and colonized.

The psychoanalyst Julia Kristeva has sought to establish a relation between the phenomenon of abjection in the individual human psyche and
the procedures of exclusion and vilification which enter into the hierarchy
of class difference. For Kristeva, the abject and its variants, such as filth,
defilement, incest, and sin, mark the boundary of the self and therefore
constitute the limits of the speaking subject:

> The abject is neither the subject nor the object. . . . It represents the
> crisis of the subject . . . insofar as it would not yet be, or would no
> longer be separated from the object. Its limits would no longer be
> established. It would be constantly menaced by its possible collapse
> into the object. It would lose definition. It is a question, then, of a
> precarious state in which the subject is menaced by the possibility of
> collapsing into a chaos of indifference. (1983:39)

Kristeva's "indifference" here is the *lack* of difference toward which there
is always a temptation to return, a temptation cut short by the laws of exclusion, such as the incest taboo, which serve to establish the structure of
the subject and a system of classification by which the subject wards off the
object and constitutes it as the Other.

A similar function of exclusion holds sway on the level of social organization. Kristeva cites the example of societies in which the religious ritualization of defilement is accompanied by a strong concern for separating
the sexes, which in practice means giving men rights over women. In such
cases women, although apparently relegated to a passive role, are held to
be untrustworthy "baleful schemers" from whom men must protect their
own identity and power. Though apparently victorious in this struggle between the sexes, the masculine sex nonetheless "confesses through its very
relentlessness against the other, the feminine, that it is threatened by an
asymmetrical, irrational, wily, uncontrollable power" (1982:70).

More problematically, Kristeva argues that in societies which fail to mark
this division of power between the sexes, there is a strong need for *other*
differences in power and social status to come into play. Thus the system of
endogamy in India, which requires that an individual marry within his or
her own group, produces, as if in compensation for this lack of difference,

a hierarchical caste system rigidly separating the pure from the impure, untouchable classes.

I do not wish to suggest that Kristeva's theory provides a rationale for colonial order as a natural consequence of normal human development. Not enough is known about the relation between the individual psyche and the structures of power inherent in any given social environment. The idea of abjection, however, offers an analogy between the symbolic structure of individual consciousness and the systems of representation at work in culture at large. Both structures appear to depend for their internal coherence on a symbolic exclusionary tactic: the horror of the Other, the repudiation of the scapegoat. In his analysis of the neurosis of modern civilization, Freud observes, "It is always possible to bind together a considerable number of people in love, so long as there are other people left over to receive the manifestations of their aggressiveness" (1961:61). Colonialism may be seen as an extreme form of this social condition, where the constant threat to a precariously established order serves to intensify, in rhetoric as well as in more material forms of oppression, the obsessive repudiation of the Other.

In connection with this threat to an established order, what I want to emphasize is the erotic element that remains present in the mechanism of scapegoating. The scapegoat, be it the maternal, the female, or the savage, represents not the object of a merely sadistic domination, but rather the object of a desire for the return to that state of undifferentiated passivity where the subject, "fluctuating between inside and outside, pleasure and pain, would find death, along with nirvana" (1982:64). The erection of a symbolic system—in social organization, in language, in ideology—establishes its terms of abjection and defilement in resistance to this terrifying desire.

In Western writing, the debasement of the Other often suggests a prohibition designed to protect the boundaries of Western cultural value against the forces of this destructive desire. On assignment from the *New York Herald* in 1873, Stanley set sail for the west coast of Africa, where he would join an expedition of the British Army engaged in subduing a tribe of rebellious Ashantis. En route to the theater of war, he stopped at Sierra Leone and recorded his impressions of African life under British colonial rule:

> If I were asked where I could find the most insolent, lying, thieving negroes, I should undoubtedly say at Sierra Leone. Through some strange caprice the English have permitted a colony of semi-civilised Africans to grow up in order to experiment, perhaps, how wild and

rank a colony of negroes can become when left to their own sinful and wicked devices, unchecked and uncurbed by the hand of law. The English will, perhaps, plead as an excuse that the climate is against the exercise of strong will; that no matter how valiant a man be in his intentions when he sets out to govern the blatant woolly-headed rabble of this colony, he will be prostrated before the unconquerable lassitude which the climate quickly engenders in him as soon as he sets foot on its shores. (1874:6–7)

Stanley's condemnation of the African is linked both to cultural necessity and to psychological danger. By criticizing a particular administration in the name of colonialism's fundamental values—civility, authority, law—he also betrays the deeply rooted fears of the European in Africa or Asia: the loss of will, the yielding to the forces of a wild and rank human nature. This nature in its most savage form lacks boundary or restraint, "unchecked and uncurbed by the hand of law." In Conrad's *Heart of Darkness*, the proof that Kurtz has been claimed by the powers of darkness is that he "lacked restraint in the gratification of his various lusts." Stanley sees a similar danger at Sierra Leone when he chastises the English for having given in to Africa's seductive and debilitating power—a power that lies not only in Africa's climate, but also in her sinful and wicked people. Aware of that influence which threatens European manhood, Stanley inverts the myth of Antaeus, whose strength was continually restored by contact with the Earth. Instead the European, as soon as he sets foot on African soil, risks prostration by an "inconquerable lassitude."

Seen in this context, the insistence on European standards of civility becomes an act of self-preservation against the danger of emasculation, while the struggle against the lotuslike powers of an unknown land becomes a defining characteristic of the discourse. Stanley constitutes the African as the abject and in doing so implies the precarious state of the European subject who is constantly menaced by the collapse into a chaos of indifferentiation. My point is that the obsessive debasement of the Other in colonial discourse arises not simply from fear and the recognition of difference but also, on another level, from a desire for and identification with the Other which must be resisted.

As one sees in Stanley's account of the situation at Sierra Leone, the principle of exclusion in rhetorical debasement has obvious political as well as psychological purposes, for the abjection of the savage has always served as a pretext for imperial conquest and domination. While this abjection had traditionally formed part of a mythic imagination, the nineteenth century elevated it to the level of scientific truth. In 1871, the first year of Stanley's search for Livingstone, Darwin published his *Descent of Man*, which included a discussion of the "low morality of savages." According to Darwin, the virtues of primitive peoples are limited to "social instinct"; their idea of good and evil does not extend beyond that which obviously affects the welfare of the tribe. They have no notion of the "self-regarding virtues" such as temperance, chastity, and physical decency, failing to perceive how the lack of these qualities indirectly affects the tribe as a whole. Thus "the greatest intemperance is no reproach with savages," and "utter licentiousness, and unnatural crimes, prevail to an astounding extent." Finally, the savage has little power of self-command, for this power has not been strengthened "through long-continued, perhaps inherited, habit, instruction, and religion" (1936:489).

As they are presented here, the immoral qualities of the savage have in common the failure to impose a series of distinctions necessary for modern civility. Individual virtue is not distinguished from the good of the tribe. Reason and passion, work and pleasure seem impossibly confused with one another. Nakedness is public as well as private, and the body itself is not kept pure of its own inner foulness. Stopping at Bahia Blanca (Argentina), Darwin finds it "impossible to conceive anything more wild and savage" than a group of Indian revelers who drink to intoxication and then, sick from drunkenness, cast up their suppers and are "besmeared with filth and gore" (1839:118). Here Darwin in his journal quotes (in Latin) Achaemenides' description of Polyphemus from Book 3 of the *Aeneid*: "The Cyclops, stuffed with food and drowned in wine, soon bowed his head and fell to the floor, a bulk elephantine, vomiting clots and bloody wine and bits of flesh as he slept."

This defilement of the self's clean and proper body, here explicitly characterized as monstrous and inhuman, marks the transgression of a crucial boundary between inside and out, between the self and that which it literally must exclude in order to maintain its difference from the Other. For Kristeva, corporeal waste, including everything from excrement to menstrual blood, represents, like an embodied metaphor, the frailty of a symbolic order based on difference. The savagery of the Indians at Bahia Blanca, like that of savages everywhere, lies in the threat that they are posing to such an order, thus making them as thoroughly abhorrent to Western civility as the Cyclops is to Virgil's readers. The lure of the savage, like the terrifying presence of the Cyclops, has a power which cannot be resisted by force alone. Rather, it can be eluded only through the craft of language and symbol. Colonial discourse thus may be understood as an evasive strategy, like the verbal ruse that delivers Ulysses from being literally swallowed up by the savage.

Darwin's theory that a higher morality has developed through evolutionary advancement is easily converted to the idea that the progress of civilization depends on the suppression or outright elimination of savage life. As a correspondent for the London *Daily Telegraph* in 1897, the young Winston Churchill covered the Imperial Army campaign against the native Mohmand tribes of the Indian Northwest Frontier. On one occasion, he finds that the enemy has disinterred and mutilated the bodies of Imperial native soldiers who had fallen in battle a week earlier. Contemplating this atrocity, Churchill invites the reader to consider "the degradation of mind and body which alone can inspire so foul an act":

> These tribesmen are among the most miserable and brutal creatures of the earth. Their intelligence only enables them to be more cruel, more dangerous, more destructive than the wild beasts. Their religion— fanatic though they are, is only respected when it incites to bloodshed and murder. Their habits are filthy; their morals cannot be alluded to. With every feeling of respect for that wide sentiment of human sympathy which characterises a Christian civilisation, I find it impossible to come to any other conclusion than that, in proportion as these valleys are purged from the pernicious vermin that infest them, so will the happiness of humanity be increased, and the progress of mankind accelerated. (1972:33–39)

The power of this genocidal rhetoric depends on the horror of the utterly abject, abjection occasioned in this case by the defilement of a sacred order. By disinterring and mutilating the bodies of their enemies, the Mohmands violate the boundaries between life and death, between the body and its dismemberment or disintegration into the indifferent chaos surrounding it. In the logic of Churchill's discourse, they have also violated yet another limit, that between the human and the animal. His final phrase seeks to restore that boundary by a rhetorical act of exclusion: having descended to the bestial, the Mohmands must be excluded from humanity, must, in fact, be exterminated altogether in order that the idea of humanity may retain its proper value.

The principles of exclusion, boundary, and difference which enter into the debasement of the primitive are connected to the fear that the white race could lose itself in the darker ones, so that the idea of "going native" has some of the powers of interdiction and attraction that one associates with the incest taboo. The supposed danger of the European's degeneration in the presence of the primitive becomes both the source and the pretext for an obsessive reprehension of the Other. Writing in 1910, W. H. Elliott of the London Missionary Society describes one Reed, a colleague who, in the early years of chartered company rule in southern Rhodesia, lived in a native hut and ate native food:

> His life presented in an acute form the experience of all missionaries to the heathen. He was pulling them up; they were pulling him down. He was a man at the edge of a horrible pit of miry clay endeavouring to rescue them that were engulfed below. By his rope of sympathy he tried to raise them to the solid ground whereon he stood; their dead weight operated to pull him into their disgusting slough. (Cairns 67)

This is colonial discourse as allegory, in which the crisis of the individual subject is elevated to the level of ideology and made into an object lesson for "all missionaries to the heathen." Reed's transgression is the betrayal of difference—not difference from the Africans themselves, represented here as capable of salvation, but from their degraded moral state. In allegorizing this tragic effacement of difference, Elliott's language simultaneously restores the terms of that difference, reestablishing rhetorically the boundary between civilization and savagery: hence the spatial opposition of ascent and descent; the nominative distinction between Reed, "a man," and the dehumanized "they" with whom he struggles; and finally, the symbolic difference between the solid ground of European civility and the debased slough of native life.

This rhetorical trope—the warning against the seductive dangers of the savage—surfaces throughout the colonial world in every form of writing: journalism, fiction, missionary narratives, and administrative reports. The year 1924 saw the publication both of E. M. Forster's *A Passage to India* and of a book by Lord Ronaldshay, former governor of Bengal, then secretary of state for India and Burma. Ronaldshay sees the attractions of primitive life as a threat to civilization itself:

> For a return to elemental life means also a return sooner or later to elemental emotions in all their crudity, and a rejection of the checks which civilization imposes upon them. Those who are incapable of bearing the burden of civilization will, if they can, wage war against it. That is why men of distorted genius who succumb to the lure of the primitive become a danger to society. (192)

Here the danger to society lies not in the primitive itself but in the perverted influence of the European who, like Kurtz, lacks restraint in the gratification of his lusts and combines a distorted genius with elemental emotion. The abhorrence of Indian life, then, involves not simply a rationale for colonial domination, but also the awareness of this in-between state, where the colonial subject threatens to become neither one thing nor the other, neither civilized nor savage, but strangely without definition.

"Abjection," writes Georges Bataille, "is merely the inability to assume with sufficient strength the imperative act of excluding abject things (and that act establishes the foundation of collective existence)" (Kristeva 1982:56). Thus from the point of view of colonial writers like Elliott and Ronaldshay, abjection consists not exactly in the condition of native life, but rather in the demoralizing crisis of *going* native, where the failure to mark the necessary bounds of exclusion is presented quite explicitly as filth and defilement. This act of exclusion, multiplied and elaborated in all its variants, establishes the foundation of a colonizing system.

If the act of going native represents one threat to this exclusionary principle, what happens when the natives, from their side, take on the manners and values of the European colonizer? In another paradox of colonial discourse, the natives are reviled for their non-Western otherness, yet ridiculed for their attempts to imitate the forms of the West. In an earlier chapter, we saw how Lord Lugard looked favorably upon Europeanized Africans or Anglicized Indians, whose knowledge of their own people made them useful as members of the colonial administration. This purely practical view, however, may be less common than that which expresses contempt for the Europeanized native, especially when the presence of such a person can be interpreted as undermining the established order.

In 1888, while Stanley's search for the Emin Pasha was providing the story of *In Darkest Africa*, Rudyard Kipling was writing about colonial life in Calcutta, "The City of Dreadful Night." At a marketplace which appears to be "the trysting place of Young Calcutta," he observes a Europeanized young Indian courting his lover:

> Pyramus carries a walking-stick with imitation silver straps upon it, and there are cloth tops to his boots; but his collar has been two days worn. Thisbe crowns her dark head with a blue velvet tam-o'-shanter; but one of her boots lacks a button, and there is a tear in the left-hand glove. (1970, 18:186)

In Kipling's exacting gaze, the native government clerk dressed up like an Englishman is not merely laughable, but a symbol of India's failure: those worn collars and missing buttons reassure him of the essential difference between these impostors and real Englishmen. In *A Passage to India*,

Forster satirizes this attitude in the character of Ronny Heaslop who, un-
aware of Aziz's sartorial sacrifice on behalf of Fielding, observes, "Aziz was
exquisitely dressed, from tie-pin to spats, but he had forgotten his back
collar stud, and there you have the Indian all over: inattention to detail;
the fundamental slackness that reveals the race" (82).

Kipling's amusement changes to indignation where the Anglicization of
the Indian involves more than buttons and collar studs. At a municipal
council debate, a long-winded Bengali representative argues for electoral
reform. Kipling comments ruefully:

> The speech continues. We made that florid sentence. That torrent of
> verbiage is Ours. We taught him what was constitutional and what
> was unconstitutional in the days when Calcutta smelt. Calcutta smells
> still, but we must listen to all that he has to say about the plurality
> of votes and the weaving of ropes in the sand. It is Our own fault.
> (1970, 18:186)

The repetition of the capitalized first person pronoun has an ironic use
here, making a proprietary claim while insisting on the essential difference between "us" and "them"—in other words, owning and disowning,
avowing and disavowing at the same time.

As the foul smell of Calcutta wafts through the Council Chamber,
Kipling expresses astonishment that the debate can even go on. Here is
where the disavowal, the insistence on the boundary, reasserts itself explicitly: "Why should Englishmen be forced to wander through mazes of
unprofitable argument against men who cannot understand the iniquity of
dirt?" The mazes of argument issuing forth in torrents of verbiage connect
the Indian's speech symbolically to the dark, winding streets of the city,
the flow of foul gutters and teeming rivers, and the flood of humanity that
populates the city. The stink of Calcutta is associated with the soiled collar of the young Indian dandy and to all the images of filth that colonial
discourse attaches to its representation of the Other.

This distancing gesture belongs to an inner economy of the discourse,
which must affirm the potential for civilization in colonized peoples while
holding them at arm's length. For Kipling, the domesticated Indian is a
kind of child of Frankenstein, both "Ours" and irremediably Other, a grotesque parody of civilized humanity. The very signs of the Indian's civility
give proof of a degraded nature, for only by seeing the Indian in this way
can the colonizer repel the challenge to ascendancy—a challenge made all
the more immediate by its presence in one of the chambers of political
power. In such instances one can see how the logic of colonial discourse

careers wildly from one position to its opposite: a colonized people is held in contempt for their lack of civility, loved for their willingness to acquire it, and ridiculed when they have acquired too much.

Despite a predominating ideology of modernization, more recent Western journalism has inherited this ambivalence over the eagerness of Third World peoples to take on the forms of the West. The desire for Western styles of consumption, for example, is seen as a natural aspiration toward a better life, while it is also treated as a sign of weakness. There is a certain contempt for non-Western peoples who appear so ready to abandon their traditions for Johnny Walker Scotch and Hollywood movies.

The journalist and novelist Shiva Naipaul, who is capable of satirizing European views of Africa, does not conceal his scorn for what he sees as the African's greed and materialism. Having just been hustled by a Nairobi shoeshine boy, he reflects on the history of the slave trade and on its stimulation of the African's "insatiable appetite" for gaudy Western goods:

> In its essence, the nature of the ties linking the African with the European has not really changed since the first Portuguese ships went sailing down the west coast of the continent: the sophisticated magic of the white man remains irresistibly alluring to the black. Transistor radios and cassette recorders have taken the place of glass beads and mirrors. (57)

For Naipaul, what distinguishes the postcolonial African from his ancestors is that he no longer fears and admires the European who has produced such wonders: "He . . . has neither wonder nor humility. He takes it all for granted. He is content with simple possession."

The theme of a frenzy for possession is applied to other non-Western peoples as well. "China Avid for Consumption" declares a headline in *Le Monde* over a story which reports on the manifestations of envy, avarice, and vandalism in a society which has just discovered the refrigerator and color television:

> With the appearance of durable consumer goods, symbols of a better life accessible to those who have money and connections, a feeling of envy on the part of the have-nots has come to light. . . . One witnesses more and more the development of a mentality according to which, if one cannot have a fridge or a t.v., there is no reason why others should have one. (June 26, 1985)

This view of the Chinese, while perhaps accurate in a limited sense, reflects a more general uneasiness over China's sudden embrace of Western things, as if the Chinese, like some tribal chieftain dazzled by mirrors and alarm clocks, failed to understand that these were *merely* things. What rough beast, the writer seems to ask, slouches behind the vision of a fully industrialized, consumerized China?

In referring to anxiety over the preservation of limit, boundary, and difference, I have in mind not only the notion of abjection, but also the fear of contamination that continually recurs as a theme in colonial discourse. In British India and Africa, European residential quarters were strictly separated from the native quarters for what were presented as sanitary reasons. In colonial Nigeria, Lord Lugard warned that yellow fever and malarial germs were present "in the blood of most natives." New townships were divided into European and native reservations separated by a 440-yard-wide buffer zone cleared of grass and scrub (called the *maidan* in India and inherited from the Moghul empire). To the charge, brought by Indians as well as Africans, that this policy of segregation was a manifestation of racial arrogance, Lugard replied that the policy favored neither race, for the European was as strictly prohibited from living in the native quarter as a native was from living in the European quarter. He added that the aim was a segregation of social standards rather than races:

> The Indian or African gentleman who adopts the higher standard of civilisation and desires to partake in such immunity from infection as segregation may convey, should be as free and welcome to live in the civilised reservation as the European, provided, of course, that he does not bring with him a concourse of followers. (149–50)

As the terms of Lugard's exception to the rule suggest, this fear of contamination is social and psychological as well as biological, a conflation that Frantz Fanon sees at the heart of negrophobia and that accounts for the colonizer's talk of "the stink of native quarters, of breeding swarms, of foulness, of spawn, of gesticulations" (1966:34). Here is the source of that entire constellation of images which, as we saw in the case of Albert Sarraut, combine social disorder, moral degradation, and epidemic disease under the name of abjection.

Sarraut and Lugard were writing at a late moment in the history of European colonialism, when Western journalists began to register alarm at the sheer numbers of people in non-Western countries, particularly in Asia, and at the prospect of mass emigrations to the West. In *La Foule d'Asie*, published in English as *Asia's Teeming Millions* (1931), Etienne Dennery writes that the end of the Great War signaled not only the decline of

Europe, but also the "twilight of the white races," which risked being over-run by the overpopulated East: "in the supply of men, Asia possessed vast reserves, masses that multiplied beyond all reckoning. Asia alone main-tained within her territories teeming races of mankind, more numerous than all the white peoples of all the other continents" (17). Dennery's prose is inspired by images of the Yellow Peril and of the stink of native quarters:

> Crowds in the great Chinese cities, half sunk in dirt and mud, swarm-ing like ants in dark, narrow, winding alleys, in which the sickening stench of decaying meat or putrid flesh ever lingers. Crowds that leave the solid ground of the towns to huddle upon the canals, rivers, and even the sea, in their little junks with their crooked sails, top-heavy with human cargoes. (19)

Dennery's language is dominated by images of malignant fusion: faces lost in crowds, crowds sinking into earth, the stink of flesh in enclosed air, ground mixing with water, the cities spilling over into the sea. This in-discriminate mixture of flesh with the unclean elements of nature is the essence of filth and defilement.

More recently, the fear of contamination that combines images of social and biological disorder has found expression even in the most well-meaning and factually conscientious writing on the Third World. Here my example is from a university town newspaper with a well-informed readership. A 1981 story in the *Chapel Hill Newspaper* (North Carolina) reports on a United Nations effort to clean up the water supply for countries in Latin America, Africa, and Asia. Drinking water in the Third World is often "teeming with microorganisms" that cause typhoid, dysentery, or cholera. Water and sanitation, the newspaper reports, are particularly poor in large urban areas such as Mexico City, Cairo, Djakarta, and Karachi, which at-tract a "continuing, massive influx" of people from rural areas who create "vast squatter communities where slum conditions make infectious dis-eases a fact of life." The United States' contribution to this international effort is a U.S. Agency for International Development project called Water and Sanitation for Health (WASH) (June 7, 1981).

No one would dispute the value of such a project for saving human lives nor the humanitarian motives of the engineers, scientists, and administra-tors who take part in it. A price for such humanitarian largesse, however, is paid on the level of representation, where the Third World is symboli-cally constructed as the site of filth and contamination. In the language of the newspaper story from Chapel Hill, the crowded populations of the Third World take on the teeming, spawning character of disease itself, with their "massive influx" into "vast squatter communities." Standard journalistic imagery here merges the human with the biological and constitutes a kind of demographic pathology in which the peoples of the Third World assume the role of a rapidly spreading malignant organism.

Within the framework of this pathology, one can reflect on the distinction between endemic and epidemic disease and on the analogy, latent in colonial discourse, with the distinction between indigenous and migrant populations. Indigenous peoples, like endemic disease, are localized, rooted in a given environment, and easily contained within controllable limits. Migrant populations share with epidemics (Greek *epi:* upon, in addition, + *demos:* people) mobility and proliferation, but also the quality of a dangerous supplement: they are *added to* a given natural or social environment, transgressing boundaries and wreaking ecological havoc. Such a description would apply, of course, only to migrant populations that have forsaken their formerly indigenous status, not to the supplemental character of the European colonizing population, whose effect on indigenous peoples tends to be seen as salutary rather than disruptive.

The association of the Third World with epidemic disease is epidemiologically sound, but metaphorically loaded. Perhaps few American journalists are more aware of such symbolic burdens than Alex Shoumatoff, yet even he manages to contribute to the traditional mythologization of Africa as the locus classicus of disease, moral disorder, and spiritual darkness. Originally published in *Vanity Fair*, his "In Search of the Source of AIDS" appears in a collection of reportorial pieces entitled *African Madness* (1988). Shoumatoff's journey is like those of Conrad's Marlow and the early European explorers of the continent, all of whom set off across the African landscape in quest of a revelatory moment, a primal scene, or a mythic origin. His purpose is to search for the historical and geographic source of AIDS somewhere in the African interior, as well as to describe the social and demographic conditions which have allowed this disease to flourish "like the plague, a living nightmare of the Apocalypse."

In keeping with the theme introduced in the book's title, Shoumatoff's travels to Kinshasa, Nairobi, Kampala, and other cities are punctuated by the same ululating cries heard in the streets at night—recurring "shrieks of madness and alienation" that connect one place to the next. Africa is a network of madness whose points are linked by the repetition, like telegraphic messages, of this primitive complaint straight out of Conrad, where Marlow hears "a cry, a loud cry, as of infinite desolation" (110). Shoumatoff's journey reaches an existential low at a place called Masaka, in Uganda:

> All the hotels are full, and we wander up and down through vermin-infested back alleys knocking on the doors of roach-infested hostelries. There is not a room to be had, but at last we find a place for me to sleep, a windowless basement pleasure dome with gaudy furniture and mirrors, probably the scene of a lot of [AIDS] transmission. "We get you one tonight?" the man at the desk asks. . . . The only place still open is a bar. We wash down chapatis with Bell beer. This is the most degenerate scene, the closest thing to Sodom I have ever seen. Guys, completely bombed, with girls on their laps, etc. Obviously nobody cares about getting AIDS. (194–195)

Dark, enclosed spaces, infestation, contamination, sexual and moral degradation: Shoumatoff invokes an ancient repertoire of images denoting evil and foreboding apocalyptic destruction. Breaking off from a coolly rational discussion of viruses and antibodies, Shoumatoff writes as if struck by a demoniacal vision: like the biblical whore of Babylon, the denizens of this godforsaken scene drink from the cup full of the filth of their fornications.

The spatial counterpart to this zero degree of moral value is the notion of an actual place to which the origin of AIDS can be traced. Shoumatoff knows the political sensitivity of this question and quotes researchers who dismiss the notion of a geographical source as both impossible to prove and irrelevant to the problem of treating the disease. Yet as if compelled by the tradition of other searches for other sources, he follows the lead of one researcher who writes that the "scientific signposts point to an origin in Africa, somewhere around the region of Lake Victoria." Thus we join our author as he travels through the Rakai district of Uganda, on Lake Victoria's western shore, which some believe is the place where AIDS originated. His path literally retraces the steps of Livingstone, Stanley, Burton, and Speke:

> The road leads on through marsh and pasture. We are dead on the equator, and the sun is incredibly hot. I imagine myself a latter-day Ponce de Leon, searching for the Fountain of Death. Or as Captain John Speke, about to discover Lake Victoria, the source of the White Nile. How curious it would be, I think, if the source of the Nile and the source of AIDS prove to be one and the same, that vast teeming lake deep in the dangerous heart of darkest Africa. (132–133)

This lyrical bow to Conrad acknowledges, however ironically, a kind of brotherhood with those other Western writers who have confronted in Africa the nadir of abjection and the face of horror. As Chinua Achebe has written of Conrad, here again Africa is presented as "a metaphysical battlefield, devoid of all recognizable humanity, into which the European enters at his peril. . . . It was and is the dominant image of Africa in the Western imagination" (788–792).

In the Rakai district, Shoumatoff passes through villages where large numbers of people are dying from AIDS. He meets the doctor of a clinic, himself weak and thin. "Shit, I realized, even the doctor's got it." The expletive seems to denote simultaneously the writer's astonishment, the stench of diarrhea in the air, the theme of filth and waste that pervades the narrative, and even, to borrow from Achebe, the metaphysical condition of the place. Shoumatoff's search for an endemic source of AIDS in the heart of Africa combines with a wide-ranging view of its epidemic proliferation. He speculates that in the early seventies, a time of mushrooming populations and tremendous social upheaval, the disease could have been "swept out of its hiding place in rural areas" and into the cities, where "new levels of promiscuity and a breakdown of health services enabled it to spread quickly," an expansion that found amplification in the homosexual bars and bathhouses of the West (139). One could say that Africa as described here is no less than a *machine* for the production of AIDS.

I do not wish to question the factual validity of the journalistic language cited here, but rather to point to the work that is carried out on the symbolic level while the reader is presented with information. In such stories, the peoples of the Third World are both reduced and magnified into the equivalent of natural disaster: influx, epidemic, inundation, the flooding of borders. The symbolic dimension of journalistic language constitutes these peoples as the source of an overwhelming and destructive vitality, while it levels and serializes the individual subject in Third World society. Mimicking the colonial view inherent in such imagery, Fanon writes of "those hordes of vital statistics, those hysterical masses, those faces bereft of all humanity . . . that mob without beginning or end" (1966:34). The fear of contamination that begins with the biological thus expands, through a scale of progression that moves both metaphorically and metonymically, into anxiety over the psychological perils of going native and finally into the dystopian view of vast social movements that threaten civilization itself. What Kristeva says of misogyny may also be said of this discourse, that it confesses through its very relentlessness against the Other that it is threatened by what it perceives as an asymmetrical, irrational, uncontrollable power.

6 NEGATION

Areas of Darkness

You see this egg
You see this egg
Well that's life on a crocodile isle.
—T. S. Eliot, *Sweeney Agonistes*

HAVING TRAVELED HALF WAY ACROSS THE CONTInent from the shores of Zanzibar in 1877, H. M. Stanley looked westward toward the Congo River, which he was about to descend in the first such voyage for a European expedition. His dispatch to the *New York Herald* contemplates a great void: "The largest half of Africa one wide enormous blank—a region of fable and mystery—a continent of dwarfs and cannibals and gorillas, through which the great river flowed on its unfulfilled mission to the Atlantic!" (1970:360). In a movement familiar to colonial discourse, Stanley combines the consciousness of absence with the structures of imagination and desire. The designation of the unexplored territory as a "wide enormous blank" gives way immediately to its transformation into mythology—"a region of fable and mystery"—as if the content of a collective fantasy were to rush in to fill the void left by Africa's essential nothingness. But in a final turning of the discourse, the temptations of both nothingness and fantasy are subsumed under the desire for conquest represented by the notion of the Congo's "unfulfilled mission." Thus the naming of an absence ultimately reveals itself as the presence of an ideological imperative.

In this chapter I explore the rhetorical strategy of negation by which Western writing conceives of the Other as absence, emptiness, nothingness, or death. This exploration leads to the formulation of two principles: first, negation serves to reject the ambiguous object for which language and experience provide no adequate framework of interpretation; second, as in Stanley's contemplation of the Congo, negation acts as a kind of provisional erasure, clearing a space for the expansion of the colonial imagination and for the pursuit of desire. In this way, the structures of discourse, in which language is divided, subordinated, and made into a working system, recapitulate the historical process of establishing and maintaining colonial rule.

The relation between absence and desire, or between nothingness and imagination, has to do with the very nature of writing. Derrida has written, "Desire desires the exteriority of presence and nonpresence." In other words, desire is connected to the principle of opposition between nonbeing and being, between lack and fulfillment. This dividedness at the heart of desire repeats itself, through language, in a series of oppositional concepts: being and nothingness, nature and its others, good and evil, innocence and perversity, consciousness and nonconsciousness, liberty and servitude, life and death (1976:167–168). This entire series or matrix, for Derrida, is writing itself, a system of distinctions erected across the otherwise empty space of the page. The writer is the original and ultimate colonizer, conquering the space of consciousness with the exclusionary and divisive structures of representation.

This metaphorical notion of the writer as colonizer ought to be considered as more than a mere figure of speech, given the practical role which writing plays in the actual processes of colonial expansion and administration. In fact the structures of writing and those of political power can never be wholly distinguished from one another, and the writer already colonizes that part of discourse which is subject to negation.

NEGATIVE SPACE

In the conclusion to his 1839 *Journal*, Darwin states that the vast, empty plains of Patagonia are among the scenes most deeply impressed in his mind:

> They are characterized only by negative possessions; without habitations, without water, without trees, without mountains. . . . Why then, and the case is not peculiar to myself, have these arid wastes taken so firm possession of the memory? . . . I can scarcely analyze these feelings: but it must be partly owing to the free scope given to the imagination. (1839:605)

Darwin goes on to compare the Patagonian plains to the ancient concept of a world surrounded by an impassable expanse of water or desert: "Who would not look at these boundaries to man's knowledge with deep but ill-defined sensations?" Darwin's discourse is at once outwardly descriptive and introspective: the question he asks is how the absence without can have such a powerful presence within him, how an inner something is created from outer nothingness. The ambiguous inner and outer spaces outlined here mark an early stage in the development of a modern trope which treats the colonized landscape as emblematic of the void which surrounds, or lies at the heart of, the human condition.

On one level, Darwin's image of a vast nothingness in Patagonia serves his official purpose, which one might call the colonization of the natural world by scientific knowledge. Through knowledge and discovery, he writes, "The map of the world ceases to be a blank; it becomes a picture full of the most varied and animated figures. Each part assumes its true dimensions." A scientific voyage like Darwin's partly satisfies "the want and craving, which . . . a man experiences although every corporeal sense is satisfied" (607). On another level, however, the contemplation of Patagonia fills the writer with a sense of the forbidden and the foreboding. Beyond the last boundaries of conscious thought, Darwin's language points to a region within himself that is "without habitation," a region of "ill-defined sensations" and feelings that can be "scarcely analyzed." These reflections come only at the very end of his journal, as if to acknowledge the limits of the positivist discourse which has brought him that far, but which cannot guide him through the indeterminate space that now opens before him.

Here Darwin anticipates Conrad's use of the savage landscape as a metaphor for modern anxiety and the unconscious. In *Heart of Darkness*, Marlow's youthful lust for adventure is fired by the "blank spaces on the earth" and in particular by "the biggest, the most blank" (70–71). As Christopher Miller notes, the name of this principal blank space is repressed in Conrad's narrative, the name of Africa being everywhere displaced by the ambiguous and portentous phrase which serves as the title of the text. By means of this displacement of the referent, Africa is no longer bound in time and space, but becomes the *figure* of darkness and nothingness. This figure serves at least two functions: it transfers historical and geographical space onto metaphysical ground while, working from the other side, it transforms nothingness into the substantial unity of time and space embodied in narrative form. Conrad's achievement is precisely this "congealing of nothingness into a figure" (Miller 1985:176).

Miller adds that a thread running through the Africanist tradition in European literature is "the writer's experience of alienation from his own meaning, of alienation as meaning itself" (182). The great emptiness signified by the blank space on the map becomes the site of a narrative colonization in Conrad's story, but also the site of the subject's terrifying encounter with his own nothingness. Conrad's insistent reiteration of absence and incomprehensibility lies in a tradition which colonizes the non-Western landscape for the purposes of an emerging modernist aesthetic: Africa serves as the spatial projection of the dark void at the heart of modern life.

The tradition is later carried forward by André Gide, whose journey to the Congo at the age of fifty-six fulfilled an ambition conceived in adolescence and fueled by the work of Conrad, to whom the *Voyage au Conqo* (1927) is dedicated. In the midtwenties the interior of French Equatorial Africa was controlled by private concessions which relied on compulsory labor for the collection of rubber and ivory. This economy depended on a system of abuses in which native Africans were beaten or imprisoned for failing to gather their monthly quotas. Those who actively resisted were often put to death.

Gide arrives on this scene as a tourist; he follows Conrad's route of 1890 up the Congo River by steamer, then sets off on foot into the interior in the manner of the Great White Explorers, with a party of approximately sixty native carriers. He learns of the atrocities being committed against the native population more or less by accident, when a local chief tells him of the massacre of thirty-two men, women, and children, inhabitants of a small village who had refused an administrative order to move their settlement to another location. Like Marlow in *Heart of Darkness*, Gide is drawn by a kind of fascination toward the horror of such deeds: "I must pass behind the stage set, to know, finally, what hides there, even if it is horrible. It is this 'horror' [*affreux*] that I suspect, that I wish to see" (97).

The psychic and metaphysical void designated by the name of horror has its counterpart in Gide's view of the African landscape as formless and uncentered, as a devouring abyss. Having arrived at a station called Berberati, he notes that

> the administrator's house where we are staying . . . is well situated on the edge of a plateau, and commands a vast prospect of the country; but, as always in this measureless land, there is no center, the lines run hopelessly in all directions, there are no limits to anything. (131)

The geography of this description serves as a metaphor for the colonial situation: the "commanding prospect" from the administrator's house is illusory, for it in fact commands nothing, but instead loses itself in the void of the surrounding landscape. Gide stands before this landscape as before the horror of human atrocity, unable to assign center, measure, direction, or limit.

This void again takes human form in Gide's description of a native dance in which about sixty persons, of both sexes and all ages, take part:

> One cannot imagine anything more dismal and stupid than this dance, unrelieved by any breath of the spiritual. To the sound of a drum and to the same musical phrase, taken up by the chorus and repeated incessantly, they all go round in a great circle, one behind the other, with extreme slowness and a fluttering of their entire bodies, as if they had no bones. . . . Such is the expression of their feeling, the manifestation of their joy! In the moonlight, this dark ceremony seems the celebration of who knows what infernal mystery. I gaze at it a long time, brooding as if over an abyss. (154)

Gide's native dancers have all the attributes of nothingness incarnate: the movements imprisoned in repetition and hebetude, the boneless bodies a fleshly counterpart to the formless and uncentered landscape, the dance itself describing an empty space in the heart of the wilderness, opening onto an abyss of ennui, like Baudelaire's allegorical figure of that name who "would devour the world in a yawn" [*dans un bâillement avalerait le monde*] (6). It seems hardly necessary to point out that this is the projection of a uniquely Western problematic onto the rituals of a non-Western people and that, as the working through of a modernist aesthetic, it conforms precisely to the deployment of a discourse in which colonized peoples are systematically represented in terms of negation and absence—absence of order, of limits, of light, of spirit. Their zero-degree of existence provides both a justification for the colonizing enterprise and an imaginary empty space for the projection of a modernist angst.

The definition of Africa as spatial nullity is of course not confined to the metaphysical. Five years after the publication of *Heart of Darkness*, Richard Harding Davis made his own trip to the Congo Free State, later known as the Belgian Congo:

> To tell what the place is like, you must tell what it lacks. One must write of the Congo always in the negative. It is as though you asked: "What sort of a house is this one Jones has built?" and were answered: "Well, it hasn't any roof, and it hasn't any cellar, and it has no windows, floors, or chimneys. It's that kind of a house." (1907:93)

Davis defines precisely the dilemma of the Western writer who, recognizing none of the familiar constructions of social reality, falls back upon the discourse of negation in writing of the non-Western world. In this case, the negative description forms part of his argument against the Belgian monopoly in the Congo at the expense of the other signatories of the Berlin Act of 1885, which was to have guaranteed free trade in the region. Davis argues for an overthrow of the Belgian administration, by military means if necessary, in order to open the Congo "to the trade of the world, and give justice and a right to live and to work and to sell and buy to millions of miserable human beings" (112). Here the discourse of negation prepares the ground for the positive exercise of Western military and economic power against the abuse of that power by a single state. In the ideology to which Davis gives expression, however, Western colonial power means more than simply the expansion of Western interests into the empty space of Africa; it also represents Africa's own coming into being, its emergence from an original nullity into the openness of the world. Understood in these terms, the colonization of Africa by enlightened interests is not conquest, but deliverance of Africa from a state of nothingness.

The metaphor of Africa as a spatial void survives in Western writing long after exploration has filled in the blank spaces on the map. An illustration for Xan Smiley's 1982 *Atlantic Monthly* article on "Misunderstanding Africa" shows a large hole in the ground in the shape of that continent. A ladder stands in the dark center of this hole, but fails to reach the surface of the earth. The implication is of disillusionment: modern Africa has failed to escape the abyss of its own nonbeing. Smiley writes:

> The numerous and much-touted future "breadbaskets" and "granaries" are still empty: the green hills and savanna of southern Sudan, for instance. The food will just not grow, so long as the political instability remains and attitudes are utterly at odds with the demands of Western technology or organizational methods. Long-term investors are probably less willing now than they were ten years ago to take risks in Africa: ideologists are less willing to practice their social experiments there. Even the strategic arguments weigh less heavily. (September 1982)

There is an interesting if not wholly consistent logic at work here: Africa's emptiness is the result of its resistance to Western technology and organizational methods, while the decline of Western interest becomes the proof of Africa's failure. Africa's intrinsic absence now is the absence of foreign investment, of social experimentation, and of strategic importance. In contrast to Stanley and Davis, Smiley looks at the dark continent from the other end of colonial history, but Africa remains nonetheless an empty space: not, this time, as the original void awaiting a fulfilling presence, but rather as a postcolonial waste land, the empty sign of unfulfilled desires.

NEGATIVE HISTORY

The discourse of negation denies history as well as place, constituting the past as absence, but also designating that absence as a negative presence: a people without history is one which exists only in a negative sense; like the bare earth, they can be transformed by history, but they cannot make history their own. The absence of history is a theme in Hegel, who finds that Africa, having no political constitution, no movement or development to exhibit, is no historical part of the world: "What we properly understand by Africa, is the Unhistorical, Undeveloped Spirit, still involved in the conditions of mere nature, and which had to be presented here only as on the threshold of the world's History" (99). History would seem to belong only to Europe and Asia, but in the case of the latter, history can only be spoken of in a negative sense. The gorgeous edifices of Oriental empires rise and fall in mere succession, without the teleological movement provided by the emergence of subjective consciousness and spirit: Oriental history, too, is "really *unhistorical,* for it is only the repetition of the same majestic ruin," each new dynasty going through "the same circle of decline and subsidence."

The absence of history is in fact a double absence—of history as written text and of history as movement toward a destiny. Hegel says of the Hindus, for example, that "it is because the Hindus have no History in the form of annals (*historia*) that they have no History in the form of transactions (*res gestae*); that is, no growth expanding into a veritable political condition" (163). Hegel sees writing not just as historical record but as a condition of the possibility of history in the teleological sense: writing fixes reality and imparts consistency to laws, manners, customs, and deeds, thereby creating the objective self-image of a people necessary for the creation of new institutions. To be incapable of writing is to have no historical destiny.

The theme of this historical lack was readily translated, if simplified, into nineteenth-century European discourse concerning newly colonized peoples. In 1874 the mayor and town council of Brighton, England, hosted a banquet in honor of Sir Samuel Baker, the explorer of the Upper Nile region who had served as governor-general of the Equatorial Nile territory. As reported in the *Times* of London, Baker told his audience that

> Central Africa . . . is without a history. In that savage country . . . we find no vestiges of the past—no ancient architecture, neither sculpture, nor even one chiselled stone to prove that the Negro of this day

is inferior to a remote ancestor. We find primeval races existing upon primitive rock formation. . . . We must therefore conclude that the races of man which now inhabit this region are unchanged from the prehistoric tribes who were the original inhabitants. (Cairns 86)

Baker's remarks may be compared to those written in 1922 by Lord Lugard, for whom the history of these same people has been "an impenetrable mystery . . . unlike the ancient civilisations of Asia and South America, the former inhabitants of Africa have left no monuments and no records other than rude drawings on rocks like those of neolithic man" (66).

In a vulgarized version of Hegel, the absence of a written or constructed record testifies to the absence of history itself. History, to put it in contemporary terms, is a matter of writing and difference. The Africans lack a history because they have failed to leave a permanent mark on the landscape—no ancient architecture, no monuments or records—nothing to bring about the transformation and construction of the environment which provide the measure of civilization. This lack of inscription becomes the sign of another failure—the failure to mark the difference between nature and its others, between present and past, between presence and absence.

The savage, in this view, lives in a continual state of self-presence, unable to leave that trace on the world which serves as the beginning of difference, distinction, opposition, and hence progress. This failure leads to the identification of Africans with the unchanged and ever self-present earth, the primitive rock formation serving as a metaphor for the silence, denseness, and historical immobility of the people themselves. This way of defining the African, as without history and without progress, makes way for the moral necessity of cultural transformation. The colonizing powers will create a history where there was none.

The example of Hegel shows that the denial of history to colonized peoples extended beyond those, like Baker and Lugard, who formed part of the machinery of imperial expansion and colonization. Karl Marx is one writer who, while abhorring the motives of European imperialism, nonetheless follows Hegel in denying history to Africa and Asia. Writing in the New York *Daily Tribune* in 1852, Marx doubts whether India has any meaningful history except as a country which has always been predestined as the prey of foreign conquerors:

India . . . could not escape the fate of being conquered, and the whole of her past history, if it be anything, is the history of the successive conquests she has undergone. Indian society has no history at all, at least no known history. What we call her history is but the history of successive intruders who founded their empires on the passive basis of that unresisting and unchanging society. (1977:322)

For Marx, then, the question is not whether the British had a right to conquer India, but whether one is to prefer India conquered by the Turk, the Persian, or the Russian, to India conquered by the British. This negation of an indigenous Indian history is necessary to Marx's larger thesis, which is that "the bourgeois period of history has to create the material basis of the new world." The building of railways and roads and factories, the development of industry and trade under British rule, have ended the isolation and stagnation of Indian economic life and prepared the way for a great social revolution in which India will take its place among the "most advanced peoples" of the world. This rationalization of European colonialism is, not surprisingly, suppressed in the discourse of non-Western Marxists, who prefer Marx's writings on European industrialization to his writings on India and China.

Marx's understanding of the colonial situation stands in ideological antithesis to the imperialist thinking of men like Baker and Lugard, but Marx shares with his fellow Victorians the need to deny a significant history to the colonized. Just as the representatives of Empire deny an African history in order to construct their own vision of an African future, so Marx must deny an Indian history for his own vision of human progress. Like Baker, Marx uses a geological image to express his idea of human history: "Bourgeois industry and commerce create these material conditions of a new world in the same way as geological revolutions have created the surface of the earth" (336). Implicit in this equation is the notion that India is the primeval earth, dormant since the beginning of time, finally to be awakened by the force of history.

The denial of history need not always have an explicitly ideological purpose. It can also represent a more ambiguous rejection, a turning away from that which resists adequate representation, so that spatial metaphors like the heart of darkness or the black hole of Calcutta have their temporal dimension as well. In 1982 Joan Didion writes of El Salvador that "history is *la matanza* [the massacre of 1932] and then current events, which recede even as they happen":

In fact El Salvador has always been a frontier, even before the Spaniards arrived. The great Mesoamerican cultures penetrated this far only shallowly. The great South American cultures thrust this far north only sporadically. There is a sense in which the place remains marked by the meanness and discontinuity of all frontier history, by a certain frontier proximity to the cultural zero. (49)

Time somehow does not pass in El Salvador. Events fail to accumulate or even to stay in the mind. Memory dries up; history vanishes.

There is a line of descent in which Didion's language can be traced historically to the high colonial period. Just as Lugard contrasts tropical Africa to "the ancient civilisations of Asia and South America," she sets El Salvador's historical void against the "great cultures" of pre-Columbian America. This idea of cultural greatness includes the sense of scale which made it possible for Darwin to rank the peoples of the world and which allows Didion to place El Salvador at the zero degree. To speak of a zero degree in this way implies a single direction for historical development. Any development must take the form of a presence supplanting this original absence, the historical zero. Thus the structure of desire, the mutual exteriority of presence and nonpresence, works its way into Didion's discourse as well as into that of earlier writers in whom the ideological cast of desire is more readily identifiable.

But a postcolonial writer like Didion differs from her predecessors in the use she makes of negative history. Her own denial has to do not only with the relative inaccessibility of a historical tradition in El Salvador, but also with a profound ambiguity regarding places like El Salvador in the modern political and literary consciousness. Such places have become, in V. S. Naipaul's phrase, "an area of darkness," a geographical and historical metaphor for the sense of absence and amnesia that pervades modern consciousness and that is privileged in the literature of high modernism. At one point, Didion meets a small group of Irish Catholic missionaries in El Salvador who have become the objects of a false etymology. The *comandante* of the local garrison is surprised to learn the nationality of the priests and nuns: "he had thought them French, because the word used to describe them was always 'Franciscan.' This was one of the occasional windows that open onto the heart of El Salvador and then close, a glimpse of the impenetrable interior" (49).

Didion here works consciously, one supposes, from Conrad, although her literary genealogy also descends from Forster, whose *A Passage to India* constructs India as a series of absences and negations: the absence of productive human relations, of meaningful institutions, even the absence, at the center of the narrative, of knowledge about what really happened in the Marabar caves.

In Forster's novel the idea of India finds its objective correlative in the horrifying emptiness of the echoing caves; as Sara Suleri has pointed out, the essence of India is represented as embodied by these mysterious inner spaces which can be described but not interpreted, so that if they have any meaning at all, they stand for the utter absence of meaning. So it is with Didion's version of El Salvador. Insofar as history is meaning, to confront the absence of history is to confront the meaningless. Her experience of El Salvador thus becomes an encounter with an emptiness that is elsewhere generalized by literary modernism as the absurdity and alienation of human experience.

The difficulty of analyzing El Salvador, Africa, or India in historic terms can be seen as a limitation of the conventions of Western discourse, rather than as a mysterious absence on the part of non-Western peoples. Simon P. X. Battestini writes of Africa that "our built-in consciousness of a [historical] continuum does not always make sense for this continent where representatives of so many of our historical categories may be observed simultaneously in any African marketplace, or in any of its modern urban settings." Africa needs to be understood in terms of pluralistic identities and spontaneous movements that lie beyond the grasp of a purely positivist awareness. One should realize that "types of 'mentalities' which are chronologically serialized in the West coexist simultaneously in any given place in Africa" (126). The concept of African history thus would be freed from the rule of linear narrative under which it has been designated as absence; instead, it would assume a more spatial form, a field in which difference is played out according to continually changing laws of possibility.

NEGATIVE LANGUAGE

For Western thought, one of the fundamental measures of a culture is the quality of its language. Language comes to be judged according to its richness and complexity, its refinement from mere cry and gesture, its capacity to make distinctions, its multiplicity of names, its range from particularity to abstraction, and its organization of time and space. Language in this view is so basic to human culture that Rousseau cannot decide which came first: was an organized human society necessary for the origin of language, or was language necessary for the origin of society (1962, 1:158)?

We know that for the ancient Greeks the *barbaros*, or barbarian, was literally one who babbled, who did not speak the language of civilized humanity. The incoherence of barbarians was linked to their lawlessness and homelessness, their incapacity to master the instincts and passions of the body. Finding the lack of this "naturally ruling element" in barbarians, Aristotle in the *Politics* compares them to slaves, and adds, "This is why the poets say 'it is fitting for Greeks to rule barbarians,' the assumption being that barbarian and slave are by nature the same thing" (36). In this early example of colonial discourse, the negation of civilized language as a faculty of the Other leads, through a series of related negations, to a conclusion which upholds the justice of colonial rule.

For Rousseau, the first human language is the primordial "cry of nature," which is gradually superseded by a process of ever more complex substitutions and combinations. A developed language, in other words, is external to nature and supplementary to the original human condition, the degree of development marking how far a people has come from its primitive being. In his *Discourse on Inequality* (the "Second Discourse" of 1754), Rousseau reflects on "how much time and experience have been required for the discovery of numbers, abstract words, verb tenses, particles, syntax, the joining of propositions, reasoning, and the formation of the entire logic of discourse" (1:158). Even where Rousseau considers language as a degeneration from the state of "natural man," he still assumes a development— in skill, in intellect, in imagination—from a primitive origin, and he identifies this development with his own European culture. Whether morally better or worse than primitive society, advanced culture is still European and is also, paradoxically, the result of natural favor. In *Emile* (1762), Rousseau finds France to be the ideal climate for education [*culture*], for the climactic extremes of the far north or far south cause the brain to be "less perfectly organized": "Neither the Negroes nor the Lapps are as wise as Europeans" (Derrida 1976:222). In the *Essay on the Origin of Languages* (1781), he makes another distinction: the French, English, and German languages "are better suited to writing than speaking, and there is more pleasure in reading us than in listening to us. Oriental tongues, on the other hand, lose their life and warmth when they are written" (Derrida 226).

This is what Derrida calls an ethnocentrism *thinking itself* as counter-ethnocentrism: Rousseau wants to validate the "life and warmth" of Oriental languages such as Arabic and Persian, holding them to be closer to an original state of divine inspiration and oral expression. In doing so, however, he appropriates the logic and precision of language embodied in writing to Western European culture. His ostensible validation of Arabic and Persian thus disguises an effective negation in which these languages are characterized by a primitive lack of rational order and culture. Europe, for all its apparent distance from a purely natural order, remains for Rousseau the preserve of science, understanding, industry, and writing.

I have cited Aristotle and Rousseau in order to provide a context for the rhetorical tradition in which non-Western peoples are essentially denied the power of language and are represented as mute or incoherent. They are denied a voice in the ordinary idiomatic sense—not permitted to speak—and in a more radical sense—not recognized as capable of speech. Throughout the history of this tradition, the degraded or inadequate condition of language signifies a corresponding degradation in the political and social order of the other.

The theme of incoherence surfaces frequently in modern colonialist writing, reaffirming language as a primary site of the effort to divide cultural presence from its opposite, which is to say clarity from confusion, articulation from silence. While encamped one night at Bundi in the Indian province of Rajputana, Kipling is awakened in his tent by a native petitioner:

> It was no robber but some poor devil with a petition—a grimy, welted paper. He was absolutely unintelligible, and stammered almost to dumbness. . . . The man clicked and choked and gasped in his desperate desire to make the Sahib understand. But it was no use; and in the end he departed as he had come—bowed, abject, and unintelligible. (1970, 17:154–155)

Forster makes the same association of incoherence and abjection in his description of the Marabar caves. The echo in one of these caves is "entirely devoid of distinction": "If one had spoken vileness in that place, or quoted lofty poetry, the comment would have been the same—'ou-boum'" (149). In the caves, the refinements and distinctions of civilized language are reduced to a single, inhuman sound. In the native petitioner, desire and the appeal to authority are likewise reduced to a confused babble. For all their differences in ideology, Kipling and Forster both create images of India that signify its inherent unintelligibility, and thus its reduction to a cultural zero degree.

The incoherence of the Oriental, in this view, is related to an incapacity to enter into the basic systems of thought that make civilized life possible. Lord Ronaldshay writes that "before the advent of Western education the average Indian was constitutionally incapable of appreciating the meaning of the word chronology," thus baffling European writers of history in their attempts to assign dates to the story of India (290–291). In 1912 Isaac Headland, an American missionary administrator in China, writes that because of deficiencies in traditional Chinese education, "reason and invention have remained dormant in the Chinese mind. They have never invented anything."

Instead, the Chinese have "stumbled upon things": they stumbled on gunpowder, on the mariner's compass, and on the printing press five hundred years before Gutenberg. But they have never improved on any of these things: "their educational system has never enabled them to make a commercial success of what might be considered their great discoveries or inventions. They therefore needed a new system" (96–97). That system was the one then being established by American religious institutions in China, such as the Canton Christian College, the Presbyterian College of Teng-Chou-Fu, the Congregationalist Girls' College of Foochow, and the Episcopal Bible School at Hankow. In Headland's thinking, the influence of American Protestantism was to awaken the Chinese capacity not only for reason and invention, but also for the more worldly benefits of entrepreneurship.

The incoherence of the Oriental is surpassed, in this thinking, only by the incoherence of the African. Georges Hardy, a principal ideologue of French colonialism, identifies six essential characteristics of the black African mind: the absence of memory, the absence of a sense of truth, an incapacity for abstraction and judgment, an incapacity for prolonged effort, a sense of respect only for force, and a gregarious instinct (81–85). While the first five of these qualities are defined explicitly in terms of lack or limitation, the sixth implies the negation of a subjective consciousness in the African: "the individual feels lost whenever he is without the support and authority of the social group" (105).

Hardy's discourse has the effect of defining the African mind out of existence in such a way that African speech also fades away, leaving no impression on the hearer except that of absence. For what does one say or hear of a speech without memory, truth, abstraction, judgment, or prolonged effort? What is left of this speech, apart from Rousseau's primordial cry, or Conrad's "dying vibration of one immense jabber, silly, atrocious, sordid, savage, or simply mean, without any kind of sense" (120)?

The denial of cultural value by the negation of linguistic capability in non-Western peoples has not ceased to play a role in more recent representations. A 1986 article on Saudi Arabia in the *Manchester Guardian* typifies this rhetorical strategy. The writer, Terry Coleman, adopts the familiar practice of evaluating an entire culture based on a brief visit during which he comes into contact mainly with airline attendants, taxi drivers, minor functionaries of the Information Ministry, and other foreign journalists.

In such cases, if the writer considers that he or she has been treated badly, the host country comes off badly in the resulting account, like the play that is panned because the reviewer was given a seat in the back of the house.

In this article Saudi culture is characterized in various instances by the failure of language, or by a language which itself denotes absence and negation. Coleman writes:

> Not one thing I asked to see, not even those suggested by the Saudis themselves, was ever arranged. Of the useful words and phrases listed in Saudia's in-flight magazine, a visitor is most in need of the following:
> It does not matter: La Yahum.
> Impossible: La Yumkin.
> There is no: La Yuu Jad. (April 20, 1986)

Ingeniously, the writer finds the negation of Arabia within Arabic itself, thereby deflecting from himself part of the critic's burden. But in other instances he testifies more directly to Saudi deficiencies in language and communication. Throughout his visit, he writes, "Not once did I get a straight answer to a straight question." He comments on the difficulty of acquiring information from government officials, the problem being that "no civil servant will dare do anything without his prince's specific say-so, and for the most part the civil servant is afraid even to ask." In other words, not only are the Arabs incapable of giving a straight answer to a Westerner; they are even incapable of talking to one another.

Coleman is probably right when he states that the Saudis are bad at arranging foreign press tours and that they do not communicate with for-eign reporters in what would be, from the reporter's point of view, an efficient manner. One wonders, however, if the "straight answer" which the Western journalist finds so elusive is considered, within the context of Saudi culture, the only effective means of communication. Could there be a legitimate way of conversing that doesn't always involve straight answers to straight questions? T. E. Lawrence, for all his extravagance, is more supple in his understanding of Arab manners. In his dealings with the leaders of the Arab Revolt recounted in *Seven Pillars of Wisdom* (1926), he empha-sizes their mastery of negotiation, with its artful blend of tact, shrewdness, patience, humor, flattery, hyperbole, exhortation, and candor. By contrast, the modern journalist's unsympathetic demand for a straight answer to a straight question seems at best an impoverished approach to his sub-ject, while at worst it combines ignorance with arrogance. The assumption seems to be that where the Western style of speaking is not present, there is no language at all.

This discussion of rhetorical negation has moved along two planes. One, which may be called the social and political, sees negation as that which denies any prior claim to a people's historical or cultural existence, in order to open a space for colonial expansion. Rather than taking the form of the substitution of one order for another, this expansion comes to be understood within its own ideology as a creation ex nihilo: civilization gives life to the places of the earth that were without form, and void.

The other plane of negation combines elements of the psychological and the metaphysical. Here I have suggested that the representation of non-Western reality as nothingness in its various forms actually serves as the projection of a more radical absence in Western consciousness. As the work of Conrad so eloquently demonstrates, there is a void at the center of consciousness that must be named or given an image in order that it be contained. The terror of this void produces the fugitive inauthenticity that Heidegger ascribes to modern existence, a constant fleeing in the face of death. Derrida as well has written that the image, or the imagination, "is at bottom the relationship with death" (1976:184)—death as the abyss at the center of representation which is spanned by the structures of imagination in the most precarious way.

The rhetoric of negation has its practical value in the political sphere, and it also has its more symbolic value in giving voice to a fear of nothingness. Are we then talking about two entirely distinct phenomena in language, or is there a way in which these two values may be seen as part of the same movement? No matter at what point we place its origin, the history of modernity has defined itself as moving simultaneously in two directions: the expansive forward movement of technological development and, along with this, the confrontation with a metaphysical nothingness which signifies the finitude of the human condition. In speaking of technological expansion, I refer to a phenomenon that is played out in the political, social, and economic spheres of modern life. But the increase of knowledge and possibility in this realm has coincided with the disappearance of the metaphysical and theological imperatives once thought to have provided the grand framework for such expansion. I would suggest that the rhetoric of negation, as I have described it here, rushes in to span this widening gap between technological progress and metaphysical regress.

In this movement, absence in the metaphysical realm is transferred onto

a plane that combines the political, economic, and cultural, thus appropriating nothingness into a context where it can be overcome by human
progress. El Salvador, the Congo, the black hole of Calcutta: as these
places are constructed in Western writing, they become more than mere
allegories for a modern sense of absence; they are also the site of a transference wherein that absence acquires a political value in the real world.
That value is set at zero, but the zero degree is already less formidable than
nothingness itself, for it implies the possibility of progress, the triumph of
civilization, and, in the language of Rousseau, the ultimate perfectibility
of man. It is hardly comforting to consider how the structures of colonial
discourse lie buried within even the most fundamental desire for human
achievement.

7 AFFIRMATION

The White Man's Burden

IN THEIR STUDY OF MASS IMAGES AND THE SHAPING of American consciousness, Stuart and Elizabeth Ewen point to a double vision in the contemporary news media. The media present an overall view of the world as chaos and disorganization; the shattered experience of the self in contemporary culture is reenacted in the fragmented world presented by the media for popular consumption: "Inner life is paraded before us, validated by a format that calls itself 'objective.'" Against the background of this daily disintegration, however, the media also present their prescription for unity within the context of established institutions, so that "policies of corporate and state authority are played out as visions of unification and order against the general mural of chaos" (269). The rhetorical economy of the media creates a demand for images of chaos in order that the principles of a governing ideology and the need for institutions of order may be affirmed.

What the Ewens say about media language in contemporary American culture is also true of that element in colonial discourse which continually returns to an idealization of the colonialist enterprise against the setting of emptiness and disorder by which it has defined the other. Colonialism must always reaffirm its value in the face of an engulfing nothingness. This perpetual need for self-affirmation, however, is more than a simple matter of propaganda; rather it is essential to all language as a symbolic activity which validates the presence, that is, the symbolizing power, of a speaking or writing subject.

This is what Derrida calls the "fundamental culpability" of writing, in which the subject, inspired by self-affection, wants to "leave a trace of itself in the world." This essential narcissism in writing necessarily involves the subordination of the world to the subject, which "gains in its power and mastery over the other to the extent that its power of repetition *idealizes itself*" (1976:165–166). What I call the rhetoric of affirmation in colonial discourse combines this theory of a fundamental narcissism in language with the Ewens' more specifically ideological theory; the rhetorical strategies of repetition and self-idealization serve to establish a political and ethical order.

This rhetoric is deployed on behalf of a collective subjectivity which idealizes itself variously in the name of civilization, humanity, science, progress, etc., so that the repeated affirmation of such values becomes in itself a means of gaining power and mastery. My choice of the word "affirmation" to denote such a rhetoric derives both from the historical use of this word, particularly in moments of the crisis of authority, and from the richness of its etymology.

"To affirm" has traditionally signified the exercise of power, or at least the desire to exercise the vestiges of an authority once held. Under the headline "Six French battleships off the coast of Lebanon," *Le Figaro* (August 24, 1989) reports: "President François Mitterrand *affirmed* yesterday that France will allow no one to dictate its policy toward Lebanon" (emphasis mine). On the one hand, the verb reflects the pathos of the statement as a whole, in which a former colonial power strives to recollect the strains of a tune once carried with more conviction. On the other hand, the verb itself is layered with meanings that connect the notions of the subject, writing, and power. To affirm is to "make firm," from the Latin *firmare:* to strengthen or support (*OED*), as well as to confirm or ratify in the legal sense. Both of these meanings have contributed to the modern definition of *firma* in several European languages as "signature," the sign of the writing subject which acquires its status in letters, legal documents, etc., only by repetition of the same essentially unvarying gesture. One may even say that affirmation is the rhetorical gesture in which the subject actually constitutes itself through repetition, allies itself with the law, and strengthens itself against imminent danger from without or within. In this chapter I shall point to several versions of affirmation, each with its own function in serving the ends of a colonizing authority.

The primary affirmation of colonial discourse is one which justifies the authority of those in control of the discourse through demonstrations of moral superiority. In an earlier chapter we saw how Darwin attributed the low morality of savages to the fact that their behavior was guided only by "social instincts," that is, those which bore directly on the immediate welfare of the tribe. In the same work, Darwin argues for the greater capacity of the "cultivated man," guided by reason, to make moral judgments *on principle,* rather than on the prospect of a mere transitory pleasure or pain: "He might then declare—not that any barbarian or uncultivated man could thus think—I am the supreme judge of my own conduct, and in the words of Kant, I will not in my own person violate the dignity of humanity" (1936:481).

We may remark in passing the rhetorical components of Darwin's affirmation. It calls attention to itself as a *declaration,* thus ennobling its rhetorical posture. It makes the obligatory *distinction* between civilized and barbarian. Finally, it appeals to the notion of the authority of the subject, "supreme judge of my own conduct," as well as to the authority of a collective subjectivity embodied in a cultural tradition—"the words of Kant"—and in the unquestioned power of phrases like "the dignity of humanity." What begins as a rational argument for moral and racial superiority thus develops rapidly into a fervent invocation of shared ideals.

In *Orientalism,* Edward Said points out that binary distinctions such as "civilized" and "barbarian" were reinforced by Darwinian theses on survival and natural selection, as well as by the rhetoric of high cultural humanism in writers like Ernest Renan and Matthew Arnold (1978:227). The passage I cite here from *The Descent of Man* shows that Darwin himself had already made the step from natural selection to cultural humanism. His "cultivated man" is a figure of ennobled subjectivity defined by enlightened *human* ideals rather than by the narrow interests of a tribe. This enlarged moral perspective serves, paradoxically, as an imperative for the establishment of European authority throughout the world.

Darwin provides a scientific and philosophical basis for a moral ascendancy which carries with it a sense of mission that must be affirmed repeatedly as the foundation, and not the alibi, for colonizing activity. The notion of the "white man's burden" as a metaphor for the civilizing mission thus becomes a recurring theme in colonial writing. In John Buchan's novel *Prester John* (1910), a young Scotsman named David Crawfurd helps to suppress a "Kaffir rising" in a region of South Africa recently settled by whites. After persuading the rebels to surrender, Crawfurd is given the task of resettling them in their native kraals and providing them with food for the winter. Contemplating this responsibility, he muses:

I knew then the meaning of the white man's duty. He has to take all the risks. . . . That is the difference between white and black, the gift of responsibility, the power of being in a little way a king, and so long as we know and then practise it, we will rule not in Africa alone but wherever there are dark men who live only for their bellies. (1910:264)

Buchan reproduces in crude form certain assumptions in Darwin. Where Darwin distinguishes between the "social instincts" of savages and the morally principled subjectivity of the cultivated man, Buchan draws a simpler distinction between the appetitive instincts of blacks and the white man's moral and political responsibilities. Buchan also reproduces some of the rhetorical features of Darwin's language. He introduces his thought with a declaration of its importance—"I knew then the meaning . . ."— before making the necessary distinction—"the difference between white and black"—while appealing to the authority of a collective subjectivity: "we will rule not in Africa alone."

I do not suggest that Buchan is consciously imitating Darwin, but rather that the language of both writers enters into a rhetorical pattern that accompanies colonialist expansion. The sense of mission implied in Buchan, however, may be considered a strategic supplement to the essentially analytic character of Darwin's thought; where Darwin simply deploys the logic of what he perceives as an inherent racial and cultural superiority, others transform that logic into the affirmation of an active colonizing rule. Buchan's character realizes that the white man's rule depends not only on the knowledge of difference between white and black but also on the translation of that knowledge into practice: "So long as we know and then practise it." Of course, when the "knowledge" of racial difference is made a condition for political power, the nature of that knowledge then becomes open to question; from a critical perspective, such knowledge loses its status as an independent, a priori basis for practice, and becomes instead a mere aspect of practice, a construct produced by the same practice it would claim logically to precede.

This consideration calls into question not only the transparent racism of Buchan's discourse, but also what I have called, for lack of a better expression, the "essentially analytic" character of Darwin's thought. The notion of an essential analytic or an analytic essence at the heart of a colonizing order is itself rhetorical, a feature of a discourse that always affirms its origins in the pure and disinterested contemplation of the enlightened subject. A critical, if not pure and disinterested, perspective on colonial discourse must question whether such an origin is not rather a kind of back-formation from colonizing practice itself.

In invoking the "white man's duty," Buchan echoes the title of Kipling's poem of 1899, "The White Man's Burden," which has elements in common with journalism as well as colonial fiction. Written in the midst of Britain's own South Africa campaign, Kipling's poem was published in *The Times* of London with the subtitle, "The United States and the Philippine Islands." The United States had entered its war with Spain the previous year and had just gained control of the Philippines with Admiral Dewey's victory at Manila. Kipling's poem is in this respect a ringing call for America to assume the same responsibilities embodied in British colonial rule. In his critical biography, Angus Wilson writes that Kipling saw the American victory as an opportunity "to replace the old worn-out colonial mercantile world of Spain and Portugal . . . with an Anglo-Saxon Imperial mission that would be wide-thinking and modern" (204).

Apart from this immediate historical context, the poem serves as a model of the rhetoric of affirmation in its techniques of self-idealization and repetition. The imperative "Take up the white man's burden" is restated as the opening line of each of seven stanzas, forming a pun on the title, which has now become the "burden" or refrain of the poem. Thus the second stanza:

> Take up the White Man's burden—
> In patience to abide,
> To veil the threat of terror
> And check the show of pride;
> By open speech and simple,
> An hundred times made plain.
> To seek another's profit,
> And work another's gain. (1989:322)

The third line has a disturbing ambiguity: presumably, the patience and plain speech of the White Man veil the threat of his terrifying power, a power invoked in the following stanza, where the "burden" entails "savage wars of peace." However, the terror may also be that inspired by the savages in the White Man himself, a fear which only continual repetition of the "burden" can conceal. In either case, the veiled burden or meaning of Kipling's poem is that the White Man's authority over and responsibility for the "silent, sullen peoples" must constantly be reiterated in order to survive: "By open speech and simple, / An hundred times made plain."

While appearing merely to celebrate the selfless humanity of the civilizing mission, Kipling in fact points to its deeply rhetorical nature, implying that in the face of the silent, sullen races, the white man's power resides in his own language. In *Heart of Darkness*, Marlow says of Kurtz, "Of all his gifts the one that stood out preeminently, that carried with it a sense of real presence, was his ability to talk, his words" (119). The white man's burden is in this sense literally his insistent refrain, uttered to affirm his own presence against a background of overwhelming silence.

Conrad writes that "all Europe contributed to the making of Kurtz" (122), implying that his report to the International Society for the Suppression of Savage Customs—one of the great fictive documents of colonial discourse—reflects a common set of Western traditions and ideals. This notion of a shared tradition conforms to my own project, which is devoted to tracing patterns of repetition and uniformity throughout the changing forms of the discourse. However, it is also possible to mark nuances and differences in emphasis among the self-affirmations of the various colonizing orders. Traditional Western ideals are shared but given a different spin as they are invoked by British, French, and American writers, respectively. The idea of the White Man, for example, is universal to European colonial discourse, but is given a distinct articulation in British writing.

Kipling's White Man seems to have been an especially British idea, for reasons of style as well as history. Said writes that for the Britisher in India, Africa, or the Arab world, there was "certain knowledge that he belonged to, and could draw upon the empirical and spiritual reserves of, a long tradition of executive responsibility towards the colored races" (1978:226). In 1900 the Americans, French, Germans, and Italians were relatively new to the enterprise of overseas colonial expansion. While the Spanish and Portuguese had even older colonial empires than the British, the spiritual reserves of their imperial traditions lay invested mainly in the Roman Catholic church. The distinctly British version of colonial discourse promoted, by contrast, a set of secular and quasi-religious ideals borrowed from the humanism of high culture: a natural aristocracy, a muscular Christianity, the racial superiority of the Anglo-Saxons, and, to use a phrase often invoked in Parliament, "the trusteeship of the weaker races."

Patrick Brantlinger has shown how medievalist novels like Walter Scott's *The Talisman* (1825) combine notions of chivalry, the Saxon "race," and Christianity against a barbarian and despotic Orient. Somewhat anachronistically, the chivalric ethos is presented in language that makes it sound remarkably like the ideas of progress and civilization which nineteenth-century Britain uses to advance its imperial role in the Near East and the Holy Land (1988:141–143). Buchan's Scotsman, with his "power of being in a little way a king" among black South Africans, belongs to the same tradition of natural aristocracy as Scott's crusaders, whose noble blood and gentlemanly character entitle them to sovereignty over the infidels of the East.

The combined motifs of chivalry, heraldry, and ancient nobility continue to serve as rhetorical figures for colonial life in the twentieth century. The British Colonial Service celebrated the chivalric tradition by conferring ancient honorary orders as a reward for loyal service. Senior colonial administrators were most often made Companions of the Order of St. Michael and St. George (CMG) or Knights of the same order (KCMG). (The initials were sometimes said to stand for "Call Me God," or "Kindly Call Me God" [Allen 162]).

The chivalric motif survived in literature and literary journalism as well. Karen Blixen's *Out of Africa*, though the work of a Danish baroness, was published simultaneously in Danish and English and belongs to a British tradition of celebrating the noble spirit of the colonial settler. She describes her friends Denys Finch-Hatton and Berkeley Cole, men of great charm and ability, as belonging to another century: "No other nation but the English could have produced them . . . but theirs was an earlier England, a world which no longer existed" (213). She writes that Cole, brilliant in wit, would have been at home in the court of Charles II, while Finch-Hatton with his many talents could have walked arm-in-arm with Sir Philip Sidney and Francis Drake in the days of Queen Elizabeth. Together their qualities were such as to inspire "the particular, instinctive attraction which all Natives of Africa felt toward Berkeley and Denys" and to cause Blixen to reflect that white men of the past would have been in better sympathy with the Africans than those of the present industrial age (215).

One day Finch-Hatton shoots a lioness suspected of having killed the cattle of the local Masai. He and Blixen return to the scene later to find a lion standing by his fallen mate: "In approaching we were a little lower than the carcass; the lion stood straight up over it, dark, and behind him the sky was now all aflame. *Lion Passant Or*" (230). The device transforms the scene into an emblem of heraldic tradition, Africa itself offering a field on which the ancient symbols of European honor and courage are emblazoned. Men born too late to walk with Drake and Sidney can still recover that lost spirit of nobility amidst the atavism of a landscape yet to be subdued. Blixen takes up the theme once more in describing Finch-Hatton's grave, which lies at a site high in the Ngong Hills overlooking valley and plain below. The Masai have reported, she writes, that "many times, at sunrise and sunset, they have seen lions on Finch-Hatton's grave in the Hills. A lion and a lioness have come there, and stood, or lain, on the grave for a long time" (360). Native tribesman and beast combine in the elegiac scene. Shiva Naipaul, as ever uncharitable toward African and European alike, remarks sardonically on this passage, "Primal Africa pays homage to the English nobleman" (149).

British East Africa of the nineteen twenties and thirties was rich ground for aristocratic nostalgia. As a visitor in 1931, Evelyn Waugh reports in *Remote People* that the English settlers there are not like the "cranks" who settled New England, nor the "criminals and ne'er-do-wells" who went to Australia, but "respectable Englishmen, out of sympathy with their own age":

> It is not big business enterprise which induces the Kenya settlers to hang on to their houses and lands, but the more gentle notion of love for a very beautiful country they have come to regard as their home, and the wish to transplant and perpetuate a habit of life traditional to them, which England has ceased to accommodate—the traditional life of the English squirearchy, which, while it was still dominant, formed the natural target for satirists of every shade of opinion, but to which now that it has become a rare and exotic survival, deprived of the normality which was one of its determining characteristics, we can as a race look back with unaffected esteem and regret. (182–183)

Waugh shares with Blixen the idea of British Africa as a twilight revival of aristocratic values which otherwise exist only in a racial memory, as well as the idea of a modern England ruled by capitalist forces that have destroyed the traditional social order. England's spirit of nobility is now to be found only in her colonies.

Waugh differs from Blixen mainly in his judgment of the East African natives. For him the Masai, far from being the noble savages suggested by their superb physiques, are "a race of bullies" given to murdering their peaceful Kikuyu neighbors. In a manner typically calculated to provoke humanitarians concerned with the "native problem," Waugh defends settlers who occasionally beat their servants by saying that such persons are merely behaving as their ancestors did toward their English servants up to the end of the eighteenth century. "The idea of courtesy to servants, in fact, only came into being when the relationship ceased to be a human one and became purely financial" (185–186). The old "human" relationship between master and servant contrasts with the new humanitarian one debased by materialism. Here, as he will do so more memorably in *Brideshead Revisited*, Waugh appeals to the social order of the past as to an aesthetic and even spiritual ideal. By representing the traditional English squirearchy supposedly surviving in Africa as an order based on such ideals, rather than on the material foundations of property and political power derived from the rule of force, he makes the colonization of Africa essential to the preservation of what is best in the English cultural tradition.

If we were to identify a characteristically American style of self-affirmation, it would have to include the notions of material prosperity and moral progress granted by a somewhat secularized Providence, often embodied in Nature. Such are the themes of Emerson's essay "American Civilization," published in the *Atlantic Monthly* in April 1862, a year into the Civil War. Fearing the nation's lapse into barbarism, Emerson seeks to define civilization and then to reaffirm its value in a specifically American context. His definition posits a zero degree of humanity which combines images of the ape and the cannibal: "a dweller in caves, or on trees, like an ape,—a cannibal, and eater of pounded snails, worms and offal" (19). Civilization is then marked by degrees of progress from this abject condition. At the other extreme, Emerson finds that "the most advanced nations are always those who navigate the most," and that in the United States the benefits of this outward-looking commerce can be seen in the building of roads, the prosperity of farms, the division of labor, the spread of knowledge, and the "multiplication of the arts of peace."

But Emerson's civilization, if materially expansive, is also deeply moral in that it draws its strength from sources that are simultaneously natural and divine: "Everything good in man leans on what is higher. . . . Thus all our strength and success in the work of our hands depend on our borrowing the aid of the elements." For Emerson, moral and material progress are inseparably bound in the same evolutionary process. This combination of moral goodness and material wealth, together with the emphasis on navigation and commerce with other nations, becomes a distinctly American understanding of civilization that is later incorporated into the discourse of empire.

The establishment of American rule in the Philippines at the turn of the century provides a case study in the deployment of this discourse. Champions of expansion had to be sufficiently persuasive to prevail over American anti-imperialists who, among their other objections, could not understand how a truly republican government could have colonial subjects. Imperialist rhetoric overrode such criticism by representing the colonial enterprise as the active extension of American civilized ideals. In 1898 the journalist Murat Halstead made what would become a familiar series of logical connections linking American investment, the development of natural wealth, and the welfare of the indigenous population: "There is profusion of the riches that await the freedom of labor and the security of capital, and the happiness of the people. Under American government the Philippines would prosper" (96). American law being superior to that of the Spanish colonial government, it would bring justice to the Filipinos (the possibility of a legal constitution created by Filipinos themselves was not considered). As for the United States, holding on to the Philippines was a matter of "finding the path of empire the path of freedom," a freedom apparently intended to be enjoyed equally by American investors and Filipino subjects (97).

In the same year, another journalist, Trumbull White, celebrates the acquisition of "our new possessions"—Cuba, Puerto Rico, Hawaii, and the Philippines. While the precise nature of American political involvement in these territories remains to be determined, White is willing to settle for economic domination with a moral purpose: "To dominate in commercial influence and in all things for the uplifting of a swarming population of alien races, is a function as worthy, and of more interest and consequence to most of our people, than the mere detail of official sway" (16). White gives expression to an attitude that historians later would blame for the ultimate failure of the United States' experiment with colonialism in the Philippines: the desire to realize material and symbolic gains without accepting responsibility for a direct and thorough colonial administration on the European model.

On the other hand, the theme of moral improvement combined with material progress anticipates the retrospective view of one David Barrows, an administrator who in 1914 evaluated the results of American rule:

> Looking back over the decade which has been here reviewed, the distinctive features of a noble and generous policy can be seen. Peace and order have been won from a long and desperate period of commotion and discontent; a judicial system has been established with codes of law which make justice prompt and effective; great material improvements have been undertaken, railroads built, navigation developed, agriculture revived, and commerce expanded to a point of importance in the world's trade. But . . . the distinctive achievement of the American administration in the Philippines is in the social and spiritual transformation of the Filipinos themselves: the pains taken to make better men. (59)

Barrows's catalog of material improvements—the building of roads, the development of navigation, the prosperity of agriculture—follows term for term Emerson's exalted vision, as does the logic of the implied argument that expanded commerce has transformed a primitive people into "better men." Such arguments have been made on behalf of European colonialism as well, but the faith in commercial expansion as a moral and even spiritual phenomenon is fundamental to the historical consciousness of a nation built on the principles of Manifest Destiny.

In more recent years this formula has been translated into a rhetoric of commercial pragmatism and strategic benevolence in the United States' approach to the Third World. At the beginning of Ronald Reagan's first presidential term in 1981, *Time* magazine devoted a dozen pages to a ponderous essay on "American Renewal." While a departure from standard editorial format, the essay was quintessentially *Time*—perfect in its self-important tone for the publication founded in 1928 by Henry R. Luce as the voice of the American Century. The essay begins by affirming what it calls "the American secular religion": "the belief in an ever better tomorrow, the conviction that obstacles exist to be overcome, and that the U.S. has a strong and beneficial role to play in the world." This faith has been shaken by, among other things, "a chaotic, largely hostile Third World," itself characterized by "mullah-led mobs," "regional brawls," and "tribal vendettas." The people of the Third World fail to understand America's benevolent intentions:

> When it has not been actively intervening, America has viewed its influence abroad as automatic, simply radiating outward through the shining example of the country's strength and goodness. If this was ever true, it surely no longer is. (February 23, 1981)

It is clear that the decline in American prestige has adverse consequences for the poorer nations of the world as well as for America itself. *Time*'s solution is a curious if nonetheless American mixture of commercial enterprise and moral resurgence. The essay argues for private-sector investment in order "to wean the poorer nations from their current paradoxical addiction: socialist nostrums at home financed by capitalist largesse from abroad." At the same time, it cautions that the need for renewal of American prestige goes beyond economics and politics: "it encompasses ethics, morale, social and spiritual values."

These values—"a respect for authority, a sense of duty, and a degree of self-restraint"—"will be restored almost mysteriously, through natural growth, as a result of millions of individual decisions and efforts." At a moment of crisis in the postcolonial world, *Time* revives a traditionally American rhetoric of self-affirmation in which authority takes the paradoxical form of individual freedom, and moral order is strengthened by Nature itself, endowed with the mystery of a secular faith. This restoration of faith will also be the salvation of the world's poorer nations who, in a metaphor mixing maternal care with the triumph of the therapeutic, must be weaned from their childish addictions.

The discourse devoted to the affirmation of French colonialism, while sharing with other powers the same fundamental logic of Western superiority, has consistently sought to create for France a separate role, a special distinction in the civilizing mission. In the 1880s France's expansion into Africa and Indochina was defended on frankly economic and strategic grounds as necessary participation in a worldwide competition for expanded markets; by the 1930s, however, partly in response to critics like André Gide, the colonial empire had been rhetorically endowed with the noblest sentiments of the French Revolution, the humanistic ideals of the Third Republic, and the historical grandeur of French civilization itself. Where Kipling sought to shift a portion of the white man's burden onto other powers, apologists for the French empire came to see that high calling as preeminently their own: Albert Sarraut thus writes in 1931 that "France, to her honor, was the first to understand the human worth of the backward races, and the sacred obligation to respect and increase that worth" (115).

This celebration of France's mission was often made at the expense of rival colonial powers, which traditionally have been viewed with a combination of envy and paranoia. A relatively late representative of this view was Georges Hardy, a historian of French colonialism and member of the Académie des Sciences Coloniales. Writing in 1953, Hardy contrasts the French "colonial conscience" and France's faith in its destiny as the "pastor of nations" to the British, who, he states, have revived the *tu regere* of ancient Rome (206). The allusion is to Anchises' prophecy in the *Aeneid* (6:851 ff), in fact a statement of classical colonial conscience and of Roman pride in generosity toward the colonial subject. His misreading of Virgil aside, Hardy's intention is clearly to compare British imperialism with the harsher side of Roman rule.

Sarraut's criticism of other empires goes beyond the British to include Spain, the United States, and Germany as well. For him the grim history of (non-French) European colonization recalls the massacres of the Incas and the Aztecs, the American slave trade, the extermination of the American Indian, and the decimation of the Herero people of German Southwest Africa. This sad record survives in "the Anglo-Saxon contempt for the 'colored races,'" itself part of a more general repudiation of the moral duties of the colonizer (115).

France's difference from other powers, Sarraut argues, derives from the tradition of thought which produced the Declaration of the Rights of Man and which, rejecting the doctrine that the nonwhite races are permanently inferior, now takes "the formless clay of primitive multitudes, and patiently models the face of a new humanity" (115). Sarraut's doctrine that colonization is the work of *fraternité* and *solidarité humaine* is presented as distinctly French in origin and spirit; it accompanies the doctrine that France's great cultural tradition has made it supremely qualified for the work of *la tutelle coloniale,* a phrase that combines the sense of tutelage with that of guardianship over colonized peoples. In Sarraut's *Grandeur et Servitude Coloniales,* a long account of France's rich cultural history including the glories of the Renaissance, the seventeenth century, and the Enlightenment, concludes with this thought:

> Our national soul has been slowly fashioned, modeled, tempered, bathed by all these influences and lights; by a sort of capillary movement, this immense moral wealth has gradually spread throughout the entire race; and thus we represent an inheritance of light that, in the colonies, comes to the aid of an inheritance of stagnation and darkness. (169)

Endowed with this purpose, France's mission is "to *affirm* everywhere the essential traits of the national tradition" (103, emphasis mine). As a recurring motif in a particular style of affirmation, the idea of French culture has a rhetorical value equivalent to the ideas of British character and American enterprise.

At the beginning of this chapter, I cited the work of Stuart and Elizabeth Ewen in order to define a rhetorical economy: the value of self-affirmation depends on the constant supply of images of chaos and disintegration, against which the principles of unity and order may be continually invoked. We have seen how in periods of established colonial rule this affirmation can take the form of a complacent reflection on how civilization has improved the formerly abject condition of the colonized. However, in times of outright insurrection, the rhetorical economy heats up, the rhythm of images opposing chaos to order intensifies, and the terms of affirmation become more strident.

In examining the role of journalism in this process, I want to look at the example of *Le Monde* in its coverage of the first two weeks of the Algerian revolution in November 1954. Although this example is taken from French colonial history, the principle which it serves to illustrate is not particularly French; the intensification of rhetoric at moments of crisis in authority should be seen as a phenomenon that applies to colonial discourse in general.

Following a series of coordinated terrorist attacks on police stations in Algeria, *Le Monde* issues a call for order on November 3:

> It is as if some invisible hand were attempting to ruin the vertical solidarities of France and North Africa at the very moment when they were capable of being strengthened. Those who have incited this work of destruction must be combatted; those who have carried it out must be revealed, pursued, and punished. But this suppression must be clear-headed and loyal if one does not want to push the population into the ranks of the outlaw. We must refuse the infernal cycle in which the enemies of Algerian France wish to enclose us.

In this passage, where *Le Monde* assumes for itself the burden of restating the terms of colonial ideology, we may recognize certain components of the rhetoric of affirmation. In its imperative tone, the statement calls attention to itself as a declaration of national purpose. The appeal is to a collective vision—the "vertical solidarities" of France and North Africa—and to the authority of the state—"suppression must be clearheaded and loyal" [*la répression doit être lucide et loyale*]. In the course of this affirmation, *Le Monde* makes the familiar distinction between "us" and "them," that is, between a collective subject united by a shared ideology and those who threaten the institutions of order and unity.

This distinction makes for a certain ambiguity, however, given the "solidarity" between France and North Africa which is restated in the name of "Algerian France." The possibility that the exercise of authority may push entire populations beyond the law [*dans les rangs des hors-la-loi*] undermines the notion of that authority as a unifying force. It is as if *Le Monde* did not know quite how to define this opposition to the ideal of unity, attributing it glibly to "the enemies of Algerian France" or, more vaguely, to some "invisible hand." This ambiguity arises from a divided purpose: *Le Monde* wants to affirm the reality of French-Algerian unity while recognizing a situation that belies such unity; unity and disunity must be simultaneously affirmed. This is the double bind of colonial discourse, in which colonized peoples are seen, quite accurately, as alternately essential to and destructive of the colonial order.

Edward Said has noted that *Le Monde* is not just a French newspaper: "it is *the* French journal of record," a collectively owned voice of the French bourgeoisie and a newspaper which "views itself as representing the world in accordance with a specific conception of what French interests are" (1981:119). *Le Monde* is capable of opposing government policy, but never of opposing the principle of France's preeminence in the arena of world affairs. In this respect, *Le Monde* serves an even greater institutional role than such newspapers as the *Times* of London and the *New York Times*.

In moments of crisis, a newspaper like *Le Monde* not only takes up the cause of national unity and order: it actively transmits the directives of the state designed to maintain authority. Thus on November 7, 1954, when the government dissolves the Algerian opposition party (Mouvement pour le Triomphe des Libertés démocratiques en Algérie), *Le Monde* cites at length the 1936 law that authorizes this measure against any association that "provokes armed demonstrations in the streets, that presents the character of combat groups or private militias, or that has as its purpose an attack on the integrity of national territory by force, or an attack on the republican form of government." This statute is quoted without a response by those against whom it is used. The voice of Algerian opposition, in fact, has no place in *Le Monde*'s coverage during this period.

Apart from citing the relevant laws brought into effect in response to the incipient revolution, *Le Monde*'s most important form of coverage is to transmit the declarations of various government authorities. This process reaches a kind of climax with the parliamentary address of the premier, Pierre Mendès-France, published by *Le Monde* on November 13:

> Several weeks ago, I affirmed the solidarity of the entire nation with the Algerian peoples. Faced with a new test, provoked this time by the criminal will of a few men—a useless and stupid test—the nation must affirm its unity and solidarity. . . .
>
> The Algerian *départements* are part of the Republic, they have been French for a long time; their population, which enjoys French citizenship and which is represented in parliament, has given too much proof of its attachment to France for France to call into question its unity. Between this population and metropolitan France no secession is conceivable. This must be clear for always and for the entire world, in Algeria, in the *métropole*, and abroad. (*Applause from numerous benches.*) Never will France, never will any parliament, never will any government yield on this fundamental principle.

These examples of coverage from the beginning of the revolution demonstrate the various forms of collaboration that are possible between a formally independent press and the authority of the state in times of crisis: in affirming the principles of authority, the press can state its own position, cite legal statutes, or reproduce the addresses of statesmen, while at the same time choosing to ignore any voices of resistance. These rather obvious facts about the relation between the press and authority have, however, a less obvious consequence, which is that the layering of journalistic opinion, statutory language, and political discourse produces a prescriptive inter-pretation of reality. The versions of affirmation reproduced in *Le Monde* not only are connected by the uniform themes of solidarity, integrity, and unity; they also aspire to what speech act theorists call the performative utterance—that which makes itself true by virtue of its being written or spoken, for example, "I salute you."

Mendès-France's "I affirm" is meant to have this same performative quality, except that, given the circumstances of France and Algeria in 1954, he can affirm a unity only by conceding its absence. This discourse takes the form of what, in another context, Homi Bhabha has described as the fundamental ambivalence inherent in positions of authority (*position* here being understood in a double sense as both the effect of disposal or place-ment within a structure of power and the rhetorical stance adopted from within that placement; thus "he is in a position to take that position"). In theory, a clear and fully present authority ("clear for always and for the entire world") would never find itself in the position of having to defend itself; there is no demand for proof when a truth is sufficiently authori-tative to be self-evident. Once authority begins to be asserted, however, there opens up a split between assertion and authority itself, in which the latter is revealed as conditional and contingent on its representation. Affir-mations of authority can now be seen as strategic devices necessary for the maintenance of that authority, rather than as simple manifestations of an unquestioned presence.

This splitting open of authority is precisely what takes place in the speech of Mendès-France: the nation "*must affirm* its unity and solidarity" only because they do not exist. The assertion that "no secession is conceivable" is made possible only because such a secession has already been conceived. Apart from this ambivalent, self-canceling quality, the rhetoric of affir-mation has this curious feature, that the intensity of its repetition—"for always," "for the entire world"—increases as its authority loses its grasp. It begins to protest too much.

After eight years of war, France formally recognized Algerian indepen-dence on July 3, 1962.

8 IDEALIZATION

Strangers in Paradise

IN WRITING ON THE RHETORIC OF APPROPRIATION IN chapter 2, I suggested that the shifting definitions of American interest in Vietnam could be traced by following the equally shifting objects of idealization in the American press. In the mid-1950s, magazines such as *Newsweek* and the *New Republic* cast President Diem as the personification of classic democratic values and described South Vietnam as a model of fledgling democratic reform. Ten years later, in the writings of Susan Sontag and other liberal-minded journalists, it was Ho Chi Minh and North Vietnam that came to embody the traditionally American values of democracy, enterprise, and discipline. In both cases, the press had simply appropriated Vietnam and redefined it in terms of classically American ideals, so that this mode of interpretation became an unconscious act of self-reflection, a commentary on the real meaning of America. The successive idealizations of Vietnam said more about American virtues and American values than about anything Vietnamese.

In this chapter I follow the practice of idealization into other arenas, in order to show not only its transformations in different historical moments, but also to sound out its essential identity from one set of circumstances to another. As always, my subject is the isomorphism of rhetorical values, the deeply rooted repetition of discursive patterns within the shifting contexts of power.

The tradition of idealizing the savage takes us back to the early stages of Western European imperial expansion and is invariably produced by a rhetorical situation in which the writer takes an ethical position in regard to his or her own culture. Montaigne's essay "On Cannibals" (1580) is occasioned by French exploration of the Brazilian coast and by the struggle between European powers for control of Brazilian territory. The discovery of savages that results from these colonialist ventures is adapted by Montaigne for his own purposes. For him the "cannibals" live in an Edenic state of purity and simplicity, "still governed by natural laws and very little corrupted by our own" (109). However, the subtext of this exotic idealization lies in Montaigne's ironic commentary on the political and social institutions of sixteenth-century France. Thus he retells the story of the three Brazilian Indians who in 1562 met with King Charles IX, then twelve years old. What these men found most remarkable about France was that so many grown men around the king should be willing to obey a child and that some men "gorged to full with things of every sort," while others went "begging at their doors" (119).

For Rousseau, as for Montaigne, savage man is less a real and living presence than an abstract ideal whose purpose lies in his symbolic value for the social and political configurations of eighteenth-century Europe. "Let us begin by setting aside all the facts," Rousseau writes in the *Discourse on Inequality* (1754); we are asked to understand his conception of the primitive not as historical truth, "but solely as hypothetical and conditional reasonings, better fitted to clarify the nature of things than to expose their actual origin" (78). Here Rousseau explicitly proposes the idea of savage as a *construct* upon which to found contemporary ideals of the "rights of man." The idea of the savage as living in a state of perfect freedom allows Rousseau, writing as a republican *Genevois* in France during the reign of Louis XV, to argue for the natural liberty and equality of human beings: "It is . . . the fundamental principle of all political right that peoples have given themselves chiefs in order to defend their liberty and not to enslave them" (125).

In *Oriental Renaissance*, Raymond Schwab offers another perspective on idealization of the primitive. In the late eighteenth century, the arrival of Sanskrit texts and their translation into European languages inspired the dream of a "revenge for Babel": people imagined that in Sanskrit the original human language had been recovered and that this was bound to lead to the restoration of an original, "primitive" people which would serve as the model for a universal society. Thus, in a movement that combined theology with political messianism, the Romantic philology of early Orientalism made the primitive into an El Dorado (168).

This phenomenon was also literary: Schwab traces the myth of "primitive poetry" to the German writer Johann Georg Hamann, who gave early expression to the Romantic doctrine that poetry is the "natural language" of humanity and that its spirit still lives in the Orient. In *Aesthetica in nuce* (1762), Hamann writes, "How then will we revive the dead language of nature? Through pilgrimages to Arabia Felix, through crusades to the Orient and the restoration of its magic" (210). Goethe would later write in the preface to his *West-östlicher Divan*, a work inspired by the Persian poet Hafiz: "Here I want to penetrate to the first origin of human races, when they still received celestial mandates from God in terrestrial languages" (Schwab 211).

The primitive is thus conceived of in space as well as time: it may be sought in the Orient, or even further, in the newly discovered islands of the Pacific, where it may be said to inhabit a realm outside of time. Herman Melville's *Typee* (1846) is one of those works that owe their visionary energy not only to the European movement described by Schwab, but also to a Romantic revolt against the utilitarian ideology of the industrial middle class. In this text, presented to the public as a nonfictional account, the spirit of merchant capitalism is embodied in the figure of the tyrannical ship's captain who doles out meager provisions of sea-biscuit, inhumanly neglects the sick, and prolongs the voyage endlessly in a futile search for sperm oil. The narrator abandons ship in the Marquesas Islands, only to fall among savages who turn out to be the human counterparts of a Romantic sublime.

Melville's story is rich in scenes of native girls bathing in cascading waters, of life lived "in an atmosphere of perpetual summer, and nurtured by the simple fruits of the earth, enjoying a perfect freedom from care and anxiety" (104). Melville finds the Typee to be governed by "an inherent principle of honesty and charity towards each other,"—by an "indwelling perception of what is just and noble," which is universal to humanity where it has not been distorted by "arbitrary codes" of unjust law (226). Melville's combination of Romantic imagery with Rousseauian moral philosophy marks his alienation from the utilitarian values of merchant capitalism, while at the same time his idealization of the savage can be understood as giving expression to a repressed desire on the part of the very same industrial middle class from which he is at pains to distance himself.

The Typee represent, in the realm of imaginary wish fulfillment, everything that nineteenth-century America is not. For an American society characterized by male-dominated social institutions, repressed sexuality, the profit motive, and the systematic destruction of native peoples and natural landscape, Melville's savages offer a visionary antithesis: a free and natural sexuality, a marriage system based on female desire, a society living in ease and abundance, and in complete harmony with its natural surroundings. The socially symbolic function of Melville's narrative may be described in the same way that Lévi-Strauss has described the graphic art of a Brazilian tribe, as "the fantasy production of a society seeking passionately to give symbolic expression to the institutions it might have had in reality, had not interest and superstition stood in the way" (176).

It is no accident that the idealization of the savage from the beginning has always accompanied the process of Western imperial expansion, for this idealization simply constitutes one more use that can be made of the savage in the realm of Western cultural production. Montaigne's idea of the savage, occasioned by real imperialist expansion, serves the purposes of his own "Renaissance self-fashioning"; it offers a pretext for distancing himself ironically from the social institutions of which he is part, and so contributes to the process by which he invents himself as a literary subject. Rousseau's purposes are more political and philosophical than personal and literary, creating the savage into a powerful symbol for the transformation of European society. Melville's ideal of the savage, notwithstanding his attacks on colonialism in the Pacific, is fundamentally more conservative than Rousseau's, as fantasy is more conservative than any passionate engagement in redefining a social order. Melville's savages are products of a Romantic nostalgia that in the end lies comfortably within the *ethos* of industrial capitalism. This primitivism is symbolically the precise reverse of American capitalism and therefore constitutes an object to be admired in the abstract—the dream of its own opposite that lives at the very heart of the capitalist imagination.

The writers I have named so far represent a certain range of positions—national, literary, political—within a Western tradition, and each produces his version of the idealized savage according to his historical situation. What unites them is that this idealization always takes place *in relation* to Western culture itself: far from being a gesture which turns its back on the West in order to accept some alternative mode of being, it conceives an idea of the Other that is readily incorporated into the fabric of Western values. Like other representations of the savage, this one stops short of crossing the boundary from one culture to the other; rather, it makes use of the savage in order to expand the territory of the Western imagination, transforming the Other into yet one more term of Western culture's dialogue with itself.

The idealization of the savage has always taken place alongside a more general idealization of the cultural Other. While Melville sojourned in the

Pacific, French writers like Théophile Gautier and Gérard de Nerval traveled to North Africa and the Middle East, gathering material for an *exotisme* that became an essential component of the Romantic aesthetic. If we are to follow this practice of idealization into the twentieth century, we must consider what happens to it with the expansion of Western economic and political interests into an ever more highly integrated worldwide system and with the increasing *rationalization* of human experience in general. This word, used by Max Weber to describe the way in which capitalism rearranges our world both economically and conceptually, has also been defined by Fredric Jameson: "The older, inherited ways of doing things are broken into their component parts and reorganized with a view to greater efficiency according to the instrumental dialectic of means and ends" (220). The world, in other words, comes increasingly to be classified according to a purely utilitarian logic of instrumentality and quantification.

With this rationalization of experience one might expect a radical demythologization of the noble savage and the reduction of idealized *exotisme* into a more banal and predictable cultural eccentricity. And, in fact, this kind of reduction does take place in a genre like the travel journalism of the Sunday newspaper, where the more bizarre and threatening aspects of the cultural Other must be domesticated and commodified for the tourist. At the same time, however, this rationalization of the Third World—the transformation of the cultural Other into simply one more component of the global system—produces a curious countereffect which ends by reinforcing the exotic and idealized qualities of the Other, as if the Western imagination harbored a secret resistance against its own movement toward a completely rational and instrumental view of the world. In this sense, the twentieth-century idealization of non-Western peoples might be understood as a "return of the repressed" within the collective consciousness of the modernized West. The simultaneous rationalization and idealization I have described here is symptomatic of *Seven Pillars of Wisdom* (1926), T. E. Lawrence's autobiographical account of his role in the Arab revolt against Turkish domination during the last two years of World War I. In a concretely political sense, Lawrence's mission in Arabia was purely strategic: the British and Ottoman empires had fallen out on opposite sides in the war, and an Arab revolt against the Turks, fostered by British influence, would not only help defeat the Central Powers, but would also assure Allied control of the Arab territories after the war. The potentially explosive power of Arab nationalism thus became a key to Britain's plans for imperial expansion in the Middle East:

> We could see that a new factor was needed in the East, some power
> or race which would outweigh the Turks in numbers, in output, and
> in mental activity. . . . Some of us judged that there was latent power
> enough and to spare in the Arabic peoples (the greatest component of
> the old Turkish Empire), a prolific agglomeration, great in religious
> thought, reasonably industrious, mercantile, politic, yet solvent rather
> than dominant in character. (56)

Lawrence's assessment here is cast in the highly rationalized language of
quantification and instrumental value, with its emphasis on numbers, proportion, and production. He rejects the notion of direct intervention by a
European power, arguing that the "standard of efficiency" is local rather
than Western and thus does not require the superior organization of a
Westernized military force. The "solvent" nature of the Arabs, moreover,
makes them all the more susceptible to Western direction.

What interests me in Lawrence is the way this rationalized language
combines with the most heightened idealization of Arab character. At the
same time that he evaluates their strategic value, Lawrence celebrates what
he perceives to be the rarefied asceticism of the Arabs. He tells of having
been taken by Arab guides to an ancient desert palace whose bricks were
made, not of water, but with the precious essential oils of flowers, so that
one could walk from room to crumbling room, sensing the odor of jessa-
mine, violet, and rose. When at last Lawrence is led into the main lodging
which opens onto the empty desert air, he is told, "This is the best: it has
no taste." The anecdote is meant to illustrate the metaphysical clarity of
Arab existence:

> The Beduin of the desert, born and grown up in it, had embraced
> with all his soul this nakedness too harsh for volunteers, for the reason,
> felt but inarticulate, that there he found himself indubitably free. . . .
> In his life he had air and winds, sun and light, open spaces and a great
> emptiness. There was no human effort, no fecundity in Nature: just
> the heaven above and the unspotted earth beneath. (38)

In this image of the human soul embracing a vast nothingness, we may
recognize a version of the modernist metaphysic of existentialism, with
its myth concerning the absurdity of human life in the face of an indifferent Nature. The mythologized Arab here stands for the existential hero
who confronts this absurdity, thus gaining an ascetic freedom from worldly
things and theological illusion.

As Jameson has pointed out in the case of Conrad, however, the existential metaphysic actually serves as a containment strategy for the writer's "acute sense of the nature and dynamics of imperialist penetration" (215). In a process that may be understood as a vertical layering or repression in the classical modernist text, the relations of power that exist in the political and economic spheres are buried or contained within the all-embracing myth of the existential void. Imperialist expansion and the calculated manipulation of Third World aspirations are made to appear trivial in the overriding context of absurdity and nothingness. This projection of a modern, Western *angst* onto the Third World landscape thus has not only a literary and philosophical value, but also has its practical uses, as suggested by the following example.

November 1917 marked a crucial point in the Arab campaign. Lawrence's army, ragged from its long sojourn in the desert, had closed in on the region of the Dead Sea, but desperately needed the support of the neighboring Serahin tribe in order to carry out the final objective in reaching Damascus. The Serahin, however, were reluctant to join in what seemed a hopeless cause in the face of overwhelming Turkish defenses. Lawrence's appeal to them is a master-stroke of metaphysical argument in the service of practical motives:

> To be of the desert was, as they knew, a doom to wage unending battle with an enemy who was not of the world, nor life, nor anything, but hope itself; and failure seemed God's freedom to mankind. . . . To the clear-sighted, failure was the only goal. We must believe, through and through, that there was no victory, except to go down into death fighting and crying for failure itself, calling in excess of despair to Omnipotence to strike harder, that by His very striking He might temper our tortured selves into the weapon of His own ruin. (421–422)

In this extraordinary exhortation, Lawrence intensifies his idealization of the Arab in order to translate that ideal into an irresistible argument for self-sacrifice. The condition of the Arab no longer stands for a mere contemplative asceticism; it has been transformed into the renunciation of hope itself, a heroic recognition of human finitude. The existential hero must actively embrace his doom as the only means of deliverance from a life lived under its conditions. This is the "choice of nightmares" made by Conrad's Kurtz, who prefers to name the horror of nothingness rather than turn away from it. The defiant abnegation of hope implicit in Lawrence's vision anticipates Albert Camus's version of the myth of Sisyphus, in which the hero achieves superiority to his fate by recognizing the eternal futility of his task. Lawrence, writing at a historical moment midway between Conrad and Camus, calls upon this metaphysic in a classic example of political rhetoric—rhetorical in its function as a mode of persuasion, political in its design for a concrete action.

Of course, the sacrifice demanded of the Arabs here in the name of an existential ideal will ultimately lead, as Lawrence can foresee, to the establishment of British and French authority in the region. This is the real purpose of Lawrence's appeal, the source of his anxiety, and the final outcome of a process that begins with the idealization of the Arab. In Lawrence's logic, the notion of Arab transcendence—of the physical world, of history—requires that the Arab must go on fighting without regard for the possibility of defeat, for fear of failure would amount to a renunciation of existential freedom. In this way, Lawrence's sublimation of the Arab serves his immediate strategic ends, as well as those of the European power he represents.

Earlier in this chapter I noted that the modern movement toward a rational and instrumental view of the world found a certain resistance in the Western imagination and that one sign of this resistance was the idealization of non-Western peoples who, in the purely rationalist view, would be regarded as sources of political instability, reservoirs of cheap labor, and potential markets for mass consumption. Idealization may thus be said to provide a *compensation* on the symbolic level for the political and economic processes that have destroyed the traditional fabric of non-Western societies; by representing individual instances of courage, beauty, and spiritual transcendence, Western writing about the Third World offers a kind of substitute gratification for what would otherwise be an overwhelming sense of loss. This compensatory gesture is what connects Lawrence's Arabia to the vision of Calcutta presented in a book such as Dominique Lapierre's *The City of Joy*.

In moving from Lawrence to Lapierre, we pass not only from an Englishman's experience of Arabia in World War I to a Frenchman's view of Calcutta in 1985. We also descend, in the scale of stylistic registers, from literary to popular journalism and from an overly refined modernist sensibility to the contagious enthusiasm of the best-seller. But the work of both writers nonetheless has in common this effect: it presents an image of non-Western society sufficiently idealized in order to "manage" the burden of the Third World on Western consciousness.

In chapter 1 we saw how Kipling accompanied the Calcutta police in order to penetrate the slums of Calcutta, a part of the city ordinarily off limits to Europeans. His journey is cast as a sort of *Inferno* in which he makes the rounds of corruption and vice in the depths of what is for him the foulest of cities. In Lapierre's book as well, Calcutta is presented initially as the object of a quest. A Roman Catholic priest seeking out "the poorest of the poor" finds them in the slums of this same Calcutta:

> It was here. He was sure it was. The exaltation that suddenly seized Stephan Kovalski, the feeling of plenitude at being at last "with them," could not be designed to deceive him. It was definitely here, in this gray, filthy, poor, sad, stinking, muddy place. In this wild turmoil of men, women, children, and animals. In this entanglement of huts built of beaten earth, this jumble of alleyways full of refuse and open drains, in this murderous pollution of sulphur and fumes, in this uproar of voices, shouting, weeping, tools, machinery, and loudspeakers. (62)

Lapierre's Calcutta shares with Kipling's the quality of being "off limits" to Europeans; the journey of the Catholic priest is described as "an experience considered impossible for a Westerner." The European in Calcutta thus finds himself in a boundary situation where, having strayed beyond the limits of civilized life, he confronts the Other as a kind of ethical absolute—only for Lapierre, this absolute is not the principle of evil, but rather its opposite: the slum dwellers of Calcutta come to represent a state of beatitude in which the spirit transcends the corruption of the diseased and hungry flesh.

In the symbolic universe of Lapierre's journalistic tour de force, the true Calcutta lies not in the depths of an *Inferno* but rather upward and outward, at the summit of a purgatory where human souls are purified and made ready to ascend heavenward. Thus *The City of Joy* recounts a series of heartwarming stories in which the poor are seen to rise above their earthly circumstances. Invited to share a meal with a family of lepers, the priest Kovalski overcomes his revulsion at "fingerless hands battling with balls of rice and marrow," to find his hosts "overcome with joy, wild with gratitude" at the privilege of entertaining a foreign guest. The slum itself is a model of human community:

> In these slums people actually put love and mutual support into practice. They knew how to be tolerant of all creeds and castes, how to show charity toward beggars, cripples, lepers, and even the insane. Here the weak were helped, not trampled upon. Orphans were instantly adopted by their neighbors and old people were cared for and revered by their children. (45)

Lapierre arrives at this utopian vision by way of a fetishization of poverty in which every starved belly, every running sore is made the object of assiduous description. In chapter 5 we saw how the abject may be constituted as the Other, and thus as the object of revilement and desecration. In Lapierre's book, however, we see that the abjection of the Other also makes him or her available to saintliness: malediction and canonization are merely opposing principles of the same rhetorical operation whereby the Other is defined as lying outside the human world of the speaking subject, or, in this case, of the Western journalist. Derrida makes the same point when he compares Lévi-Strauss's idealization of the Nambikwara to the moralizing descriptions of an American anthropologist who finds in the same natives nothing but surliness and lack of civility. "In fact," Derrida writes, "these two accounts are symmetrically opposed, they have the same dimensions, and arrange themselves around one and the same axis" (1976:116). The axis is that of ethnocentrism, although in the case of Lévi-Strauss as well as that of Lapierre, an ethnocentrism that sees itself as its own opposite.

Lapierre's moral abstraction of Calcutta is also, of course, a deflection from politics: he helps to manage symbolically the human crisis of the slum dwellers by showing that they have taken the spiritual path out of their misery. In keeping with this strategy of containment, political activists in *The City of Joy* are represented as terrorists or as left-wing *Babus* who turn their backs on the poor. Political engagement invariably ends in failure and disappointment. Kovalski's own decision to become a missionary is made after his father, a revolutionary Marxist, hangs himself in prison. In Calcutta a rare strike by the rickshaw pullers fizzles out amid empty speeches by union leaders. One of the striking workers remarks, "All these speeches had prevented us from earning our living that day" (201). This sublation of politics is consistent with the process of fetishization which seeks to remove poverty from the context of power relations and which seeks, simultaneously, to represent poverty as the way to human and spiritual fulfillment. The "joy" of Calcutta thus serves to compensate for the great inequality between the Third World and the modernized West; it enables a Western audience to feel compassion and even to see the poor of that other world as living out the realization of some of the West's most ancient ideals.

Hayden White has remarked that concepts like "wildness," "savagery," and "barbarism" belong to an area of modern consciousness not yet colonized by scientific knowledge: such knowledge does not necessarily touch the levels of psychic anxiety where images of the Other have their origin (153).

This is true not only of debasing concepts like savagery, but also of concepts that idealize the Other; Lawrence's existentially authentic Arabs and Lapierre's saintly Indians may be seen as reactions to a more rational, scientific knowledge that would prevent one's vision of Arabia or India from being elevated to the level of an ethical or metaphysical abstract. This resistance to the purely rational is also a resistance to the purely *rationalized*— to a view of the social order which, for example, defines Arabs or Indians in terms of their instrumental value in the cause of technological progress and economic development. In this regard, the idealization of the Other can be understood as symptomatic of modern alienation and as a mark of profound self-doubt in the collective consciousness of the West.

One of the more striking examples of such idealization in recent journalism came with the discovery, in 1971, of an apparently Stone Age tribe on the remote Philippine island of Mindanao. This seemingly isolated tribe of hunter-gatherers, called the Tasaday, became an international media sensation. They were the subject of a *National Geographic* special on CBS television and of breathless accounts in newspapers and magazines. They made their way into textbooks on anthropology and into the *Encyclopedia Britannica*'s 1973 *Yearbook of Science and the Future*. According to *Time*, the "lost tribe of the Tasaday" had been untouched by contact with the outside world and had remained unchanged for aeons in their way of life. They had no knowledge of agriculture and were unfamiliar with rice, corn, salt, and tobacco. The *Time* account continued:

> The tribesmen also have no metal technology, no domestic animals and no permanent dwellings. Though situated on an island, they live in a mountainous, thickly wooded area of rain forest, have never seen the sea and have no word for it in their strange Malayo-Polynesian language. (October 18, 1971)

We have seen how in writers like Stanley the rhetorical strategy of negation is used to designate the Other as absence and emptiness in order to clear a space for colonialist expansion. In this case, however, the same strategy indicates a presence; the repeated negatives are used as if to strip away layers of history in the excavation of a primitive ideal which is still there, fully present in its hothouse isolation, its wholeness uncompromised by social difference, by knowledge, by time.

In an operation which Derrida would recognize as part of a recurring Western fantasy, the Tasaday are symbolically constructed in the media as humankind in its original, undivided state. The *National Geographic* (August 1972) describes the Mindanao rain forest as "the wilds of a primitive Eden" and asserts that the Tasaday "live much as our ancestors did thousands of years ago." This way of life is characterized by a total lack of conflict and contradiction. The Tasaday, we are told, have no weapons and no word for war. "There is no division of labor; each man does what he can do best." There is no special sense of property—tools, for example, are shared by all. There are no divisions of authority; a tribesman says quite simply, "We decide things together."

A story in the *New York Times Magazine* pursues this desire for an original innocence into the realm of popular metaphysics. Here the Tasaday are said to have a "vagueness . . . with regard to time, space, and past events." Until recently, according to the *Times*, the Tasaday could not count. Sheltered by the thick foliage of the forest, they had no occasion to check the monthly cycle of the moon or the changes in season. The *Times* writer asks rhetorically, "Why measure the length of pregnancy when a woman delivers her child when it comes, and the husband simply waits till the afterbirth has appeared to cut the umbilical cord?" The Tasaday have not only escaped the divisions of time, space, and numerical abstraction; they also appear to have avoided the metaphysics of good and evil: "Though little is yet known of their religion or myths, they have not yet peopled the world with a mass of malevolent spirits" (October 8, 1972). Here is truly that Rousseauian being captured in his essence, undivided by notions of good and evil, then and now. This being, who for Rousseau was little more than a hypothetical concept, has now come to life in the pages of *Time*, *National Geographic*, and the *New York Times*.

Although the idea of having discovered one of the lost tribes of Eden may have a special urgency for the late twentieth century, the rhetorical figures which the press brings to bear on the subject are anything but new. The accounts of the Tasaday have their origins in nineteenth-century adaptations of Rousseau such as Melville's writing on the Pacific islanders. The *New York Times*, for example, finds that in the Tasaday's uncorrupted disregard for time and space, "very similar days in one settled place flow, without dramatic interruption, into one another." Melville likewise observed that "Nothing can be more uniform and undiversified than the life of the Typee; one tranquil day of ease follows another in quiet succession" (171). Where the *Times* finds a "remarkable harmony" of social life which avoids even the exchange of harsh words, Melville found a society of "smoothness and harmony unparalleled" by the most "refined and pious associations of mortals in Christendom" (226).

Perhaps the most attractive of all the Tasaday's qualities is that, although they apparently have dreams, they claim what can only be interpreted as a blissful ignorance of the meaning or importance of dreams. A Tasaday tells the *National Geographic*, "We do not know what dreams are." The Tasaday thus take their place in a recurring Western dream of a world without dreams, without, that is, the division of the conscious from the unconscious, and the fundamental concealment of the self from itself. Christopher Miller has traced this dream of dreamlessness back to Homer, Herodotus, and Pliny, who wrote that the Ethiopians "are not visited with dreams like the rest of us" (63).

Miller compares such representations to what Freud calls the "perceptual identity" of the dreamer with the dream content. Given his theory in *The Interpretation of Dreams* that a dream is a fulfillment of a wish, one kind of fulfillment occurs when the dream is taken for perception itself, is "taken for real" in order "to reestablish the original situation of satisfaction." Freud assigns this kind of fulfillment to a "primitive state of the psychical apparatus . . . in which wishing ended in hallucinating." Miller points out that this primitive state of wish fulfillment, where the dream is not distinguished from perception, is how Europe conceives of African thought: "as a free reign of fulfilled desire" (63).

Freud opposes perceptual identity to "thought identity," where thought substitutes for hallucination in the fulfillment of desire and the subject remains aware of the distinction between dream and reality. The dream itself, however, is neither thought nor perception, but is constituted by the free play between these two opposing forms of wish fulfillment (64), that is, between the identity of perception and the difference of thought.

The early reports of the Tasaday ascribe to them in their ignorance of dreams a perceptual identity with wish fulfillment; they dwell in the same free realm of fulfilled desire earlier ascribed to Africans. At the same time, such reports conceive of the West in terms of thought identity: only in the divided and hence more complex Western mind does thought intervene to distinguish dream from actual experience. But later stories about the Tasaday suggest that the early reports had a hallucinatory quality of their own and that the idea of a people innocent of divided consciousness itself belonged to the form of wish fulfillment that identifies the dream with actual perception.

Since the mid-1980s it has become increasingly likely that the phenomenon known as the Tasaday was in fact a hoax created by members of the regime of Philippine President Ferdinand Marcos. Most anthropologists, both in the West and in the Philippines, now believe that the Tasaday are neither Stone Age nor even a tribe in themselves, but are rather members of already well-known indigenous tribes of Mindanao Island. Their skepticism focuses on traditional criteria (language, diet, implements, refuse heaps, population count) for establishing the "authenticity" of an isolated and self-sufficient human society. In three international meetings held between 1986 and 1989, anthropologists argued that the Tasaday story was a fraud, evidently staged to deflect international attention from Marcos's domestic policies and to provide Philippine history with an acceptable alternative to the *negritos,* the black race heretofore considered the most ancient of Philippine peoples (*Science News,* May 6, 1989, and November 25, 1989; *Science,* December 1, 1989). The Tasaday would appear to stand beside another hoax, Melville's Typee, whose way of life has since been revealed as largely a product of the author's fertile and archetypal imagination; both instances of the primitive ideal fill the same demand. If the Tasaday had not existed, they would had to have been invented, and it appears that they were.

A few anthropologists have defended the authenticity of the tribe on some of the same grounds mentioned above, while skeptics have been attacked as leftist intellectuals eager to discredit the Marcos regime for its "sponsorship" of the Tasaday. Even defenders of the Tasaday, however, have retreated from the position that the tribe has always existed in isolation from other human groups. They claim instead that the Tasaday represent a splinter group, divided from a larger tribe a century or two ago. Amid this scientific and political controversy, events took a bizarre turn in 1988, when four members of the Tasaday filed suit in Manila against two Filipino anthropologists who dispute their authenticity, one of whom had called the Tasaday the most elaborate hoax perpetrated on the anthropological world since the Piltdown Man scandal of 1908 (*New York Times,* October 29, 1988). In Freudian terms, the Tasaday may be said to have already passed from the primitive psychic condition of perceptual identity to one of thought identity with the dream; they are now caught in the vortex of political and legal institutions from which their authenticity can only be thought of in the abstract, its substantial reality destroyed by the very means used to recover it. What is at stake for our purposes, however, is not the authenticity of the Tasaday, but the idea of authenticity itself, traditionally advanced by anthropology as a way both to validate its object and to reinforce the distinction between "socially authentic" communities—those based on an oral tradition—and the "inauthentic" condition of societies corrupted by writing, courts, political factions, etc., yet also seen as more advanced because of this complexity. The case of the Tasaday has become a parody of that distinction, as the notion of authenticity is flung back at anthropology by the very people who have served as its object. Despite the lingering power of the primitive ideal, authenticity and inauthenticity have collapsed into a space not defined by binary distinctions of this kind, but marked instead by a more complex interplay of loosely connected subjectivities.

Michel Leiris foresaw something of this collapse more than thirty years ago in a now famous essay on ethnography and colonialism. After pointing to the various ways in which the history and methods of ethnography coincide with the European colonial enterprise, Leiris argues for a kind of ethnographic writing which would recognize not only this complicity, but also the ways in which colonialism itself has in part constituted those societies that form the object of ethnographic inquiry:

> If we wish to be objective, we must consider these societies in their *real* state, i.e. their actual state as societies subject in some degree to the economic, political, and cultural empire of Europe—and not by appealing to the idea of some sort of integrity, because it is obvious that the societies in question have never known such an integrity, even before being colonized; there is really not a single society that has ever lived in complete isolation, without any relations with other societies and thus without receiving from the outside a certain amount of influence. (359)

The myth of social integrity or authenticity is combined, according to Leiris, with the idea that certain human communities are "happier" if left apart than if mingled with our own: "We tend to see as happy those peoples who make *us* happy when we look at them, because of the poetic or aesthetic emotion evoked by their appearance [*spectacle*]" (364).

Instead of an ethnography based on ideal categories of social integrity and structural unity, Leiris argues for the study of the most culturally compromised members of colonial society, the native-born but European-educated *evolués* (a term itself reflecting the desire both to isolate and to overcome the primitive). In these persons, removed from the more superficial aspects of their social origins, one might observe certain surviving characteristics that constitute the particular way of being a man belonging to that culture [*la façon particulière qu'on y a d'être un homme*]. It is here, however, that having rid himself of the myth of authenticity, Leiris lets it reenter through the back door. The *evolué*, like an experimental "control" from which variable factors can be eliminated, constitutes the sign of a human essence specific to a certain culture. Authenticity is thus resurrected in an aesthetic and poetic way in order to identify a source of cultural difference even more deeply rooted in myths of essence than one based on principles of social and historical continuity.

The logical move which Leiris appears ready to take, and yet steps back from, is one which would see the *evolué* as neither more nor less authentic than either the indigenous "bush-native" or the European *colon*. Questions of authenticity must be put aside in order to see each of these groups as existing only by virtue of continual negotiation with the other two, a process that inevitably blurs the lines of demarcation that distinguish one group from another in an ideal sense. From this perspective, culture itself is no longer a unified and coherent construct, but rather an ongoing phenomenon in human relations arising out of the dialectical play between forces of homogeneity and heterogeneity. The encounter between one culture and another cannot finally be distinguished from any given culture's continued confrontation with its own ruptures and discontinuities.

9 INSUBSTANTIALIZATION

Seeing as in a Dream

GÉRARD DE NERVAL'S *VOYAGE EN ORIENT* (1851), THE massive first-person account of his travels in the Near East, contains this description of the hallucinatory effects of hashish:

> Delivered from that clumsy jailer of a body, the spirit escapes, like a prisoner whose guard has fallen asleep, leaving the keys at the door of the cell. Joyful and free, it wanders through regions of space and light. . . . With a light stroke of its wings it travels through atmospheres of indescribable bliss—all this in the space of a minute which seems an eternity, so rapidly do the sensations succeed one another. (404)

These words are spoken by a character in an ancient tale told by a Druze sheikh whom Nerval has sought out in Beirut. They appeal not only to Nerval's interests in hashish and in Oriental romance, but also to a symbolist aesthetic which seeks the liberation of the spirit through the transcendence of time and space. In the particular context of the *Voyage*, however, this passage belongs to an oneiric language which applies everywhere to Nerval's experience of the Orient, returning the reader continually to what Edward Said has called Nerval's "quintessential Oriental world of uncertain, fluid dreams multiplying themselves past resolution, definiteness, materiality" (1978:183). On his way back to Europe at the end of his journey, Nerval laments, "I return to the land of storm and cold, and already the Orient seems but one of those morning dreams that are quickly dissipated by the worries of the day" (696). Despite the prosaic conventions of travel narrative followed by the *Voyage*, Nerval's Orient is a region of the visionary imagination, a series of dreamlike sensations whose rapid succession releases him from the weight of historical and material reality.

Said places Nerval in a historical line of writers—Chateaubriand, Lamartine, Flaubert—for whom the Orient was less the object of direct observation than a literary topos, a site upon which each writer's imagination confronted those of his predecessors. But this placement of Nerval suggests a still larger context that I want to explore—that of an entire tradition of Western writing which makes the experience of the non-Western world into an inner journey, and in so doing renders that world as insubstantial, as the backdrop of baseless fabric against which is played the drama of the writer's self.

As a rhetorical gesture, this insubstantialization is close to what I have elsewhere called aestheticization, but with the difference that instead of being ordered by the material unity and coherence of an aesthetic model, in this case the object of representation is seen as an immaterial counterpart to the dissolving consciousness of the subject, a dissolution which can be joyful, as in Nerval, or profoundly disorienting. The emphasis here is on a certain phenomenology of consciousness deployed in relation to the non-Western world, rather than on the aesthetic qualities assigned to that world.

The irony of a disorienting Orient has been noted by Steve Attridge, who cites two alternatives to the familiar use of "Orient" as a proper noun. In Samuel Johnson's *Dictionary* (1755), Orient appears as an adjective: "Bright; shining; glittering; gaudy; sparkling." The *Oxford English Dictionary* (1928) includes the following figurative use of Orient as a verb: "to adjust, correct, or bring into defined relations, to known facts and principles. *refl.* to put oneself in the right position or relation; to ascertain one's 'bearings,' find out 'where one is.'" These diverging senses of the word come from the differing ways in which the notion of the Orient has been used in Western writing: as a space against which the West defines or orients itself, and as a source of dazzling, disorienting brilliance—Nerval's regions of space and light. The two meanings come together when one considers how the "defined relations" and "known facts and principles" of Western thinking are constituted in antithetical opposition to the perceived lack of such knowledge and definition in the Orient. One "finds out where one is" by putting the Orient, with its undefined categories of subjective and objective experience, over *there*.

Hegel's procedure in defining the fully realized subjectivity of Western consciousness is first to show how the conditions for such consciousness are totally lacking in "the Oriental World." Thus India is "an enchanted World . . . a region of phantasy," whose Spirit exists only in the amorphous form of a dream-state. The fantastic quality of India refers both to its image in the Western mind and to the actual state of consciousness (or lack of consciousness) represented by the "dreaming Indian." For Hegel, the Indian view of things dissolves the world into a space of infinite confusion; the sensuous object

> is not liberated by the free power of the Spirit into a beautiful form . . .
> but is expanded into the immeasurable and undefined, and the Divine
> is thereby made bizarre, confused, and ridiculous. . . . *Things* are as
> much stripped of rationality, of finite consistent stability of cause and
> effect, as *man* is of the steadfastness of free individuality, of personality,
> and freedom. (141)

Hegel's dreaming Indian anticipates Freud's figure of a primitive psychic state defined by the dreamer's perceptual identity with the dream; but Hegel's figure is one of enslavement and annihilation (*Vernichtung*) rather than fulfilled desire. The Spirit of the Hindu finds no rest and can content itself only in ever more extravagant and wild reveries, "as a man who is quite reduced in body and spirit finds his existence altogether stupid and intolerable, and is driven to the creation of a dreamworld and a delirious bliss in opium" (167). This self-oblivious dissolution makes Hegel's Indian incapable of either writing or creating a history, as we saw in chapter 6; the dream-state thus describes not only consciousness but an ontological condition as well. On the other hand, the objectification of this dream-state by the self-conscious mind, its comprehension in rational connection with other objects, is for Hegel precisely what makes history, writing, and the writing of history possible for the West (162–163). The history of the West *as* the West arises out of an orientation that understands the Orient as a space of disorientation.

If for Hegel the ontological instability of the Orient serves this antithetical purpose in the construction of knowledge, it serves other writers as an escape *from* the Hegelian dialectic into the unexplored regions of the self. Raymond Schwab quotes an 1888 letter from Stéphane Mallarmé to Jean Lahor, an Orientalist who had written a history of Hindu literature:

> What is wonderful to me is that your Orient arises completely from
> your soul, because that is your nature, and you have simply juxta-
> posed an exotic malady against your own thought, as a proof or
> illustration; but even your voice, and a certain rich monotony that

veils your lyricism, elucidates this remoteness in ourselves—entrancing, sad, broad—that loses itself in the sacred river of annihilation
[*anéantissement*]. (421)

Hegel's *Vernichtung*—annihilation as enslavement to the fantastic productions of a fevered imagination, has become Mallarmé's *anéantissement*—
annihilation as release from the rational world of finite relations. Mallarmé constructs the Orient as a remote inner state alternately conceived as
the decadence of "exotic malady" (*un mal exotique*) and the purity of the
"sacred river."

The relation of this Orient to rational consciousness, however, is essentially destabilizing, a subversive and entrancing presence that dissolves into
absence, a "remoteness" that invokes presence *as* absence, and leads to the
annihilation of the boundary distinguishing these conceptual categories.
Mallarmé's use of "voice" contributes to this effect of destabilizing the subject, for by this word he seems to mean something more occult than the
individual tone or style of Lahor's expression. The voice, whose rich mo-
notony "veils" the speaker's lyricism as it "elucidates" an inner remoteness,
has become a medium of both concealment and illumination, a faltering,
fading voice that signals the breaking up of consciousness itself. Mallarmé's
internalization of the Orient thus depends not so much on a spatial metaphor as on a phenomenological language of veiling and unveiling, nearness
and remoteness, thought and entrancement.

The destabilizing of the subject entailed in this quest for an ephemeral
inner Orient has its counterpart in travel writing devoted to stories of disguised identity and hallucination. Such writing often involves a surrender
of the self to the powers of the Other in what is represented as a dangerous
transgression of boundaries. In 1888, the year of Mallarmé's letter to Lahor,
a Frenchman named Camille Douls wrote an extraordinary account of his
travels in the Western Sahara. Fluent in Arabic and disguised as a Moslem,
he is captured by warlike nomads and eventually becomes "a brother of the
tribe," joining in their raids on caravans. Though ostensibly undertaken
for purposes of geographical exploration, Douls's journey has the quality
of a calculated flirtation with the possibilities of enslavement, madness,
and self-annihilation.

Emblematic of Douls's narrative is his experience of a hallucination
brought on by the extreme conditions of desert travel and called the *ralgue*
by the nomads. Suddenly the desert appears to Douls like the shining surface of a lake; he feels alone between heaven and earth on this "resplendent
plain" and hears sweet, melodious voices:

For all this time my sense of perception had completely disappeared;
I submitted to a sort of hypnotism. . . . —But the expression on my
face must have revealed what was happening, because a Moor, seeing
my hallucinated stare fixed blindly on the horizon, shook me by the
shoulder and cried, "wake up, wake up, you have the *ralgue,* you will
go mad!" (14)

Whatever the lived experience on which this passage is based, it belongs
to a recurring scene in Western writing: the spell of the Orient leads to a
sublime madness which betrays itself in the *look* of the speaker and which
causes those around him to recoil in alarm. In Coleridge's "Kubla Khan"
these witnesses to Oriental madness cry, "Beware! Beware! / His flashing
eyes, his floating hair!"; in Walter De La Mare's "Arabia" they say, "He is
crazed with the spell of far Arabia, / They have stolen his wits away." The
perilous submission to a dream-state is presented ambivalently, as an entrance to an enchanted space of fulfilled desire, but from which the attempt
to return can be fatal.

This dynamic of penetration and submission goes beyond moments of
hallucination or madness and applies more generally to narratives in which
the space of the Orient or Africa itself is presented in terms of visionary
experience. A spectacular follower of Douls was the French writer Michel
Vieuchange, who became obsessed with a place in the Western Sahara
called Smara, still a mystery to Europeans in 1930, and said to be the center of brigandage and fanaticism for the nomadic Moors. Determined to
reach this forbidden city, Vieuchange disguised himself as a Berber woman
and traveled for two months among the nomadic tribes south of Morocco.
Fearful of being discovered in the company of an infidel, his guides would
conceal him in a wicker hamper on the back of a camel. As in the case
of Douls, these acts of concealment and disguise are part of a symbolic
transformation of personal identity which the writer chooses to undergo
in pursuit of an ephemeral goal. The transformation and the pursuit, however, may be regarded as part of the same rite of passage: Vieuchange
divests himself of gender, of nationality, and even of open physical presence in his search for what Mallarmé calls that remoteness in ourselves (*ce
lointain de nous*) that loses itself in annihilation.

Vieuchange's narrative is remarkable for the manner in which the desert
city is made to objectify the longing for visionary transformation. When
after great hardship he reaches Smara, he discovers it to be a ghost town of
stone buildings abandoned in the middle of the desert landscape; its silence,
isolation, and absent glory only enhance its phantasmagoric quality:

> Smara, town of our illusions . . .
> As ravishers we press towards thee,
> But also as penitents we come.
> And to the friend, or to one who questions us on the way,
>   we shall say, "I know you not."
> We travel towards that bourne
> Which the dawn floods to overflowing
> And purifies. (17)

The combination of ravisher and penitent follows the pattern of penetration and submission we have noted elsewhere; it may be seen in a larger context as a rhetorical movement which extends itself into ever more remote territory, even as this extension represents itself as surrender and abandonment.

Camille Douls returned to France to tell of his life among the nomads. A year later he returned to the Sahara; while trying to reach the Niger River from Tafilalet, he was murdered by his guides (Vieuchange 11). Michel Vieuchange died of dysentery on the return journey from Smara.

In the foregoing discussion I have assembled a group of texts in which the movement into exotic geographical space is understood as an inner exploration of the boundaries of consciousness. In following this expansion of European experience both inward and outward, we are led to the intersection of colonial discourse and literary modernism and to the question of how these two systems of symbolic order may be seen as related to each other in their responses to the same overall set of historical circumstances. Two extraordinary works of nonfiction which lie squarely at this intersection are Lawrence's *Seven Pillars of Wisdom* and Gide's *Voyage au Congo*. Both works, published in the mid-1920s, are essentially about the modernist sensibility and its effort to comprehend what may loosely be called the colonial situation.

In chapter 6 I discussed the way in which Gide projects a uniquely Western problematic onto the African landscape when he sees it as an abyss of nothingness and ennui. Here I want to concentrate on the way in which his African experience is represented as psychic disorientation and disintegration. The characteristic mode of what Georg Lukács has called the ideology of modernism involves the disintegration of the subject as a coherent, rational entity, and a corresponding attenuation of outward reality which makes narrative objectivity impossible. In this double disintegration, Lukács says, "Man is reduced to a sequence of unrelated experiential fragments; he is as inexplicable to others as to himself" (26).

Gide's narrative conforms to this mode at moments where an otherwise consistent point of view gives way to extreme disorientation. As he moves further into the great forest of Oubangui, Gide traces the unhinging of his own state of consciousness: "Each day we sank a little further into strangeness. I lived all day in a state of torpor and semi-consciousness, *as though of hemlock I had drunk,* losing all notion of time, of place, of myself" (122). The quotation (in English) from Keats' *Ode to a Nightingale*, which in turn recalls the death of Socrates, is part of a strategy Gide employs throughout the narrative in order to mediate his disorientation by interpreting it within the context of a literary and intellectual past. At other stages of his journey, we find him commenting on passages from Bossuet or Bergson. These texts, which Gide has brought with him, perform the same symbolic function as *An Inquiry into Some Points of Seamanship,* the book that Conrad's Marlow comes across in the midst of the jungle and which, unlike his actual surroundings, gives him "a delicious sensation of having come upon something unmistakably real" (108). For Gide, it is as if his subjective disorientation could only be made real by reference to a literary model.

The feeling of disorientation soon extends to Gide's relations with the native population. In a part of the country not controlled by the *grandes compagnies,* the expedition is received by the native population with a celebration bordering on what appears to Gide as delirium. Scores of people follow his party from one place to the next, ceremoniously bidding him farewell, only to overtake him and greet him anew at the next village. Under the pressure of this unceasing jubilation, Gide begins to lose his hold on reality. At the village of Pakori, he writes,

> The number of children is unimaginable. I try to count them; at 180 I give up in dizziness [*pris de vertige*]; they are too many. And the whole population envelops you, presses in on you for the joy of shaking the hand you extend, all with shouting and laughter, a sort of lyricism in their demonstrations of affection. It is almost cannibalism. (129)

The word *cannibal* derives from *Carib* or *Caribes,* the West Indian tribe encountered by explorers in the sixteenth century. In the language of Shakespeare (*Othello*), Montaigne (*De Cannibalis*), and Defoe (*Robinson Crusoe*), the word refers more generally to savages who eat human flesh, particularly in those parts of the world that are being annexed by the great European powers. Thus at the precise moment when he begins to lose control of his powers of observation, Gide invokes a word which entered the modern European languages as part of the colonization of Africa and the New World and whose history recalls the fear of being consumed by the object of conquest.

Gide's sensory consumption of the African landscape—"as though of hemlock I had drunk"—becomes the occasion for an ironic reversal when the tasting, consuming subject experiences the fear of being eaten alive. The thought of being devoured by cannibals, with its images of bodily dismemberment, provides a physical counterpart to the disintegrating psychic state in which the subject loses all notions of time, place, and self. In *Heart of Darkness*, Marlow hopes that his own flesh might look more appetizing to the local cannibals than that of his "unwholesome" fellow voyagers—an absurd conceit he attributes to "the fantastic vanity which fitted well with the dream-sensation that pervaded all my days at that time" (112). In Gide as in Conrad, the characteristic *vertige* of the modernist sensibility leads dangerously to the colonizer's thoughts of being devoured by that which is so precariously subdued. The specifically ideological nature of this sensibility can be seen where the inner conflict of the subject displaces those conflicts taking place outwardly, in the actual arenas of human practice.

This recurring tension between inner and outer worlds against the background of colonialism is what unites Gide with Lawrence, two writers ordinarily understood as having very different projects. I have already noted Lawrence's tendency to project a specifically Western and modernist anxiety onto the Arabian landscape. Here I want to pursue this aspect of Lawrence a little further, in order to show how he presents himself as caught in a crisis of self-identity.

The disintegration of subjective identity which Lukacs identifies as a primary component of modernist ideology takes place in Lawrence as a crisis of cultural identity. In reflecting on his experience of Arabia, Lawrence writes of his efforts "to live in the dress of Arabs, and to imitate their mental foundation." This effort releases him from his English self and "destroys" the West and its conventions for him. At the same time, however, his effort to imitate the Arab mentality is "affectation only . . . I had dropped one form and not taken on the other." Lawrence thus occupies a terrifying in-between state, no longer English, but not yet Arab either, in which the foundations of reality and the motives for action suddenly lose their meaning. This absence of any firm identity takes the form of a split in which his "reasonable mind" looks critically upon the actions of his bodily self: "Sometimes these selves would converse in the void; and then madness was very near, as I believe it would be near the man who could see things through the veils at once of two customs, two educations, two environments" (30).

Seven Pillars of Wisdom has relatively little to say about Arabia or the Arabs; it is rather a modernist version of *Robinson Crusoe*, in which the subject is systematically stripped of all existing relationships, then confronted with the awesome but undefined presence of the Other. For Crusoe, the unknown landscape inspires fear and the desperate attempt to reconstruct a remembered domestic and theological order. Lawrence, on the other hand, has moments where he gives in to the void, transforming the landscape into the agent of his own purification: "The abstraction of the desert landscape cleansed me, and rendered my mind vacant with its superfluous greatness; a greatness achieved not by the addition of thought to its emptiness, but by its subtraction" (524). What unites Lawrence not only with Gide but with Defoe, Nerval, and others finally is his treatment of the colonial situation as the occasion for an inner, spiritual quest involving both the dissolution of the subject and the abstraction of its material surroundings.

In *Tristes Tropiques* Lévi-Strauss writes of a puberty rite he has observed in certain tribes, where young men subject themselves to long periods of solitude, to physical pain, and to delirium in hopes of communicating with the supernatural. They deliberately venture into "hazardous marginal areas where social norms cease to have any meaning"; they move along the unstable border areas of consciousness, flirting with the danger of death or permanent madness (29). The point of this flight from ordinary living and thinking is to be able to return to one's normal social surroundings with the prestige of having confronted the unknown. Thus the conscious repudiation of the social order has as its final object the improvement of one's own standing within that order. The quest for the unknown takes place simultaneously as an individual quest for power within the framework of an order that is already known intimately.

Lévi-Strauss sees a parallel to this rite in the relationship that exists between contemporary Western society and its explorers of exotic territories: "A young man who lives outside his social group for a few weeks or months, so as to expose himself . . . to an extreme situation, comes back endowed with a power which finds expression in the writing of newspaper articles and best-sellers and in lecturing to packed halls" (31). What matters in these cases is not contribution to scientific knowledge or to art, but rather the simple fact of having braved the extreme, of having walked on the edge of a cultural, psychological, or physical Otherness, and having lived to tell about it.

This particular value placed on certain forms of narrative is one way to account for their emphasis on the unreality of the situations they portray, a radical uncertainty which applies to inner consciousness as much as to the outer world. *Heart of Darkness* draws its compelling power not from the events that comprise an objective narrative, but from the narrator's insistence on their unreal, dreamlike quality, on what Conrad calls "that notion of being captured by the incredible which is the very essence of dreams" (95).

Similarly, very little actually happens to Joan Didion during her trip to El Salvador in the summer of 1982—a series of official interviews, a visit to a village near the front, a few social gatherings in the capital. The power of her narrative comes not from the nature of these incidents, but from the sense of extreme disorientation which the country produces in her mind. The North American who enters El Salvador plunges directly into "a state in which no ground is solid, no perception so definite that it might not dissolve into its reverse" (13). As she endeavors to make sense of her surroundings, Didion finds that "the place brings everything into question . . . that this was a story that would perhaps not be illuminated at all, that this was perhaps even less a 'story' than a true *noche obscura*" (35–36). The allusion is to St. John of the Cross and the spiritual journey recounted in his *Dark Night of the Soul*, though it is only ironically that her experience may be compared to that of the sixteenth-century mystic, for her discourse lacks the theological framework that gives coherence to his work. Hers is not a true *noche obscura,* but a fevered dreamwork for which El Salvador serves as the shadowy texture. My purpose is not to doubt the accuracy of Didion's observations nor the sincerity of her personal responses. It is rather to question the consequences of her presentation, which allows the reader to see the war in El Salvador as *grand guignol,* or as a particularly sinister hallucination. This use of an essentially colonial situation as a way into the darkest recesses of the writer's mind, as an inner *Voyage au bout de la nuit,* constitutes yet another recolonization of Latin America in the realm of the North American mind.

Up to this point, I have treated the problematization of the self, and of its tenuous relation to objective reality, as the product of chiefly literary sensibilities. Writers like Nerval, Gide, Lawrence, and Didion are, by virtue of an artistic vocation, naturally concerned with creating a language that sounds out the possibilities of imagination, even where that language is applied to the chronicling of events, be they the momentous occasions of war or the ordinary experiences of the traveler in trains and hotels. Near the end of his own great chronicle, Lawrence confesses, "I had had one

craving all my life—for the power of self-expression in some imaginative
form—but had been too diffuse ever to acquire à technique." The Arab
revolt gave him that power—"a theme ready and epic to a direct eye and
hand, thus offering me an outlet in literature" (565).

But what happens to this expression when it leaves the domain of the literary and takes the form of newspaper articles and best-sellers? How does
this dramatization of the self and the attendant transformation of reality
come to be a subject for the popular press? One way of answering this
question would be to take the figures of Nerval, Conrad, and Lawrence as
literary prototypes for certain *gestures* in the press toward reproducing the
crisis of the Western subject in the non-Western world. According to this
model, Nerval would represent the power of fantasy, Conrad that of terror, and Lawrence that of irony—fantasy, terror, and irony being alternate
ways of undermining the reality of one's surroundings.

I name these writers somewhat arbitrarily—not to give them special
historical importance, but merely to designate certain qualities which are
present in the work of any number of nineteenth- and twentieth-century
Western writers on the colonial world. As I hope to have demonstrated,
the rhetorical figure of transforming the Orient into a fantasy was common
in travel writing of the high colonial era, as well as in popular English and
French novels set in the East. Attridge quotes the popular novelist Flora
Annie Steel, whose *On the Face of the Waters* (1897) was one of several fictional treatments of the 1857 Indian mutiny. She offers this image of the
king's palace in Delhi:

> The outer court of the palace lay steeped in the sunshine of noon. Its
> hot rose-red walls and arcades seemed to shimmer in the glare, and
> the dazzle and glitter gave a strange air of unreality, of instability to
> all things. (62)

This particular descriptive strategy typically moves from the outer world
inward, starting with the unreal aspect of an exterior scene, then extending
the principle of unreality or instability to the writer's own thoughts, and
thus to all he or she may behold.

The effectiveness of this device as a literary and journalistic convention
has hardly been diminished by the changing political relations between the
West and the formerly colonial world. It remains one of the figures of colonial discourse that a journalist will invoke when writing colorfully about
the Third World. In an "Essay" on Africa in *Time* (February 23, 1987), the
correspondent Lance Morrow describes a "gray-purple rainstorm" moving
across the East African plain "like a dark idea." He adds, "Wildlife and

landscape here have about them a force of melodrama. They are the Book of Genesis enacted as an afternoon dream." A few paragraphs later the dreamlike qualities of Africa combine with a case of jet lag to destabilize the writer's own sense of reality:

> The visitor's soul vibrated. He thought of a soap bubble's elongation when its iridescent membrane is drawn swiftly through the air by a child. His soul began to float slow-motion in the strange, bright medium of Africa. He felt suspended, drifting through layers of time.

The image of distortion is apt, for if there is a real Africa it has dissolved in the heat of this overrich prose, reduced to a medium for the writer's communication with what he takes to be his soul and with the myths of his own cultural past. Nerval's spirit wandering through regions of space and light is reincarnated here as the soul of a *Time* correspondent "drifting through layers of time." When such rhetorical figures have filtered down from the rarefied symbolist imagination of the nineteenth century to the mass-market journalism of the twentieth century, it shows how firmly established they have become at all levels of Western culture.

In Morrow's language the sensation of dreaming is combined with that of being transported to an ancient past—a combination that is characteristic of the genre I wish to define here. We have seen this, too, in Nerval, whose experience of the Orient is mediated not only through a visionary language, but also by continual reference to an exotic antiquity. At the center of Nerval's travel narrative, there lies an inner narrative, the so-called "Tale of the Caliph Hakim" told by the old Druze in Beirut, a story itself set in the fourth century of the Moslem era (circa 1000 A.D.). This tale of hashish, passion, and intrigue Nerval claims to be "based on authentic traditions"; and indeed for him it embodies the authentic, true Orient, as if his own disorientation in that world could only be managed by a *re*-orientation of experience within the framework of a distant historical era.

This association of the dream-sensation with the historically remote takes place casually in the popular press, as suggested by the example of the *Time* essay. An article in *L'Express*, the French news magazine, takes a similar approach toward the lands of the "silk route," the ancient path followed by Marco Polo across Central Asia. Here a desert village in western China is self-consciously rendered in images of the Holy Land:

> The roads of the oasis were crowded with donkey-carts transporting families of peasants; with sheep to be slaughtered the next day; with camel-drivers and horsemen riding to the bazaar. Women carried

water. Old people, sitting cross-legged on open-air bedsteads, chatted or daydreamed. Biblical. (August 8, 1986)

Like the *Time* correspondent who sees the African plain as the Book of Genesis reborn, the *Express* correspondent invests his subject with the myth of ancient origin. These vast, isolated regions of central Asia exist for the Western writer principally for their power of suggestion, for their capacity to evoke an inspired reverie. Hence the disillusionment of the writer who finds, in one of the same ancient places, anti-American and pro-Khomeini graffiti: "End of the route of dreams!" It is natural that the expression of a modern political sentiment would seem absurd in the context the writer has created, for his vision is abstracted from any sense of history that would take into account the actual, lived reality of central Asia in its own terms.

If Nerval can serve as a symbol for that tradition whereby the non-Western world is made an object of fantasy, then the name of Conrad might serve to signify the tradition in which that same world is made the object of terror—specifically, the terror of the unreal and the abyss. We have seen how writers as different as Gide and Didion may be said to belong to this tradition. Now I want to look at an example from the daily newspapers.

In an earlier chapter I quoted a 1981 story in the *Washington Post* which treated anti-Marxist Angolan rebels as standard-bearers of civilized Western values. However, in one of the contradictory turns that colonial discourse often takes, this attempt at domestication alternates with the portrayal of Africa as the site of a disturbing subjective disorientation. Having accompanied the rebels to one of the provincial outposts, the *Post* correspondent describes the place in this way:

Mavinga itself could be the stage set for a colonial melodrama. It sits on a barren, dusty plain, surrounded by nothingness. I could imagine becoming very violent and depraved after a few years under this broiling sun. Joseph Conrad could do it justice. (July 21, 1981)

Apart from its self-indulgence, this language shrewdly combines the effects of strangeness and familiarity. The image of subjective depravity created under the pressure of an objective nothingness emphasizes the extreme strangeness of the writer's situation, as if he stood at the outer limit of an existential order. But at the same time the situation is made familiar, and even cause for a self-deprecating irony, by reference to a tradition of "colonial melodrama." The writer may see himself as surrounded by the unreal or the insubstantial, but the anxiety of such an experience is diminished by its placement within an existing discourse. What makes for the fatuous quality of this particular passage is that, unlike Conrad, the *Post* correspondent invokes the ideas of depravity and nothingness without being able to speak seriously about them. This fundamental lack of seriousness extends to his portrayal of Africa itself, which, even in the passage I have cited here, is reduced to a scene of terror in caricature. It is the same Africa that Barthes finds in a *Paris-Match* story, where the African appears as a bizarre object whose function is to divert the European visitor by his "vaguely threatening baroque" (1979:37).

The ironic mode adopted by the *Post* correspondent belongs as much to colonial discourse as does his avowed fear of madness. There is, for example, the irony of Kipling, who writes of the Chinese Boxer Rebellion of 1849 through what he calls "the medium of a fevered imagination": "It would be quite right to wipe the city of Canton off the face of the earth, and to exterminate all the people who ran away from the shelling. The Chinaman ought not to count" (1970, 17:253). Kipling caricatures his sinophobia partly in order to shock his Victorian audience, but also as part of an ironically conceived construction of his own persona. Despite their differences in ideology and historical situation, Kipling and Lawrence have in common this ironic preoccupation with personal style. Both writers admit to seeing things through the medium of a fevered imagination; but fevered as it is this imagination is still more real to them than the world it interprets.

Modern journalism has inherited, often in degraded form, this convention which makes the Western writer's encounter with the non-Western world a pretext for the presentation of a personal style. Writing in the British magazine *Granta* (Winter 1986), Leonard Frank writes of his service as a Canadian development officer in Pakistan:

> I'm tired of this mission. I don't like Moslem countries; they make your life difficult. All over the world men are much the same: you can unwind them in bars, talk about money and politics and women. Here they don't drink in public and don't admit to lust. The will of Allah suddenly comes into the middle of a business discussion. A meeting stops because it's time for the chief secretary to pray. The whole place seems slightly out of focus. (242)

The persona of the weary, disillusioned colonial has its origins in the period of imperial decline to which Kipling and Lawrence belong. To invoke it remains one way in which Western writers try to make sense out of how they experience the non-Western world—or rather a way of conveying the fact that for them the experience does not make sense. The persona includes a measure of self-directed irony; in the passage quoted above, the statement that the writer doesn't like Moslem countries because "they make your life difficult" mimics the colonial persona and thus creates a slight ironic distance between the subject and his discourse. The writer also confesses to something like inadequacy as well as to a general ennui.

It is precisely this minor self-dramatization, however, that has consequences for the portrayal of "Moslem countries," whose people are seen as mysterious, unpredictable, "out of focus." In discussing other writers, I have noted how the phenomenon of insubstantiality moves from the outer scene inward when the unreality of a given situation produces disorientation in the reader's mind. But here we can see how the process moves in the reverse direction as well. In a journalistic version of the pathetic fallacy, the writer's subjective disintegration is projected onto the outer scene, so that the scene itself becomes the locus of confusion and disintegration. The Western writer, literary or journalistic, is after all a kind of Prospero who transforms the non-Western world into a series of enchanting or disturbing visions, as easily dissolved as they are conjured up.

10 NATURALIZATION

The Wilderness in Human Form

THE CONCEPT OF "NATURE" HAS BEEN FOR COLONIAL discourse the occasion for a fundamental equivocation. On one hand, nature is opposed to culture and civilization: primitive peoples live in a state of nature. On the other, nature, or "natural law," is also that which grants dominion over the earth to more advanced peoples; the land shall belong by natural right to that power which understands its value and is willing to turn it to account. Colonial discourse thus naturalizes the process of domination: it finds a natural justification for the conquest of nature and of primitive peoples, those "children of nature."

The notion of naturalization that I wish to invoke here has its sources both in structural anthropology and in literary theory. For Lévi-Strauss, naturalization as a mode of mythical thought is the opposite of totemism. Totemism refers to the practice of interpreting nature according to the language of human institutions, such as kinship and ancestry. Naturalization does the reverse: it represents the human in terms of natural species and natural phenomena. Lévi-Strauss cites the seventeenth-century sketches of Charles Le Brun, who drew men with owl-like or fox-like faces, as if to reveal their essentially animal nature (1962:chap. 5).

In literary theory, naturalization refers to the process whereby a theory about how the world works is assumed implicitly by a text, as what is "natural" within the system of cultural values which the texts represents. Jonathan Culler thus defines naturalization in literature as the entire range of operations by which what happens in a novel, a poem, or a play is made intelligible and plausible (*vraisemblable*) (chap. 7). Homer takes great care in preparing for Odysseus' slaughter of the suitors on his return to Ithaca;

in the system of values which the *Odyssey* embodies, this otherwise problematic act of revenge must be made to seem natural for a king, a father, and a husband.

Colonial discourse may be said to naturalize in both of these senses: while it identifies a colonized or primitive people as part of the natural world, it also presents this identification as entirely "natural," as a simple state of what is, rather than as a theory based in interest. The elements of naturalization as a rhetorical mode applied to the representation of non-Western peoples are to be found not only in overtly imperialist ideology, but even in the writing of those, like Rousseau and John Stuart Mill, who have contributed to modern Western ideals of liberty and justice. For like other components of colonial discourse, the concept of nature and its relation to "less developed" peoples is so deeply imbedded in our language that it transcends ideology and is so pervasive in the system of representations by which we know the world that it tends to disappear every time we try to locate it.

Let me nonetheless begin that effort with a reflection on Rousseau. In his *Essay on the Origin of Languages* [published posthumously, 1781], Rousseau remarks on what he sees as the softness and sonorousness of languages spoken in Southern climates. He attributes these qualities to the relative ease of life in natural surroundings of mildness and abundance: "The passions of the warm countries are voluptuous, relating to love and tenderness. Nature does so much for people there that they have almost nothing to do. Provided that an Asiatic has women and repose, he is content" (1968:133). Rousseau conceives of a natural alliance between the Asiatic, or any native of a non Northern, non European climate, and the benevolent state of nature. The inhabitants of the tropics are closer than the European to nature in at least a double sense: they are literally surrounded by the fruits of the natural world, while their way of life is itself more "natural," more immediate and spontaneous than the European's, and more given to the expression of passion and desire.

For Rousseau, of course, this natural condition constitutes an ideal insofar as it represents an original freedom and the absence of artifice, dissimulation, or repression. In the North, by way of contrast, "the idleness that nurtures passion is replaced by work, which represses it" (131). Yet the Rousseauian ideal is easily stood on its head and made into the basis for a natural European superiority. The voluptuous Asiatic, wholly content with idleness and the satisfaction of carnal desire, is a stereotypical object of contempt in the Western imagination of Rousseau's age as well as our own. That natural abundance which Rousseau attributes to the southern climates turns out to be, even within the boundaries of his own discourse, a fateful lack when considered in the light of human progress.

In his commentary on the "Second Discourse" [*On the Origins of Inequality*] of 1754, Paul De Man reads Rousseau as implicitly criticizing the type of "fetishism" that reduces history to nature, that is, that sees the historical condition of humanity as purely the effect of natural causes. This error holds sway not only in the science of language, but also in studies of ethical judgment (Hobbes) and the development of technology (De Man 192). In the later *Essay on the Origin of Languages*, however, Rousseau would appear to have been seduced by the same fetish: differences in natural surroundings now account for moral differences between peoples.

Rousseau finally stands within a European tradition which identifies non-European peoples with the forces of nature and then places nature in opposition to culture. Derrida, commenting on a distinction that connects the Greek idea of nature to our own, has described this conceptual opposition as "an unquestioning faith in the entire system of differences between *physis* and its other," adding that the series of "others" has included at various historical moments art, technology, law, institution, and society (1976:103). On a level deeper than any merely political ideology, this fundamental system of differences connects Rousseau unexpectedly with the apologists of Empire who define primitive peoples as those who have yet to acquire art, technology, and meaningful social institutions.

The philosopher R. G. Collingwood has made the following distinction between Renaissance and modern ideas of nature: in Renaissance thought, the created world of nature is like a machine, devoid in itself of intelligence and life. Instead, the order which we perceive in the natural world is the work of a Divine Creator and Ruler who acts upon nature from a higher level of being. The movements of nature are imposed on it from without, and their regularity is due to "natural laws" also imposed from without. The modern view departs from this in two important respects: it sees the world as a great organism endowed with a life of its own, and it projects that life onto a historical framework. The structure of nature is resolved into natural functions, natural change is seen as progressive rather than only cyclical, and the ancient concept of *telos* reenters scientific thought, although on a scale entirely different from the Greek model (4–15).

Foucault, in reflecting on this great shift from the Renaissance to the modern view of nature, has noted another consequence: the invention of "man" as a subject, apart from nature, of epistemological consciousness (1970). Man no longer stands at the center of the natural world in microcosmic relation to the universe. Rather, human history is now distinct from natural history, although its origins lie in natural phenomena, and it can even be understood according to the model provided by the study of nature. Human history, in other words, follows natural laws while it also progresses away from natural origins. The inconsistencies of a discourse which alternately idealizes and reviles the savage may be seen as part of this larger ambivalence surrounding the unstable concepts of nature and man. This instability, in turn, can be traced to a division or a splitting off in the discourse surrounding the idea of nature: alongside the idealization of nature and of man in his natural state represented by Rousseau, there arises a countermovement toward the subordination of nature to human use and improvement.

Mill's essay on "Nature" (1873) represents an important nineteenth-century attempt to clarify the distinction between nature and man; it does so in such as way as to provide groundwork, in the realm of moral philosophy, for Victorian ideals of social and industrial progress that come to be applied to the colonialist enterprise. Taking issue with what he understands to be Rousseau's position, Mill disparages the ideal of mankind in its natural state; nature and natural instinct are precisely what humanity must learn to discipline. For Mill, human progress is the history of the great triumphs of art over nature: the building of bridges, the draining of marshes, the dragging to light of the minerals that nature has buried deep in the earth. "The ways of Nature are to be conquered, not obeyed" (20).

The ways of nature that constitute the object of this conquest have their human form as well, in the manifestation of natural instinct that defines certain classes of humanity. Mill uses the examples of non-European peoples to demonstrate either the imperfection of nature itself or the moral weakness inherent in the failure to control nature. God must have intended for us to improve on His creation; otherwise we would have to suppose that "the best He could do for His human creatures was to make an immense majority of all who have yet existed, be born (without any fault of their own) Patagonians, or Esquimaux, or something nearly as brutal and degraded." One of the signs of victory over natural instinct is the power to sacrifice a present desire to a distant object or a more general purpose. Even this simple sense of virtue is "unnatural to the undisciplined human being," as one may see by its absence "in savages, in soldiers and sailors, and in a somewhat less degree in nearly the whole of the poorer classes in this and many other countries" (41–50).

As for the Rousseauian notion that man in his natural state is innocent of the artifice required for deception, Mill finds this "a mere fancy picture, contradicted by all the realities of savage life. Savages are always liars. They have not the faintest notion of truth as a virtue." To selfishness and deception as natural instincts that must be disciplined by civilizing influence, Mill adds what we would now call sadism: "This kind of cruelty is not mere hardheartedness, absence of pity or remorse; it is a positive thing; a particular kind of voluptuous excitement. The East, and Southern Europe, have afforded, and probably still afford, abundant examples of this hateful propensity" (57). Throughout Mill's discourse, non-Northern or non-European peoples are the locus of an unregenerate human nature. His image of the despotic, sadistic Oriental can be set alongside Rousseau's image of the indolent, carnal Asiatic. These complementary ideas of the East unite Rousseau and Mill in a common Eurocentrism despite their differences in ideology and philosophical formation. This Eurocentrism is actually only one element of a more universal binarism that derives ethical value from an entire series of polarities: the Orient vs. the West, southern vs. northern Europe, primitive vs. modern, nature vs. civilization.

If we imagine this system of binary divisions as a kind of geometrical model for a central tradition of nineteenth-century thought, we can also see it as a dynamic model, set in motion by certain basic principles. There is, for example, the principle of slippage or substitution, by which one term of a binary pair trades places with its counterpart from another pair: the conceptual oppositions between nature and civilization, and between Oriental and European, thus merge into new oppositions between (civilized) European and nature, or between (instinctual) Oriental and civilization.

Apart from this internal dynamic of substitution, the whole system of differences is set in motion by a dynamic of progression which sees history as a great struggle between the opposing forces of nature and culture, instinct and reason. This concept of a universal historical dynamic carries with it an implied justification for the European colonizing mission. Although Mill warns against the "instinct of domination," again finding this evil most prevalent in the relatively uncivilized regions of southern Europe and the Orient, his philosophy is above all an active, practical one which finds man's calling in the transformation of nature toward civilized ends. "The paramount duty of man upon earth is to amend himself," he writes, but this implies "the additional duty of amending the world, and not solely the human part of it but the material; the order of physical nature" (26). We have seen how Mill's discourse conflates the order of physical nature with the nature of primitive peoples. The duty to amend the world thus extends logically, and by means of this conflation or substitution, to the

European's duty in civilizing those races that have yet to free themselves from nature's power.

While the ideology of colonialism has its foundation in a moral philosophy which calls for the conquest of nature, it also derives support from nineteenth-century scientific theory, which sees the colonizing process as a counterpart, in the development of human society, to natural evolution. Classical evolutionism, as the historian George Stocking has noted, brought together a series of interrelated assumptions: that human social phenomena are essentially *natural* phenomena, and thus follow laws that science can discover; that cultural development arises out of the interaction between human nature and an external natural environment; that different human societies can be classified hierarchically according to how well they control external nature: and finally, that any given society progresses independently, at a greater or lesser rate, in the single direction of more advanced development (170).

Yet in addition to all this, Darwinian theory implies at various points that the active *intervention* of one society in the life of another—for example, the intervention of culturally advanced peoples that either transforms or displaces primitive peoples—is also part of a natural evolutionary process. In the journal written during the voyage of the H.M.S. *Beagle* (1839), Darwin observes, not without regret, that "the varieties of man seem to act on each other in the same way as different species of animals—the stronger always extirpating the weaker" (520). In *The Descent of Man* (1871), Darwin writes that the extinction of human races follows chiefly from "the competition of tribe with tribe, and of race with race." Apart from local natural causes, such as famine and epidemic disease, a greater degree of civilization generally allows one race to prevail over another, so that "when civilized nations come into contact with barbarians the struggle is short, except where a deadly climate gives its aid to the native race." Civilized races, because they have experienced a greater variety of climates and conditions of life, are able to "resist changes of all kinds better than savages," who are likely to become either sterile or "weary of life" with any radical change in their environment (542–543). Oscar Peschel, a German ethnologist and contemporary of Darwin, applies the theory of natural selection to the struggle for the American West in 1874:

> The opening of the great western railroads to California will greatly
> accelerate the extinction of the Bison tribes and the other remnants
> of the Indian race, and the next century will not find any Redskins
> in the United States, or at most as domesticated curiosities they may

drag on a miserable existence for a few years. This process by which the beings of a past age pass away ought to be no mystery to us. (150)

No mystery, that is, once it is understood that the displacement of one race by another is part of a natural process, analogous to the gradual substitution of weaker species by stronger ones throughout the evolutionary history of the natural world. Thus the principle of natural selection filters down from scientific theory to journalistic accounts of progress in the colonial world. Richard Harding Davis, writing on the east coast of Africa in 1907, celebrates the engineers building the railroad from Cape Town to Cairo, and ends his account by affirming the "interest which the East Coast presents in its problems of trade, of conquest, and of, among nations, the survival of the fittest" (1907:219–220).

If writers like Davis derived confidence in the colonizing mission from the theory of natural selection, others expressed anxiety over the debilitating effects of a tropical climate which, in their view, had created a permanently inferior race. Writing in 1910 for *United Empire*, the publication of the Royal Colonial Institute, L. W. Lyde addresses a contemporary debate over the physiological and genetic consequences of "naturalisation," by which he means the permanent settlement and propagation of the white race in the tropics. Lyde argues that the fundamental inferiority of the Negro can be attributed to specific physiological processes arising from the climatic conditions of the tropics. Borrowing from the Victorian science of anthropometry, he claims that these conditions produce ossifying and "mineralising" elements that petrify the cranial sutures; this prevents the brain-pan from expanding beyond a certain size and so abruptly arrests intellectual development. This lack of mental capacity, according to Lyde, made traditional forms of African slavery relatively tolerable:

> It was just because Negroes never attained an "age" when personal dignity or self-respect became conscious beyond the degree in which they are conscious in the average child, that slavery was a matter of *relatively* little moment to them as long as they were kept in a typical tropical climate. (Emphasis Lyde's, 767)

New generations of slaves in North America, however, have become increasingly unhappy with their lot, since the temperate climate allows for the development of greater mental capacity. The danger Lyde foresees is that, for similar climatic reasons, successive generations of Europeans in Africa will gradually *de*generate to the condition of native Africans. The cost of permanent naturalization is thus too high, for eventually it would efface the racial difference between European and African: "The penalty is racial identity, and the price is prohibitive" (772). Thus while one movement in colonial discourse sees nature as an ally in the colonizing mission, another sees it as a force of racial extinction. These conflicting views may be compared to a more general ambivalence in philosophy and literature, which saw nature as a force to be harnessed for purely instrumental ends, while they also looked to nature for a spiritual regeneration they no longer found in the Church.

Considering the various points of intersection joining scientific theory, moral philosophy, and political ideology in the nineteenth century and after, it seems no accident that scientific expeditions have often marked an early step in the colonizing process. Theodore Roosevelt's *Through the Brazilian Wilderness* (1914) is an account of his expedition on behalf of the American Museum of Natural History in New York. Originally concerned only with mammology and ornithology, the scope of the expedition expanded to geographical exploration when it joined forces with the Brazilian Telegraphic Commission, which was establishing a strategically important telegraph line connecting the federal capital to the northwest frontier. In Roosevelt's own view, the most significant accomplishment of his expedition was solving the mystery of the so-called River of Doubt (Rio da Duvida), which, after seven weeks of "hard and dangerous labor," he ascertained as the major affluent of the Madeira River and hence an important tributary of the Amazon. In a ceremony complete with the erection of a sign post and cheers for the governments of the United States and Brazil, the river was renamed the Rio Roosevelt (267).

We may see this incident as emblematic of how nature is both established and conquered by the combined forces of knowledge, writing, and political power. In the mystery of the river's course, nature is posited *as* doubt, as an area of darkness which includes the "ephemeral villages" of the Nambikwara tribe. The signpost bearing the title Rio Roosevelt marks the white man's inscription of himself onto the landscape, an act here made quite literal by the use of Roosevelt's own name. This self-inscription represents the expulsion of doubt and suggests—to any reader of Foucault or Derrida—that all knowledge of nature, or of the Other, is but an elaboration of the process of inscribing one's own name onto the unknown. Writing—writing journals, scientific papers, maps, or documents of colonial administration—all of this writing illuminates the darkness with the light of the writer's own countenance, while at the same time it sets up, once and for all, the logical oppositions between writing and blankness, knowledge and doubt, culture and nature, civilization and savagery. Here one is reminded of Derrida's assertion that writing is fundamentally the act of "drawing lines": the establishment of a system of difference, of classification, and of names. For Roosevelt, the work of discovering, classifying, and naming new specimens of birds and mammals conformed perfectly with the mapping of new territory for the Telegraphic Commission; the study of nature and the extension of technical mastery over it became the same (writing) project. Here, as elsewhere in post-Rousseauian thought, the concept of nature itself—made into an object and polarized in a system of value— plays a crucial role in the discourse of an essentially colonialist expansion.

Let us consider for a moment the fate of this telegraph line, which, through its recurring image in a series of texts, connects the discourses of journalism, science, and criticism. For Roosevelt, the establishment of the line was a way for the Brazilians "to open this great and virgin land to the knowledge of the world and to the service of their nation." Contemplating the line that has already been built as far as the highland wilderness of western Brazil, Roosevelt envisions a railroad to follow it, there being "no serious natural obstacles." Once this is done, he predicts that the land will offer extraordinary opportunities to "enterprising businessmen" and other "settlers of the right kind." The Indians, like the landscape itself, present no serious obstacle. The chief of the Telegraphic Commission, by providing them with the rudiments of civilization, is "raising them by degrees— the only way to make the rise permanent" (183).

Twenty-five years later Lévi-Strauss sets out along the same line in search of the Nambikwara, but finds the line itself in hopeless disrepair:

> The telegraph wire . . . sags between posts which are not replaced when they collapse, through having been either eaten away by termites or destroyed by Indians, who mistake the characteristic hum of the telegraph wire for the buzzing of a hive of bees at work. In places the line either trails on the ground or has been carelessly hooked onto nearby shrubs. Surprisingly enough, the line adds to, rather than detracts from the surrounding desolation. (304)

In *Tristes Tropiques*, from which this passage is cited, Lévi-Strauss tends to revive a Rousseauian ideal, seeing the Nambikwara as uncorrupted children of nature. Yet even in this passage we can see how his discourse shares the conceptual structure of Roosevelt's pragmatic rationalism. The organizing principle of Lévi-Strauss's image is that of a struggle between nature and culture, the telegraph line representing a forlorn trace of human civilization amidst the desolation and destructive force of the wilderness. The Indians are represented as part of that wilderness, syntactically and metonymically interchangeable with the forest creatures that attack the line. The fact that the Indians mistake the hum of the wire for the buzzing of bees merely emphasizes their immersion in nature, and their distant remove from any civilizing influence. Like the elements, they are unconscious of their destructive force. The nature-culture axis which runs through this discourse also divides the concept of modern humanity from that of the primitive. In this particular slippage, primitive peoples are substituted for nature in opposition to culture.

Citing this same passage from *Tristes Tropiques*, Derrida compares Lévi-Strauss's writing, and indeed all writing, to the *line*—the stroke of rupture, division, arrangement, and of a colonizing penetration (1976:108). It is noteworthy that the telegraph line, basically an instrument of communication, is also the principal forerunner—the front line—of the effort to establish a cultural domination. The line stands as a metaphor for the way in which writing—critical, scientific, journalistic—inscribes difference, but in a system of differences which itself institutes the will to power.

Calvin Coolidge once remarked that the principal products of Latin America appeared to be earthquakes and revolutions. The joke here comes out of the tradition in which primitive peoples are seen as extensions of the landscape, as the wilderness in human form. Coolidge's remark, however, introduces a twentieth-century version of the tradition: the violence and social upheaval of the Third World are seen as a natural state of affairs, endemic to less civilized peoples, and removed from the rational course of history. As its name implies, the proverbial "banana republic" is only half-formed as a legitimate human polity and remains entangled in the rank and uncertain motions of natural process. Hence a rhetorical posture in modern journalism: the interchangeability of natural and social phenomena as applied to the Third World survives from its earlier manifestation in nineteenth-century natural and moral philosophy.

It has often been observed that modern Western reporting on the Third World tends to favor images of violence. Esther Parada's study of news photographs in the *New York Times* points out that stories from the Third World are frequently accompanied by wide-angle crowd shots depicting "the people," often as chaotic, irrational mobs. Stories from the developed world, on the other hand, favor close-up head shots of well-groomed individual leaders identified by name and portrayed as rational even in crisis. The leaders of the great powers—almost all men in suits and ties—are "grown-ups," in graphic contrast to the milling throngs of "children" in the non-Western world.

The language of Western news reporting suggests that a source of this contrast lies in the notion that human chaos and disorder are somehow a natural condition of the Third World, on the order of monsoons, tidal waves, and volcanic eruptions. A *Time* headline on Sikh terrorism in India proclaims "A New Cycle of Violence" (May 20, 1985). After describing the most recent terrorist strikes, the *Time* story places them in the context of widespread disorder:

> The latest violence added to an epidemic of turmoil that has broken out in several parts of the country in the last two months. In the western state of Gujurat . . . 91 people were killed and many homes and shops burned in rioting to protest job and education quotas for disadvantaged castes and tribes. . . . To the north, in the states of Jammu and Kashmir, a general strike called by opposition parties erupted into violence. About 100 people were injured and arrested as a result of the disturbances.

The story groups together a number of different incidents, involving different issues among different classes of people in different states, under the single rubric of a "cycle of violence." The authority of such a rubric is reinforced by a vocabulary borrowed from the language of natural disaster: an *epidemic* of turmoil has *broken out;* a strike *erupted* into violence. This vocabulary combines with the use of passive constructions—"were killed," "were injured as a result of the disturbances"—to create the impression of an entire subcontinent bursting into spontaneous combustion. My purpose here is not to question the accuracy of *Time*'s reporting nor the terrible reality of the events it describes. It is rather to point out the qualities of a discourse that represses historical perspective in favor of an apocalyptic imagery more suited to the mythic role of India in the Western imagination.

In the logic of this discourse, events in the Third World, caught up in "endless cycles" of bloodshed, lie beyond any principle of rational causation, a condition which prohibits realistic hope for the future. A reporter for the liberal *Nouvel Observateur* of Paris writes of a village in El Salvador: "For more than a year, Tenancinango has been muddling through, between fear and hope, as if peace could not quite take root in this blood-soaked soil" (May 22, 1987). A figure of speech: peace and war do not literally spring from the earth like the race of Titans in Hesiod, but the metaphorical value of the figure is nonetheless grounded in a tradition that naturalizes war in the Third World; as nature is substituted for history, human conflict becomes an inherent feature of the landscape. The casual metaphors of modern journalism have their source in the same mythology that informs Marlow's view of the natives in *Heart of Darkness*, a group of whom appear suddenly "as though they had sprung up from the ground" (134). This modern rhetorical tradition concerning the Third World can be related to earlier philosophical and scientific traditions in two ways: first, it produces new versions of the Rousseauian idea that primitive peoples exist in a state of nature and that their relations can be understood primarily as manifestations of natural law. Second, it shares with evolutionary theory the notion that primitive peoples reside with nature at one end of a historical continuum that measures the difference between nature and culture, instinct and reason, savagery and civilization. The evident lack of history attributed to primitive or non-Western peoples confirms, within this discourse, the truth of history as the process by which human society becomes rational and productive.

This identification of Third World peoples with the forces of nature relates to the belief in *essences* that govern the behavior of one people or another: the essence of the Arab character, the (inscrutable) essence of the Chinese, etc. A headline in the feature section of the *Chicago Tribune* (December 6, 1981) proclaims "Violence, the Islamic Curse." The article by Raphael Patai, an academic specialist in the Middle East, attributes the assassination of Egypt's President Anwar Sadat to "the darkest side of the Moslem-Arab personality" and to "the Moslem proclivity to settling differences with the sword, the gun, or the bomb." This essentially violent nature is traced back to a pre-Islamic "heritage of belligerence" among Arab peoples which has survived throughout the centuries as a "proclivity toward conflict" common to all Islamic peoples. Patai's article seems designed to lend historical and intellectual legitimacy to the journalistic practice of naturalizing violence in the Arab world. For him, the assassination of Sadat has virtually nothing to do with actual political conditions in the Middle East, but rather with those qualities of "Arab national character" which have "succeeded in causing a dangerous turbulence in the flow of global history." Arab conflict is thus represented as a sort of tidal wave in the otherwise regular current of historical progress. As if to emphasize the identity of Arab aggression and natural disaster, the *Tribune* illustrates Patai's article with a drawing: in the foreground, a line of men in Arab dress walk one behind the other, each man holding a knife in the back of the man before him. In the background, dark and turbulent clouds gather over the desert horizon.

An article in *The New Republic* (June 6, 1981) ascribes a similar violence by nature to the Pathans, the people of southern Afghanistan who have fiercely resisted Soviet invasion. Here we learn that "war and honor are the Pathans' proper business, and if they had not been invaded by the Russians they would doubtless be killing each other in innumerable blood feuds." Violence is so ingrained in the Pathan character that disputes over land, livestock, women, personal injury, or insult "can only be settled by blood-shed." Pathan women are known for committing "unspeakable atrocities" on enemy wounded. Pathan poetry is "shot through with images of vio-lence, even when speaking of love." There is of course satisfaction in the thought that these demons have been unleashed against the Russians, a position which recalls T. E. Lawrence's plan to release the "latent power" of Arab nationalism against the Turks. In both cases, it is as if the West had forged an uneasy alliance not with reasonable men and women, but with the terrifying forces of the natural world.

In his introduction to the anthropological work of Marcel Mauss, Lévi-Strauss speculates on the nature of *mana*, a Polynesian word used in the art of magic and in other contexts. According to Lévi-Strauss, *mana* is one of those notions, something like algebraic symbols, that represent "an indeterminate value of signification, in itself devoid of meaning and thus susceptible of receiving any meaning at all; their sole function is to fill a gap between the signifier and the signified." The *mana* is, in other words, a "floating signifier," a "semantic function whose role is to enable symbolic thinking to operate despite the contradiction inherent in it" (1987:63). It stands for nothing and everything at once; rather, it *stands in* for an entire system of values over and above what it ostensibly designates.

The concept of nature, whether implied or explicit, performs just such a function in Western writing on the Third World. It stands for an empty space in the discourse, ready to be charged with any one of a number of values: nature as abundance, as absence, as original innocence, as unbridled destruction, as eternal cycle, as constant progression. These meanings, which lie layered in the discourse, fill in one for the other as the occasion requires. As I have noted elsewhere, however, the internal inconsistencies of colonial discourse are necessary in order that it be able to function con-sistently in the service of power. The concept of nature must be available as a term that shifts in meaning, for example, by idealizing or degrading the savage, according as the need arises at differing moments in the colo-nial situation. If in the language of the colonizer what is natural means one thing today and something else tomorrow, then the mobility of the

concept only increases its practical value. Thus an idea like "nature" desta-
bilizes itself in direct proportion to the constancy of its practical function
in colonial discourse, which is always that of designating difference and of
assigning hierarchical or ethical value to the distinctions that inhere in the
structures of power.

11   EROTICIZATION

The Harems of the West

Licence my roving hands, and let them goe
Behind, before, above, between, below.
Oh my America, my new found lande,
My kingdome, safeliest when with one man man'd,
My myne of precious stones, my Empiree,
How blest am I in this discovering thee.
—John Donne, "Elegie: To His Mistris Going to Bed"

IN *THE HISTORY OF SEXUALITY*, FOUCAULT IDENTIFIES
the "hysterization of women's bodies" as one of the great strategic unities
that have informed the Western discourse of sex since the eighteenth century. For Foucault, hysterization is the process whereby the feminine body
is "thoroughly saturated with sexuality," in such a way as to define a set of
specifically feminine biological and moral responsibilities: duties of regulated fertility, of devotion to family, etc. (104). Within such a system of
representation, the woman is constituted as her body, and her body as its
sexual nature. The essence of woman is located in the womb (Greek *hys-
tera*), a reductive process that also has its integrative function, establishing
the feminine role within the mechanisms of knowledge and power.

Foucault is concerned not with the female body per se, but with the
manner in which the body is constructed as an erotic and (re)productive
sign within the discourse of sexuality. I wish to borrow Foucault's notion
of a rhetorically constructed body for that strain of discourse which represents the colonized world as the feminine and which assigns to subject
nations those qualities conventionally assigned to the female body. What
I shall call the eroticization of the colonized refers to a set of rhetorical
instances—metaphors, seductive fantasies, expressions of sexual anxiety—
in which the traditions of colonialist and phallocentric discourses coincide.
As Yvonne Kniebiehler and Régine Goutalier remark in their study of colonial women, "Everything takes place as if the colonies were the harems of
the West" (21).

Charles Allen's glossary of Anglo-African slang tells us that among
British colonial officers the euphemism for an African mistress was "sleep-

ing dictionary" (164). Colonial officers were required to learn native languages, and native mistresses could provide a relatively painless form of language instruction. Beyond this prosaic etymology, however, the metaphor suggests an entire series of unstated connections between the sexual and the lexical. It suggests, for example, that the African woman is a text to be opened and closed at will, and whose contents allow entry into the mysteries of African language; that this language, and by extension African culture, is itself both contained within and revealed by the female body; that sexual knowledge of her body is knowledge of Africa itself. The body as text, however, is read only as a series of lexical fragments, without regard to history or narrative. In yet another sense, the "sleeping dictionary" evokes Africa as a dormant or sleeping text, which can only be awakened and brought into definition by the intervention of the European reader. And finally, the metaphor suggests that the colonizer's own language derives from his erotic relations with "her," the pronoun in this case designating both the African continent and the African woman.

In *The Green Hills of Africa*, Hemingway defines his relation to the landscape as one of insatiable erotic possession:

Now, looking out the tunnel of trees over the ravine at the sky with white clouds moving across in the wind, I loved the country so that I was happy as you are after you have been with a woman that you really love, when, empty, you feel it welling up again and there it is and you can never have it all and yet what there is, now, you can have, and you want more and more, to have, and be, and live in, to possess now again for always. (72)

The simile of sexual union is elaborated in terms of the dynamics of male desire, here represented as an infinite movement of appropriation and physical possession unbounded by limits of time and space, yet entirely palpable and available in the present moment: "there it is." The fluid syntax and ecstatic repetition of this passage correspond to the larger structures of Hemingway's narrative, which is devoted to an alternately triumphant and frustrated hunt for ever bigger and more varied game. Hemingway shares with other writers the fascination with Africa as a mistress who is somehow both completely available and never wholly possessed.

The allegorization of colonized nations in terms of the female *figure* (bodily, rhetorical) has been a cliché of colonial history. Jean Lorrain's *Heures d'Afrique* (1899) describes Algeria as "a cunning and dangerous mistress," who distills "a climate that envelops with caresses and torpor." Another French writer of the same era sees Laos as "swooning like a lascivious lover, between the arms of her river and her stream, drunk with pleasure [*volupté*] at the flanks of her burning mountains" (Kniebiehler 40). The erotically charged language of these metaphors marks the entrance of the colonizer, with his penetrating and controlling power, as a natural union with the subject nation. Colonial domination thus is understood as having a salutary effect on the natural excesses and the undirected sexual energies of the colonized.

Kipling, always a rich source of figurative language concerning life in the colonies, makes essentially the same point in a reference to the battle of Omdurman. Traveling through the Sudan in 1913, he recalls the battle sixteen years earlier, in which the Anglo-Egyptian forces had put down the revolt of the Mahdists:

> It was—men say who remember it—a hysteria of blood and fanaticism; and precisely as an hysterical woman is called to her senses by a dash of cold water, so at the battle of Omdurman the land was reduced to sanity by applied death on such a scale as the murderer and the torturers at their most unbridled could scarcely have dreamed. (1970, 19:303)

According to Foucault, the negative image of the "nervous woman" has constituted the most visible form of the hysterization of women's bodies. Kipling not only makes use of that image in order to characterize a revolution; he also translates the difference between colonizer and colonized into a conventional distinction between rational man and irrational woman. In opposition to images of feminine excess and disorder—hysteria, fanaticism, blood, unbridled nature, and the dream—Kipling erects a male ethic of reason and repressive order: sense, reduction, death "applied" systematically, precision, and memory. In this rhetorical strategy, differences in power are reformulated as gender difference, and colonization is naturalized as the relation between the sexes. Colonial domination thus is seen to have a beneficial, cathartic effect, like the dash of cold water in the face of the woman who has lost her senses. Kipling's curative metaphor anticipates the "surgical strikes" of the American war in Vietnam—operations of penetrating swiftness and precision on a country also characterized as having abandoned reason for a passionate fanaticism, and often represented in images of prostitutes and "dragon ladies."

The feminizing metaphors persist even in the postcolonial, post-Vietnam era of Western journalism. A *Chicago Tribune* reporter visits Vietnam in 1983 and finds the symbol of postwar Saigon in Madame Dai, a woman of former wealth and influence now fallen on hard times: "Saigon is an aging dowager mistress, pining for her lost youth, yet still capable of firing the imagination with gestures that hint at the elegant temptress she once was" (November 27, 1983). The *Tribune* correspondent later encounters a group of Amerasian children begging in the streets. These children surround Western visitors, asking for soap, money, and cigarettes: "'I am American, I am American,' they repeat over and over. One small child looks hard at one foreigner and asks, 'Are you my father?'" Although this incident is reported without irony, it can be read as a commentary on the stock colonialist image of Saigon as an "elegant temptress," the power of naming sexual roles now having passed into the mouths of babes. In a kind of rhetorical crisis, the cavalier metaphors of seduction give way to the disquieting metonymies of genealogy, suggesting the currents of sexual guilt and anxiety that flow just beneath the rhetoric of eroticization.

SEDUCTION

The rhetorical gesture in which an entire people is allegorized by the figure of the female body has its sources in fantasies of seduction, in imaginary scenes representing the fulfillment of sexual desire. Such fantasies in their endless variation date from the early stages of European discovery and dominion over the non-Western world. In his *Supplément au Voyage de Bougainville* (1796), Denis Diderot purports to uncover a forgotten appendix to Bougainville's account—a dangerous supplement, in other words, which reveals the repressed sexual content of the *Voyage*.

In Diderot's version, a French chaplain from Bougainville's ship is confronted by naked Tahitian woman vying for the privilege of going to bed with him. Thia, the youngest and most beautiful, clasps him by the knees and implores him to make her a mother. An ensuing dialogue between the flustered chaplain and the girl's willing father develops a Rousseauian theme on the subject of sexuality, in which the Tahitians demonstrate their happy freedom from sexual taboos, in contrast to the unnatural inhibitions of their European visitors. In a comic denouement, the chaplain, having yielded to Thia on the first night, lies on succeeding nights with each of her sisters and finally with her mother:

> The father and mother having implored him to sleep with their second daughter, Palli appeared in the same déshabille as Thia, and the chaplain cried out several times in the night, "But my religion!" "But

my calling!" On the third night he was troubled by the same remorse with Asto, the eldest, and on the fourth he submitted respectfully to the wife of his host. (49)

In telling this story, Diderot's larger purpose is a philosophical one, to establish his concept of natural reason in opposition to the hypocritical moralities of eighteenth-century European society. However, my observation has less to do with Diderot's philosophy than with the rhetorical phenomenon by which an eroticized idea of Tahiti is freely constructed and appropriated by philosophical and literary discourse. Diderot enters into a distinct rhetorical tradition by presenting the newly discovered territory as the site of seduction, both in the immediate, erotic sense and in the sense that the idea of Tahiti provides the scene of imaginary access to the outlawed "other" of institutional morality and conventional reason. The discovery of this Tahiti of the imagination is also a discovery or uncovering of the body; it is where the body accedes to the gratification of repressed desire.

In his discussion of Flaubert's Oriental writings, Edward Said notes both Flaubert's search for a "visionary alternative" to the ennui of the French moral landscape and his presentation of the Oriental woman in terms of "dumb and irreducible sexuality." Said sees this aspect of Flaubert, which combines a visionary with an erotic sensibility, as representative of a recurring motif in Western views of the Orient: "the Orient seems still to suggest not only fecundity but sexual promise (and threat), untiring sensuality, unlimited desire, deep generative energies" (1978:188).

While it may not be possible to explain why the Orient plays this seductive role in the Western imagination, one can at least suggest ways in which these fantasies of seduction correspond to certain structures within colonial discourse as a whole. For example, two elements in Flaubert's Oriental writings recall moments in Diderot. The first is the *unveiling* of the female body. In Diderot we learn of the prototypical Tahitian girl, "eager that her mother, authorized by her puberty, will remove her veil and lay bare her breast" (16). Again, the Tahitian host presents his unclothed wife and daughters to the French chaplain, saying, "Here is my wife; here are my daughters" (21). The second such element is that of serialization or *repetition*: the chaplain sleeps with each of the women in turn, as if to signify both the abundance of sexual gratification in its infinite possibilities for renewal and the absence of individuation among the objects of this gratification. These scenes of unveiling and repetition create a specifically erotic context for certain fundamental qualities of colonial discourse: the removal of the veil serves as a visual metaphor for ideas of opening and discovery everywhere implicit in the discourse, including the "visionary alternative" of Flaubert and his contemporaries.

To the serialization of pleasure in Diderot, one can compare the reductive metaphors that Flaubert applies to Oriental sexuality. On his return from the East in 1851, he writes reassuringly to his French mistress, "The Oriental woman is no more than a machine: she makes no distinction between one man and another" (1973:270). In both writers, the language of serial repetition corresponds to those rhetorical (and administrative) operations whereby members of colonized populations are regulated, made uniform, and deprived of a subjective personal identity. These erotic fantasies are emblematic of the larger colonialist enterprise in their variation on the alternate yet complementary dynamics of reduction and seduction.

The principles of unveiling and repetition come into play perhaps most distinctly in the forms of colonial discourse produced for popular audiences. In newspaper stories, travel posters, advertisements, and the like, these structuring principles do not lie buried under the prevailing ground of a literary aesthetic or a philosophical argument; rather, they push through the surface of discourse, exposing the raw energy of a colonizing desire.

In an unusual work of documentation, the Algerian writer Malek Alloula has gathered the picture postcards of Algerian women produced and sent home by the French in Algeria during the period 1900–1930. In these photographs, the veil acts quite literally as an organizing principle: one passes from pseudo-ethnographic pictures of completely veiled women to those of women in the act of removing their veils, and finally to those who, like Diderot's Tahitian girls, have laid themselves bare to the viewer. On another level, the postcards enact the ritualistic unveiling or penetration of the private space occupied by women. One series depicts women peering through barred windows, where they are understood to be imprisoned by their husbands; another is devoted to women in their interior quarters; yet another takes the viewer inside the harem itself, where women lie in luxuriant undress. The gradual removal of the veil corresponds to the progressive conquest of interior space.

Alongside this dynamic of unveiling, the colonial postcards establish an equally forceful dynamic of repetition which depends on the complete anonymity and interchangeability of the female models. Dressed in "traditional" costumes provided by enterprising photographers, women appear in groups to reenact exotic rituals or appear singly in a series devoted to ethnic types, identified only as "Kabyl woman," "Moorish woman at home," "'Uled-Nayl woman," etc. Often the same model poses as different ethnic types. By describing these postcards in such detail, I wish to suggest the ways in which they serve as a synecdoche for the greater structures of colonial discourse, and even for the colonizing process in general. First, their staging of exotic ritual is a bogus repetition, a false appropriation of Algerian traditions for the minor amusement created by commodity production. As such, it corresponds to that aspect of colonial discourse in which an indigenous culture is reinterpreted under conditions determined by the observer, resulting in a presentation of indigenous life that merely reflects the framework of values imposed by the colonizing eye.

Second, the serialization of Algerian women produced by the postcards mirrors the serialized conditions of the viewer, who must constitute himself passively as part of a class (of colonials, of Frenchmen, of Europeans), that is, as *other* than himself, in order to reduce the Algerian to an interchangeable object. The denial of a subjective identity to the Algerian is a sign that the colonizer has already relinquished that identity in his own case, in the process of assuming the colonizer's role. As Jean-Paul Sartre has argued, the reductive phrases by which the white colonial characterizes the native "have never reflected real and concrete thinking; they have never even been the *object* of thought." Instead, one must see these phrases as reassuring gestures of solidarity. They are addressed by the colonials to themselves "as members of a series,"—phrases which serve to signify the colonials *as* colonials "in their own eyes and in the eyes of others, in their collective unity" (406–409). Put simply, the serializing formulas of colonial discourse reflect a loss of subjective freedom—a freedom that the colonizer, by virtue of his position *as* colonizer, has given up.

Finally, the penetration of the veil which takes place in the postcards can also be seen in larger context. Alloula points out that the veil constitutes a challenge to the photographer (and to the colonizer), not only by denying the power of his gaze, but also by making him the object of the woman's gaze: she sees him but cannot herself be seen. The unveiling photograph thus enacts "a symbolic revenge upon a society that continues to deny him access and questions the legitimacy of his desire." Even more fundamental than this motive for revenge is the desire for transparency, for overcoming the resistance that Algeria presents to European knowledge and authority. By seeming to dissolve this actual resistance, Alloula writes, "the colonial postcard offers a view of a pacified reality, restored to the colonial order, which presently proceeds to draw up an inventory of it" (64).

This business of unveiling seems to combine two contradictory impulses of the colonialist imagination: the domesticating force of the postcards operates alongside the illusion of initiation into a world of exotic sexuality; the inspiration of a visionary alternative in Diderot or Flaubert is counteracted by language which reduces its object to a ritualized repetition. These two movements—the visionary and the domesticating—though contradictory, are fused together within the framework of the discourse. There is confirmation of this double movement in Fanon's description of European attitudes toward the Algerian woman: "Unveiling this woman is revealing her beauty; it is baring her secret, breaking her resistance, making her available for adventure" (1967:43).

FEAR AND LOATHING

The undercurrent of violence implicit in these metaphors of unveiling moves toward that aspect of the discourse in which the colonized territory represents not only sexual promise, but sexual danger as well. Within the ambivalent terms of the discourse, the symbolic rending of the veil invites erotic adventure, but it also threatens to release hidden and uncontrollable energies. In *Heart of Darkness* Kurtz's African mistress—a "wild and gorgeous apparition"—serves as a classic figure of sexual adventure, standing in synecdochic relation to "the colossal body of the fecund and mysterious life" that is the wilderness itself. Yet this same erotically charged wilderness is the site of a "fantastic invasion" where Kurtz destroys himself in a madness of unrestrained lust (133–137). In Conrad's symbolic working through of the dynamic interaction between colonization and desire, the representation of Africa as both seductive and destructive occurs as a projective mechanism, originating in the colonizer's fear of forces within the self.

Stanley, whose journalism anticipates much of the psychic terrain for Conrad's fictional exploration, shares Conrad's sense of the lethal dangers inherent in Africa's seduction. As if staging a recurring inner drama, Stanley continually prepares the ground for betrayal by establishing Africa as a figure of erotic attraction. Sighting the Saharan shore from shipboard en route to the Ashanti war of 1873, Stanley quotes this apostrophe to Africa by the German Romantic poet H. F. Freiligrath:

> Oh zone so hot and glowing,
> Queen of the earth art thou;
> Sand is thy mantle flowing,
> The sun doth crown thy brow.
> Of gold, thou queenly woman,

> Are all thy clasps and rims,
> That fasten with fiery splendour
> The garment to thy burning limbs.
> (1874:4)

Freiligrath's verse serves as the paradigm for an erotic vision of the landscape which Stanley elsewhere translates into his own language. On a later expedition through the interior, Stanley refers to Africa as "still a virgin locked in innocent repose" but envisions the surrounding tropical forest as a loving embrace: "Nature did its best with her unknown treasures, shaded us with her fragrant and loving shades, and whispered to us unspeakable things sweetly and tenderly" (1891, 1:231).

Elsewhere, however, the desire to possess these unknown treasures inspires confusion and dread. Here, for example, Stanley presents the geographical enigma of the Congo River as an ominous resistance to the unveiling gaze:

> Darkness and clouds of ignorance respecting its course everywhere! What a terrible dread thing it is that so pertinaciously prevents explorers from penetrating and revealing its mysteries! It struck me thus also, as though a vague indescribable something lay ahead. (1970:360)

In an earlier chapter I noted Stanley's implied fear of emasculation by the physical and moral climate he encounters at Sierra Leone. This fear at times extends to the impenetrability of the landscape itself, which frustrates the invasive energy of the eye: "It is the unbroken expanse of foliage that baffles the eye, subdues its power and vitality, and compels the mind to an indolent and careless observation of the whole" (1874:162). In the dynamic of unveiling that gives form to the colonizer's desire, the "colossal body" of the wilderness is symbolically bound to the body of woman, while the impotency of the gaze amounts to a kind of castration.

For Stanley, the unmanning effect of Africa extends to a taboo on African women, whose sexual attraction he sees as literally a threat to the white man's life. In 1871 Stanley's assistant John Shaw had set out "in superabundant health" on the search for Livingstone, but soon after he "lost courage and health." Stanley warns that the same fate awaits his other white assistant, Farquhar, as well as the members of any African expedition actuated by no higher motives than to "indulge their lust" (1970:44).

The psychosexual anxiety inspired by the colonial situation is nowhere more manifest than in the writings of T. E. Lawrence. I have already spoken of Lawrence's tendency to idealize the asceticism of Arab life; yet his discourse (Latin: *discursus*: a running to and fro) is always capable of veering wildly toward images of filth and sexual defilement. In a passage headed "Morality of Battle," Lawrence tells of how his Arab followers scorned the "raddled meat" and the "sordid commerce" of public women in favor of homosexuality. He goes on to describe this phenomenon in strangely ambivalent terms:

> Later, some began to justify this sterile process, and swore that friends quivering together in the yielding sand with intimate hot limbs in supreme embrace, found there hidden in the darkness a sensual coefficient of the mental passion which was welding our souls and spirits in one flaming effort. Several, thirsting to punish appetites they could not wholly prevent, took a savage pride in degrading the body, and offered themselves fiercely in any habit which promised physical pain or filth. (28)

On one level, Lawrence's complex and troubled attitude toward Arab (homo)sexuality is obviously a private case; in a language which alternately yields to and reviles the passions it describes, Lawrence expresses a subjective anxiety over the forces of his own desire. It would be a mistake, however, to treat this language as merely idiosyncratic, as simply the product of an individually guilt-ridden sexuality; the lesson of Foucault is that all such language is conditioned and penetrated by cultural value and that it acquires meaning within an arena defined by relations of power. In the sentence immediately following the paragraph just quoted, Lawrence reminds us that he writes of the Arabs as one "charged by duty to lead them forward and to develop to the highest any movement of theirs profitable to England in her war." In this respect, his description of their sexuality compares with already-established patterns in colonialist writing. Arab women appear here, and throughout Lawrence's narrative, as prostitutes—reduced metonymically to the raddled flesh of their bodies or to the serialized and interchangeable currency of a sordid commerce. There is no notion of Arab women as the wives, sisters, and mothers of Lawrence's own passionate followers. As for these men themselves, their "hot limbs in supreme embrace" recall the "fiery splendour" and "burning limbs" of Freiligarth's allegorized Africa. The "yielding sand" of Lawrence's image suggests that an uncontrolled human sexuality finds complicity in the Arab landscape. Finally, the images of bodily degradation carry on the theme of sexual violence and cruelty we have seen in other writers. Whatever the nature of Lawrence's own sexuality, his discourse shares in the Western tradition that symbolically constructs the Orient in terms of sexual danger.

In writers like Stanley and Lawrence we find individual and complex examples of an anxiety which surfaces in various discursive modes through the history of European colonialism and which finds its expression in language that, either explicitly or symbolically, refers to non-Western peoples as given over to unrestrained promiscuity and debilitating sexual excess. Sir Richard Burton, the Victorian explorer, travel writer, and expert on Oriental erotica, merely affirms the conventional wisdom of his age in claiming that "in damp-hot climates . . . the sexual requirements of the passive exceed those of the active sex; and the result is a dissolute social state, contrasting with mountain countries, dry-cold and damp-cold, where the conditions are equally balanced or reversed" (1:379). Writing in this case on Zanzibar, Burton establishes a familiar correlation connecting tropical geography, the ascendancy of female sexual desire, and corruption in the social sphere. His language demonstrates not only the myth-making function of colonial discourse, but its strategic value as well: by joining sexual excess—especially female—to the decadence of non-Western peoples and their institutions, he implies the need for European intervention as a regulating force.

The anxiety over the sexual passions of colonized peoples historically has been heightened by a more concrete fear of their procreative energies. Writing on South Africa in 1903, John Buchan sounds the alarm:

> The Kaffir, south of the Zambesi, already outnumbers the white man by fully five to one, and he increases with at least twice the rapidity. . . . What is to be the end of this fecundity? Living on little, subject apparently to none of the natural or prudential checks on over-population, there seems a real danger of black ultimately swamping white by mere gross quantity. (1903:296)

In Flaubert's *Temptation of St. Anthony* (1874), the third-century mystic is visited by a nightmarish vision of "pygmees," verminlike little men who proclaim defiantly, "We are burned, drowned, and crushed only to return, all the livelier and more numerous—terrible in our quantity!" (265). In a rhetorical phenomenon recalling the tale of the sorcerer's apprentice, the reduction of colonized peoples to mere ciphers leads to their infinite multiplication, returning to haunt the colonizer with a vengeance. This serializing strategy combines with the conventional imagery of the native quarters as foul and breeding swarms, as swamplike spawning grounds of unnatural fecundity. If the eroticization of Africa or the Orient at times evokes the lure of earth and fire—of yielding sands, burning limbs, and fiery splendour—it is equally capable of drawing its vision from the crude, viscous material of filth and degradation. Insofar as it conceives its object as both sexual and feminine, the colonialist imagination swings wildly between two extremes: the gorgeous apparition of the African queen and the raddled meat of the camp follower.

As I have suggested, these features of the colonizing imagination survive in the postcolonial era, although transformed and adapted to a modern usage which is sometimes indirect in its reference to traditional myths. During the period of media attention focused on the Ethiopian famine in 1985, a syndicated Wright cartoon appeared on the editorial pages of many American newspapers. This cartoon consists of four frames devoted to the monologue of a starving black child—the figure of shriveled limbs, bloated belly, and hollow eyes which has become a kind of media icon. Facing the reader in a series of helpless gestures, the child speaks. First frame: "Africa's problem is very simple. We make babies and they starve to death." Second frame: "We make more babies and they starve to death." Third frame: "We repeat the cycle over and over again." Fourth frame: "This is called the rhythm method" (*Chicago Tribune*, August 19, 1985).

The newspaper cartoon, with its reliance on caricature, cliché, and the simplest common denominators of popular mythology, often serves as the perfect medium for the dissemination of a colonialist ideology. In this instance the editorial cartoon is adapted to the serial form of the comic strip in a device that promotes the idea of an endless and uncontrolled repetition of African sexual activity, a sexuality bound inexorably to death. The punch line of the cartoon relies on a *triple entendre* spectacular in its racist overtones: on one hand, the reference to the "rhythm method," a practice of contraception and sexual regulation related to the concept of sin, emphasizes the difference between Western restraint and African profligacy; on the other, the phrase evokes the eroticizing stereotype of Africans who "have rhythm," whose expression takes the unique form of bodily movement and sexual gesture. And finally, the generation of human life in Africa is reduced to the inexorable rhythms of nature itself, what Eliot calls "Birth, and copulation, and death" (80). In an earlier chapter we saw how writing on the AIDS virus had constructed Africa as a machine for the production of that disease. A similar metaphorical construction operates in this case: the African, defined solely as body and caught up in an endless cycle of overreproduction and starvation, is a machine of sex and death.

One may compare this image of African sexuality to the one conveyed in V. S. Naipaul's 1984 article in the *New Yorker* on the Ivory Coast. There Naipaul's informant is a black woman from Martinique named Arlette, who "was to make me understand many things about the country." Citing this source, Naipaul writes that prostitution is a kind of sport among female students in Abidjan. University "girls" sleep with men in the government in return for gifts and money, while the *lycéennes* do the same with male university students: "This kind of behavior was acceptable, because Africans believed in independence in relationships, Arlette said. They didn't look for or expect sexual fidelity" (May 14, 1984). Naipaul presents this analysis in his capacity as the *New Yorker*'s "reporter at large," a role which by convention allows him to combine personal impressions and casual knowledge in a style of literate sophistication. This particular journalistic form is also capable of both reviving and concealing a colonialist mythology. By writing that prostitution is a "sport" among Africans, that it constitutes "acceptable behavior" for everyone from government officials to high school girls, Naipaul effectively consigns African society to a state of degradation which recognizes no scruple or taboo in its limitless corruption of desire. The representation of an African society prepared to accept prostitution as "independence in relationships" revives the myth that either idealizes African sexuality as "natural" and unfettered by social constraint or execrates it as a sign of bestiality. In both cases, African (or Indian or Tahitian) sexuality, like nature itself, is held in opposition to civilization; it is literally exotic, lying outside the realm of a social order which commands the observance of things like sexual fidelity.

Here again, my purpose is not to argue the correctness of Naipaul's impressions of African society—which in any case are of dubious value—but rather to consider the effect of these impressions on his audience and their place within a history of interpretation that defines the non-Western world in visions of excess, as an uncharted, undivided territory of death and sensuality. In an essay on the nature of eroticism, Georges Bataille has described the Western principle of individuation—the subjective "consciousness of self"—which finds its most formidable opponent in the barrier-destroying urge toward bestiality. According to the theology that erects this opposition, "the being yielding to that urge is no longer human but, like the beasts, a prey of blind forces in action, wallowing in blindness and oblivion" (105). Sexual excess can thus be understood as the loss of individuation, as the death of the human subject through the transgression of the boundaries by which it is defined. Precisely this transgression produces the horror and ecstasy connected with bestiality, as Western writers have testified, from de Sade and Flaubert to D. H. Lawrence and T. E. Lawrence. Within a tradition that opposes sexual excess to the rationally ordered subject, the role of colonialist writing has been to project this opposition onto the arena of the confrontation between cultures. The nature of this projection, I believe, accounts for the peculiar double-sidedness of the discourse, by which the non-Western world stands for sexual debasement and death as well as sexual adventure. Both these representations may be traced to the destruction of barriers—to the transgression of human borders common to eroticism and colonization.

12 RESISTANCE

Notes Toward an Opening

> "For I ain't, you must know," said Betty, "much of a hand at
> reading writing-hand, though I can read my Bible and most print.
> And I do love a newspaper. You mightn't think it, but Sloppy is a
> beautiful reader of a newspaper. He do the Police in different
> voices."—Charles Dickens, *Our Mutual Friend*

THE FOREGOING CHAPTERS PERFORM AN INVENTORY:
they take stock of various rhetorical configurations that language has stored
up in the extension of modern technology known as the colonialist enterprise. My metaphor here is borrowed from Heidegger, for whom language
shares with technology the power of enframing reality, of ordering forth
the world in such a way as to establish a claim over it, and to secure it as
a "standing reserve," a supply depot for the operations of knowledge (18).
It is as if Heidegger's own discourse, with its talk of unconcealing, setting
claims, and establishing reserves, drew its inspiration from the history of
Western colonialism, which has proceeded through the stages of discovery,
claiming territory, and setting up the Third World as a reserve of labor and
natural resources.

Heidegger offers a global perspective on the relation between language
and power, but he also reminds us that this relation is "forever restructuring anew": there are always cracks in the edifice; language is constantly
sabotaging the very structures it supports. Foucault has translated Heidegger's theories on language into a study of *discourse* in order to show the
uses of language within a particular field defined by relations of power:
penal institutions, the treatment of madness, sexuality, etc. He acknowledges that it is in discourse that power and knowledge are joined, but this
juncture is imperfect; discourse can be not only an instrument or an effect
of power, but also a point of *resistance*. "Discourse transmits and produces
power; it reinforces it, but also undermines and exposes it, renders it frag-
ile and makes it possible to thwart it" (1980:101). Just as law establishes
itself by defining the outlawed, so the very nature of discourse as a frame-

work involves principles of limitation and exclusion and therefore creates the possibility for alternative ways of speaking. The critique of colonial discourse is thus made possible by those aspects of the discourse that lend themselves to a pattern formation—to a structuring and hence limiting view of the world.

The first step toward an alternative to colonial discourse, for Western readers at least, has to be a critical understanding of its structures; and this understanding would be an insider's because we read the discourse from a position already contained by it. The logical operations we perform in such a critical project—for example, those of classification, analysis, objectification—are those we have learned from the same critical tradition that produces the discourse of colonialism. We are constituted *as* readers by the very principles we would call into question, and we do not escape the West merely by constructing it as an object of critical interpretation. Referring to the modern West not just as a geographical and temporal entity but as a psychological category, the Indian scholar Ashis Nandy writes, "The West has not merely produced modern colonialism; it informs most interpretations of colonialism. It colours even this interpretation of interpretation" (xii). Against the danger of enclosure within this hermeneutic circle, however, Nandy points out that an element within the Western tradition has been an "ongoing revaluation," an "other self" of the West which invites an alliance, however tentative, with the non-West.

Heidegger's "restructuring," Foucault's "resistance," and Nandy's "revaluation" all point to a dynamic of difference and alterity within colonial discourse, such that it never resolves itself into a stable, unified structure. To these names we may add that of Homi Bhabha, for whom "resistance" in colonial discourse is not necessarily a politically motivated act of opposition, but rather the effect of an "ambivalence" produced within the dominating discourse as it struggles with its own displacement and distortion throughout the highly differentiated scenes of colonial presence. Inevitably the discourse becomes transformed into a hybrid, into something other than the transparent manifestation of a uniform collective authority which theoretically constitutes its origin (172).

The internal resistance being described here can be seen in practically every enunciation of colonial discourse, including those I have used in earlier chapters simply as instances of one or another colonizing trope. For now, however, I will cite two anecdotes from Charles Allen's oral history of the British Colonial Service in Africa. The first is told by Richard Turnbull, a career colonial officer who served as a district commissioner in Kenya. According to Turnbull, the tribe known as the Kipsigis were "a stock people—brilliant herders of cattle and devoted to them—and of course, stock-thieving was their metier. It was their way of improving their herds and passing the time." This stock-thieving reached such proportions in the 1930s that the acting governor held a special meeting to tell them that they were ruining the country's economy and disgracing their own names.

> The leader of the Kipsigis listened to what he said very carefully and then came forward and said they recognized the error of their ways; that owing to what he'd said this blinding light had flashed upon them and from that day forward they would steal no stock and become model citizens. The Governor was really extremely pleased. He said nothing but you could see him smiling to himself and reflecting upon what a word or two from the great would do. That night the Kipsigis came into the station and stole the entire government herd. (92)

Turnbull's story is a good example of what Bhabha calls the mimicry and mockery of authority—doing the police in different voices—that characterize the classic colonial situation. In claiming to have received the governor's words as an epiphany—"this blinding light had flashed upon them"—the Kipsigi leader mimics the fantasy of a colonial power that, in Bhabha's words, demands that *"the space it occupies be unbounded,* its reality *coincident* with the emergence of an imperialist narrative and history, its discourse *nondialogic,* its enunciation *unitary,* unmarked by the trace of difference" (176).

In fact the story unravels the fabric of this originary myth: colonial authority is shown to be localized and contingent, its reality something other than what an imperialist narrative would dictate, its discourse dialogical only in the sense that it invites a camouflaged response from members of the colonized population, and its enunciation split between the governor's complacent "word or two from the great" and the ironic commentary of Turnbull, the district commissioner. The story shows how the terms of authority, once given voice, are far from having a direct and unambiguous effect; on the contrary, they can be reappropriated by the colonized and used against the institutions from which they emanate. In the ironic mode which forms an alliance of the speaker and the tribal leader against the governor, the story also suggests that this split between two official representatives of colonial authority could also be a split within the colonial subject and that colonial discourse in general is, at some level, always divided against itself.

The second anecdote is told by Nancy Robertson, who came out to the

Sudan in 1926 to join her husband, an officer in the Sudan Political Service. In the remote outpost of Geteina, she becomes the object of curiosity among the local Sudanese women. These women were

> very kind, very inquisitive people who knew nothing about the British. One of them said to me, "Why is it that the Turks"—and that is how they addressed us—"are always so rude, and why do they smell so bad?" And from then on I realized that to these people we smelt disgusting, because we were meat-eaters and we smelt like death." (112)

Again one suspects that a rather elaborate joke is being played on the representatives of colonial order. When the Sudanese woman identifies, perhaps disingenuously, the British with the Turks, she effectively negates any difference between the former and the present colonial administrations. From the Sudanese point of view, the British are simply the latest in a history of foreign occupiers. Then, in the form or guise of an *innocent* question ("kind . . . inquisitive"), the Sudanese woman attributes to the colonizing race the very qualities of barbarism and bodily abjection with which colonial discourse traditionally constitutes the other. In another ironic reversal, the terms of the discourse are reappropriated and turned against their source.

The annals of colonial history offer relatively few such encounters between women, and it may be that gender has created here a marginal space in which something like an actual dialogue is possible between British and Sudanese. In any case, the point of the question is not lost on Robertson, who suddenly sees the limited and contingent nature of a colonialist perception: "We might not like their rancid oil smell but our smell was as bad for them as theirs was for us." Her story has in common with Turnbull's the manifestation of difference and ambivalence within the voice of colonialist authority, a manifestation which allows us to see both colonizer and colonized—not as equally burdened—but as sharing in some measure a sense of entrapment within the structures of power.

How does any form of writing find its way out of this entrapment? Given the degree to which a colonizing discourse penetrates Western writing that deals in representations of the non-Western world, I have suggested that this writing also contains at least the seeds of resistance to the pressures of that discourse and to the temptations of a totalizing authority over the objects of representation. The question remains whether this resistance, identified as latent and marginal within the texts of colonial discourse, can be converted into a conscious authorial strategy without simply recycling the conventional tropes of ideological opposition. Put another way: do the possibilities for written description and representation of other cultures extend beyond the theoretical space occupied by the Western discourses of power?

In recent years this question has been raised, by critics such as Pierre Bourdieu, Clifford Geertz, and James Clifford, with regard to ethnography. By now it is a commonplace that classical ethnographic writing modeled on the tradition of "participant observation" enacts, in Clifford's words, "a specific strategy of authority" determined by "multiple subjectivities and political constraints beyond the control of the writer" (25). These constraints include the professionalization of the discipline of anthropology, its historical coincidence with European colonialism, and its position within the institutional complex of universities, museums, and foundations. The response to this recognition has been a search for alternate forms of interpretation embodied in experimental ethnographic writing.

In a review of the historical forms of ethnographic authority, Clifford characterizes this experimentation as pursuing principles of *dialogue* and *polyphony*. Dialogic ethnography focuses on the context of research and the situations of interlocution: it reproduces a dialogue between two individuals who ideally negotiate their way toward "a shared vision of reality." As Clifford points out, the problem with this model is that it merely displaces an older model of monologic authority; the ethnographer remains in control of the *representation* of the dialogue. Polyphonic ethnographic writing is inspired by Mikhail Bakhtin's notion of heteroglossia, which opens up the textual field to a plurality of voices. Again, the problem encountered here is that even a text built up out of direct quotations from different sources ultimately confirms the "virtuoso orchestration" of various discourses by a single author. Clifford can only imagine a sort of utopia in which authorial control over ethnographic texts would be shared by members of different cultures, and even readership would be more plurally defined, the text no longer addressing "a single general type of reader" (50–52).

Despite their limitations, the ethnographic experiments cited by Clifford have at least the virtue of an awareness of the problem of authority and the desire to challenge the conventions of representation without abandoning it altogether. Christopher Miller faces a similar problem in the interpretation of African literature, which in his view cannot be done responsibly without ethnographic knowledge. Warning against a radical self-reflexivity that disavows all knowledge of cultural and historical context, he writes, "if description and representation themselves are renounced, if the focus of ethnography shifts completely from observed to observer, then its use value as an interlocutor for the criticism of African cultures will have been lost." Miller argues persuasively that for Western readers, "attentive[ness] to difference" is an *ethical* imperative from which one is not excused by theoretical objections to the representation of cultures (1990:27–31).

Let me try to apply some of the recent lessons of ethnography to other forms of writing committed to the description and representation of non-Western cultures. Although writers can hardly break free from the basic cultural presuppositions that give their work meaning, there are nonetheless ways of writing that resist the imposition of value inherent in any colonizing discourse. Here I refer not merely to writing which opposes specific colonialist policies. There is a history of dissent which has sometimes formed an effective counterdiscourse in relation to the prevailing deployment of colonial power; yet we have also seen how such writing can simply reproduce in inverted form those same distinctions (civilized vs. savage, good vs. evil) upon which the logic of power depends. Rather, I want to consider a kind of writing which takes itself as the object of its own critical examination without giving up the task of describing and representing a world that lies outside of Western subjectivity. Examples from journalism seem particularly appropriate here because of the way in which journalism, like ethnography, is a direct response to the experience of a specific cultural or historical actuality.

In trying to imagine what a "theoretical" journalism would look like, I find signs of it everywhere in the interstices of discourse, in those places where journalists call into question, however briefly, the underlying assumptions that govern their work. This *mise en question* is relatively easy for persons who write critical studies of colonial discourse, and who have the advantage of being able to contemplate the problem from an abstracted perspective. The journalist who wishes to confront the same questions, however, must treat them as an *event*; he or she must find them in the immediate context of the moment. With these conditions in mind, one can cite a few ways in which Western journalists have begun to loosen the hold of colonial discourse. These gestures of resistance may be characterized as a set of critical or interpretive problems which certain journalists have tried to address.

1. *The question of language*. Writing from the United Nations in 1984, a correspondent for the *Christian Science Monitor* reports on a debate over the meaning of "terrorism." The story quotes African and Asian diplomats

whose idea of terrorism includes South African apartheid, government-supported death squads in Central America, and International Monetary Fund policies which, in their view, "starve children and lead men to despair in Third World countries." The *Monitor* reporter adds,

> Many governments . . . feel the French resistance fighters who gunned down Nazi occupiers, Jews who blew up British soldiers in Palestine before Israel became an independent state, and the assassinations by Italy's Red Brigades, for example, cannot be lumped together under one heading and labeled "terroristic." (May 3, 1984)

The *Monitor* story does two things which are the exception rather than the rule in Western reporting. First, it reports the views of representatives of Third World countries as it would typically report those of Western officials, that is, as the views of serious, even thoughtful men and women. Second, it examines the nature of a word, "terrorism," that has become part of the predominant Western view of the Third World, and it does so in a way that raises the question of the relation between what is called terrorism and political power. The effect of this examination is what Bhabha, borrowing from Freud, calls *Entstellung*—"a process of displacement, distortion, dislocation, repetition" (166). In a striking example of reappropriation, what Western readers ordinarily understand by terrorism has been disfigured beyond recognition, to the point where we are asked to consider the International Monetary Fund as a terrorist organization. Subject to a polyphonic play of difference, the familiar word is displaced simultaneously onto so many different contexts that it loses its authority as the name for a specific phenomenon and is instead revealed as an instrument of rhetorical and political strategy.

The question of language is similarly raised in a *Harper's Magazine* story (January 1988) on life in Iran under the Ayatollah Khomeini. Here the reporter reverses the usual direction of questioning by quoting a senior official in the Iranian hierarchy: "You westerners . . . why do you always talk about us as having power struggles while you yourselves merely have politics?" The question causes the reporter, John Simpson, to reflect on the fact that while Khomeini's political power is based on his personal influence as leader of the revolution, he also holds a constitutional position as supreme authority, or *faqih*, on all matters that touch upon Islamic law, an authority that "derives from the Shi'ite concept of an Islamic jurisprudent who will be in overall charge of affairs until such time as the twelfth Imam returns to earth." Simpson departs from usual journalistic practice by entering into a kind of dialogue with a representative of that phenomenon most alien to the Westerner, the Islamic revolution. In this case the interrogation of an otherwise ordinary distinction—the barbarism of "power struggles" versus the relative civility of "politics"—leads to an unfamiliar territory of discourse in a process intended not to defend the revolution in Western terms, but to see what it is that an Iranian might see in it.

2. *The conditions of observation.* In his essay on "Shooting an Elephant" (1936), George Orwell notes that what one sees in the colonial world depends on the circumstances which allow one to be in the position of an observer. Writing about his days as a police officer in Burma, Orwell recalls that his distaste for the excesses of British rule was compromised by his own role in maintaining that rule; with part of his mind he thought that "the greatest joy in the world would be to drive a bayonet through a Buddhist priest's guts" (149). Feelings like these are "the normal by-products of imperialism," because the maintenance of authority depends on an inherent enmity, a constant vigilance for signs of resistance among the colonized. The signs of resistance in *oneself* are alternately repressed and expressed in irrational ways.

Orwell's story, in which he is trapped by his official role—or at least Burmese expectations of it—into needlessly destroying a valuable beast of burden, is rife with ambivalence toward the colonial system and those whom it rules. On one hand, Orwell can observe lucidly that "when the white man turns tyrant it is his own freedom he destroys" (152). On the other, his imprisonment within the perceptual framework of colonial rule reduces the local population to "a sea of yellow faces" whose childish will he feels compelled to obey. As Nandy points out, Orwell brings to the surface the symptoms of a cultural crisis in the West: the reification of social relations, the instrumental view of nature, the "created loneliness" of the colonizer, the perpetual need to display masculine authority before a colonized population perceived as children, and the "suppression of one's self for the sake of an imposed imperial identity" (40). The value of Orwell's essay lies less in its political opposition than in its inside knowledge of colonialism's perceptual and psychological costs. Orwell allows us to see the history of colonialism as a loss for the West as well as for the Orient.

Of course, it is not only the colonial officer whose perception is skewed by political circumstances. Orwell's essay "Marrakech" (1939) is unusual as travel writing in its analysis of what the European is likely to *see* in a country like Morocco:

> In a tropical landscape one's eye takes in everything except the human beings. It takes in the dried-up soil, the prickly pear, the palm tree

and the distant mountain, but it always misses the peasant hoeing his patch. He is the same colour as the earth, and a great deal less interesting to look at. (184)

The hiatus of perception is literally a matter of interest; one sees what it profits one to see, what one has a share or stake in, a claim upon. To a Frenchman, Morocco means "an orange grove or a job in Government service." To an Englishman, the country presents itself in images drawn from films and popular romance: "camels, castles, palm trees, Foreign Legionnaires, brass trays, and bandits" (184). Orwell's writing, both here and in longer journalistic works like *The Road to Wigan Pier*, plays an adversarial role in relation to the familiar categories of colonial discourse by attempting to expose the fundamental economics of perception.

3. *The consciousness of interest.* In raising the question of interest as one of the conditions of observation, I wish to consider under the realm of journalistic practice a problem familiar to the philosophical study of language. Following Foucault and Hans-Georg Gadamer, Edward Said has written that "there is never interpretation, understanding, and then knowledge where there is no *interest*" (1981:157), a truth often denied in the name of a disinterested objectivity. There are writers, however, who have taken the risk of examining their own interest in writing about some aspect of life in the non-Western world and have shown how this examination can deepen the meaning of *reportage*, even as it undermines the conventions of the genre.

Precisely this disruption of convention accounts for the relative absence of such writing in the daily newspapers, and for its appearance mainly in "alternative" newspapers of limited means and audience or in magazines like *The New Yorker*, where a degree of critical self-consciousness is made possible by the tradition of a literary journalism. Writing for this magazine in 1982, John Hersey manages to combine the genres of autobiography and travel writing in a story that questions his own interest. Hersey returns to the city of Tientsin, in northern China, where he was born in 1914 as the son of American missionaries. As he revisits the scenes of early youth, he struggles with a kind of double vision. The glowing memories of childhood spent in imperial days—Boy Scout outings, Charles Kingsley's *The Heroes*, schoolboy productions of "The Mikado"—form a nostalgic overlay that is continually disturbed by the drab actuality of modern China; the former Anglican All Saints Church now houses the No. 1 Tientsin Sewer Management Team.

Among Hersey's virtues as a writer is the honest examination of his own interest in returning to Tientsin and the effort to place that interest in a perspective that would do justice to the Chinese. Seeking out the house where he was born, he finds it now occupied by seven families, each with its own story, its own examples of courage and endurance. His tour of the house is organized as a series of dialogues with members of these families, each adding to his knowledge of Chinese society and family life. One resident, Mrs. Fu, is so moved by his recollections that she impulsively invites him to move in with her family: "You were born in this house. You belong here." Hersey concludes by putting his nostalgia into what might be called a postcolonial perspective:

> The fragmentary memories that had flitted in and out of my mind in the house, as I went from room to room, were of things that had no real connection with China—with either the China that had surrounded us boys back then or the China that lived in the house now. I realized how much we missionary children in Tientsin had been isolated from the hard realities of our natal country. (May 10, 1982)

The use of "natal" for "native" subtly acknowledges the writer's ambivalent search for his own origins; he cannot call his own the country in which he was born and recognizes this fact with a mixture of regret and humility. The world in which he grew up is newly localized, displaced from the center of consciousness by the encounter with other subjective realities. This modest realization marks a conscious transformation of the writer as subject, not so much diminishing that subject as preparing the ground for an enlarged area of experience, a new set of terms by which the subject may be defined. The consciousness of interest thus moves from nostalgic confinement toward a wider possibility of understanding.

4. *Other voices*. If the problem of Western writing about the non-Western world is that of a historically colonialist conception of the other, a solution would appear to lie in the simple substitution of one discourse for another: let us hear, in unmediated purity, the testimony of those who are the objects of colonization and exclusion. The barriers to such a solution include those of translation, not merely in the literal sense but in the political sense as well: who is "representative" of any non-Western culture? In what context can the speech of the Indian or African be made relevant to a Western understanding without betraying its origin? And given Nandy's assertion that as a psychological category "the West is everywhere, within the West and outside; in structures and in minds" (xi)—who exactly is not of the West? These questions arise not only in the case of the "anthropological war" between traditionally different cultures—the Vietnamese and the

French, for example—but also in the class struggle between peoples, such as in Central and North America, who have much in common in their history and in their understanding of the world. Even where the anticolonial discourse of Central Americans is translated from Spanish (itself a colonial language) and quoted directly by North American writers in English, such citation does not take place outside of a surrounding framework of presentation, analysis, and qualification—that is, other layers of interpretation added to that of linguistic translation.

There have been writers who attempt to resist the imposition of power through a kind of stance which seeks both to represent other voices and to recognize the difficulties inherent in this representation. T. D. Allman, reporting on El Salvador for *Harper's*, encounters a group of revolutionary guerillas who, while devout Christians, are also men who cannot read or write and thus have their own views on the value of North American journalists:

> "It is good that journalists come to El Salvador," one of the men with machetes said, "but you should not just visit our country. You should live here." I agreed that journalists wrote much better stories when they lived in the countries about which they wrote, but that had not been what he meant. "If you lived in El Salvador," he explained, "you could hide Christian people in your house and the Guardias could not find them, and you could bring us food and medicine and guns in your car." (March 1981)

The reporter's interest in writing "better stories" is abruptly displaced by a discourse based solely on the concrete demands of revolutionary struggle. This displacement effectively calls into question the writer's own discourse, one founded on the belief in an objective, politically disengaged style of reporting and on the primacy of the written word. In the reporter's own words, the guerillas are "illiterate" and thus defined by their lack of access to the written word, while the advantage of the resident correspondent over the visitor lies in the ability to *write* better stories. Allman allows this ideology of the letter to be both exposed and neutralized by the momentary vision of a struggle carried on entirely outside the boundaries of what is ordinarily called writing. Even if such a vision turns out to be illusory— what human activity, what part of the world remains untouched by writing?—it yet serves to reveal a difference—in ideology, in culture, in the very foundations of social reality—that would otherwise stay concealed.

These examples are not only brief and incomplete but, as one could have predicted, their gestures toward a shared vision of reality produced through dialogue and self-reflexivity ultimately produce only a displaced version of monologic authority: a single writer, under the constraints that govern publication, remains in control. As an epistemological order backed by political reality, Western subjectivity is powerful enough to absorb a certain amount of interference. Incorporating the sounds of other voices only enhances the richness of a Western orchestration. And yet the passages I have cited here still have in common some gesture toward an *opening*, a movement fundamental to theory itself. I wish to end as I began this chapter, by considering some implications of theory for the possibility of resistance to colonial discourse.

The language of postmodern theory from Heidegger through Derrida is continually inspired by ideas of the open, of opening, and of openness. In *The Order of Things*, Foucault calls for a theory that will put into play "a perpetual principle of dissatisfaction, of calling into question, of criticism and contestation of what may seem, in other respects, to be established." Such theory moves "in a region where representation remains in suspense, on the edge of itself, open, in a sense, to the closed boundary of finitude" (1970:373–374). Foucault here refers specifically to the possibilities of psychoanalysis and ethnology, but his spatializing metaphor applies equally to any theoretical practice which both defines and resists ideological closure and which sees the mechanisms of that closure operating in established systems of representation.

For Derrida, thought itself is conceived as an "opening" into the indeterminate space where new meaning has yet to be decided and from which established meaning already belongs to "a past epoch . . . that is open to view" (1976:93). A journalism or an ethnography that would seek to incorporate the work of thinking, then, would have to do more than simply stand in ideological opposition to the prevailing discourses of power. Rather, it would have to remain open to the possibility of new and other forms of interpretation in its approach to social reality. This writing would act as a kind of guerilla resistance to the discourse of colonialism: evading the power of that discourse by harassing its encamped position, by exposing its logic to view, and by maintaining a perpetual openness to the unexpected, to the chance disclosure of some truth that would otherwise remain closed off by the boundaries of discourse.

Julia Kristeva speaks of precisely this need for a decentering of discourse and a readiness for the aleatory in her own writing about the women of China. She sees herself as confronted, to begin with, by the *otherness* of

China, by an irreducible strangeness that opens up as an abyss in the understanding of the Westerner. Some try to fill this abyss by rewriting China for Western purposes—a rewritten China that will serve some revisionist or liberal cause, for example, by proving that the Chinese are like "us," against us, or simply to be ignored. Others will create a China against "them," that is, those whose ideology does not conform to one's own. This writing "for" or "against" is, for Kristeva, the familiar tactic of the militant committed merely to defending a position: "what is lost is the chance that the discovery of 'the other' may make us question ourselves about what, here and now, is new, scarcely audible, disturbing" (1977:12–13).

It is fitting that Derrida and Kristeva in particular should share this sense that established forms of meaning belong to a past epoch, while at the same time these two theorists hold forth the possibility of a writing that would open itself to the realities of the other. Both writers have their personal origins in places that define the outer limits of Western European culture: Derrida in colonial Algeria, where the French empire fades into the great open space of Africa; Kristeva in Bulgaria, crossing-ground of the Crusades and the historical territory of contention between Christianized Europe and the Ottoman Empire. In such places it is possible to live both in and beyond the West, knowing the boundaries of its language, and looking southward or eastward as if toward regions of the unthought.

In a recent essay Derrida speaks of himself as a cultural half-breed (*métis*), as "someone who, beginning with the schooling of French Algeria, has had to capitalize on the old age of Europe while holding on to a little of the imperceptible, impassive youth of the other shore," that is, the African shore of the Mediterranean. Thoughts of his own culturally hybrid identity lead to the reflection, reminiscent of Leiris, that every culture is a hybrid, that there never is a single origin, and that the "monogenealogy" of culture is itself a mystification in the history of culture. But Derrida carries this logic one step further than Leiris: if a culture is characterized both by a hybrid origin and by the myth of a single origin—by difference and by the discourse of a unitary nondifference—then the distinctive property of culture is to identify itself as other than what it is—to have an identity that is, in a sense, always other than itself (1991:13–17). If this is true, then there is nothing more "proper" to culture than the displaced identity belonging to its margins; Paris shares with Algeria and Bulgaria the danger and the freedom of the boundary situation. An awareness of this difference-from-itself within culture is the opposite of an ethnocentrism, a xenophobia, or a racism that sees cultural purity as threatened from the outside, and such an awareness may allow the writer to negotiate more openly the border region between what we must continue to think of as one culture and the other.

In citing these writers who come literally from the boundaries of Europe, I do not intend to identify a geographical cause or origin for their ideas, but rather to offer a geographical metaphor for the obscure space, both in and outside of familiar modes of discourse, that one enters into through the radical reflection on language that characterizes our time. This study of language is essentially an act of resistance. In the words of Foucault, it seeks "to destroy syntax, to shatter tyrannical modes of speech, to turn words around in order to perceive all that is being said through them and despite them" (1970:298). For Derrida, what comes of this reflection is astonishment *at* language as the origin of history, rather than as a mere consequence of historical forces. This continuing surprise now activates our thought, although in the irony of the moment, the destiny of this thought is "to extend its domains while the boundaries of the West are drawn back" (1978:4).

The language of postmodern theory which I have invoked both here and in preceding chapters has only begun to be applied to questions of cultural difference in the postcolonial world; not surprisingly, its value in addressing such questions has been most vigorously debated by Western or Western-educated critics living in newly decolonized parts of the world. One such writer is Simon Battestini, an American who taught in Africa during the last years of colonial rule and the first two decades of independence. Battestini argues that the critical practice known as deconstruction is a logical consequence of the historical process of decolonization that followed World War II. It is a natural and positive intellectual response to a world of "fragmented and constantly reassembled environments," a "pluralistic," "open-ended" world subject to the free movements of the mind and to the perpetual renewal of meanings (122–124). There is possibility here for a new Western understanding of Africans, who—as their identities, language, patterns of thought, and modes of behavior change according to immediate situations—seem to be living out the intellectual project of deconstruction. Battestini sees African consciousness as liberated by this heterogeneity of experience and thus as providing a model for the postindustrial West.

Despite the attractiveness of such a theory, some problems come quickly to mind. One is the extent to which Battestini's vision of Africa resembles yet another idealized projection of Western philosophy. The liberated African, embracing *différance* and living out the free play of deconstruction, is not far removed, conceptually or historically, from the noble savage of European Romanticism. Another problem is that Battestini's theory of subjective freedom lacks an analysis of the relations of power that belong to specific contexts of African life: is the African's changing identity spontaneous and free, or is it a necessary series of adaptations determined by differing and localized structures of authority?

Similar questions are raised in the writing of Karin Barber, of the University of Ife (Nigeria), who examines the parallels between deconstruction and African oral poetry. According to Barber, deconstructive criticism proposes a view of literature in general that seems fortuitously suited to an understanding of oral literature. This view is essentially an attack on conventional notions of literary unity, as traditional ideas of the "authentic text," of the literary work as a coherent whole, and of the single, synthesizing authorial mind are replaced by notions of textual instability, decenteredness, intertextuality, and indeterminacy. Barber finds that these challenges to literary unity in fact describe various aspects of Yoruba *oriki* or "praise poetry," the stylized and highly figurative appellations used to address persons and spiritual beings at ceremonial gatherings. *Oriki* are characterized by constant variability and improvisation, by interchangeability with one another as textual units, by the lack of any definable corpus, and the absence of any single authorial voice, as audience members freely intervene to change the direction of the performance in medias res.

Barber finally rejects deconstruction as a way to knowledge of the *oriki* because of what she sees as a double movement which simultaneously demobilizes the critic as it activates the text. On one hand, the deconstructive critic, trapped within the dominant metaphysic of Western culture, is "reduced to impotent self-reflection" by the lack of any alternative cognitive framework. On the other hand textuality is decentered, but also made universal, to the point where Derrida can write, "Il n'y a pas de hors-texte" (1976:158) (There is nothing outside the text). Barber finds that this view of textuality rules out the questions of power and ideology raised by the *oriki*: "It is a view that could only have been entertained in a culture where texts are divorced from both producer and consumer and can therefore appear to exist as a vast system in their own right, pushing human participants into the margins. In other words, a literate culture" (514). In an apparent gesture toward Marxist criticism, she calls instead for an approach to the *oriki* "based on the conception of literature as social practice" (515).

The critics to whom Barber refers (Derrida, Barthes, J. Hillis Miller) probably would not recognize themselves in her essay, which presents deconstruction as a "view of literature" on the order of, if opposed to, the

New Criticism of the 1940s and 1950s. They would argue that deconstruction neither comprises nor imposes a solidified point of view; it is rather to be understood primarily as a critical practice, a way of reading specific texts that does not commit itself to a series of positions or pronouncements. Equally disputed would be the version of deconstruction which divides textuality from human participation. The idea that there is nothing outside the text is meant to imply not the divorce of texts from human subjects but, on the contrary, the inseparability of textual from human activity. Finally, Barber's distinction between "oral" and "literate" cultures would come under question, as it does most notably in Derrida's critique of Lévi-Strauss. Rather than comparing the *oriki* to a generalized idea of literature supposedly advanced by deconstructive critics, Barber might have compared deconstructive *activity* to the *oriki* performance, which Barber describes as a string of units combined somewhat arbitrarily, united by habit, thematic drift, and a consistency of style, yet formally disconnected and subject to abrupt shifts "governed by social, rather than formal requirements" (509). Barber is right, however, in pointing out that deconstruction is the product of a Western literary and philosophical tradition, that it has had little to say about oral literature (an exception is the work of Henry Louis Gates), and that its strategy of reading appears more suited to exposing the overwhelming power of Western metaphysics than to identifying the exercise of power inherent in concrete human activity, especially in non-Western settings.

The positions represented here by Barber and Battestini reflect a larger critical debate over the role of theory in the critique of colonial discourse. In a wide-ranging review of this debate, Benita Parry divides its participants into two loosely assembled camps: those critics who seek to identify the ideologies embedded in texts as the expression of political forces themselves operating outside of language, and those who see discourse itself as the primary form of social practice and who seek to expose the nature of ideology by "stirring up and dispersing the sedimented meanings dormant in texts" (32). The difference is basically between two views of the relations between power and language: one sees language as the effect of power, the other sees power and language as practically (i.e., virtually and in practice) the same.

Parry points out that neither approach has succeeded in producing an alternative discourse to displace the dominant system of knowledge belonging to Western imperialism. Where writing is seen as the mere instrument of material and social conditions, there is no theoretical space for the emergence of new forms of discourse to construct conditions not yet in existence (50). Where discourse is universalized as power, "there is no point outside of discourse from which opposition can be engendered." Instead, critics engaged in this kind of project (the reference is to Bhabha and Gaya·tri Spivak) seem destined "to place incendiary devices within the dominant structures of representation and not to confront these with another knowledge" (43). If both approaches have arrived at a theoretical cul-de-sac, it may be that alternative discourses and new structures of knowledge await the intervention of forces outside the West. Not that Western knowledge can simply be replaced by existing non-Western forms, but that one can look for new structures that combine and transcend what already exists. In that case the task of the writer, critic, or journalist would be one of continued questioning, not only of the Western tradition but also, in the manner of one disposed to learning, of non-Western traditions and their transformations in a postcolonial world. To avoid intellectual quietism, this writing would have to run the risk of epistemic violence encountered in all striving toward new knowledge.

As the foregoing discussion suggests, there is yet to be created either a tradition or even a recognizable style that would reflect an actual dialogue between the West and what is called the Third World. The Moroccan writer Abdelkabir Khatibi observes that the decolonization of the Third World has not brought about a corresponding decolonization of thought which would be, apart from a simple reversal of colonial power, the "affirmation of a difference," an openness to plurality and a free subversion of the powers that inhere in discourse (1983:47). The work of deconstructing colonial discourse is even greater than that of dismantling the massive systems of colonial administration; it is work that has only just begun, to say nothing of the creation of entirely new discourses. Yet some encouragement may be found in the thought that in a sense this has always been the task of writing. Again, Khatibi reminds us that the *untranslatable* is not only what forms a barrier between one language and another, or between a culture and its other (1987:204). The untranslatable is also a condition of writing itself, where writing is understood as the consciousness of difference (difference as temporal, sexual, social, linguistic, national, or cultural) and as an attempt to bring the unthought and unsaid into the realm of the sayable.

How can I say, now, what it is like to turn from this theoretical discussion to the scene outside my open window, where the intervention of the non-Western world seems already at hand? It is a summer day in a working-class, "ethnic" neighborhood on Chicagos's North Side. Mexican vendors selling coconut-flavored *helados* ring little bells on their pushcarts. The smell of strong coffee wafts through the air from the Assyrian cafe. Women in pastel-colored saris stroll in the park, where Vietnamese families are cooking outdoors. From here one can go down the street past the "Luyong" Filipino bakery, the "Yasmin" Driving School (instruction in Arabic), the Korean Methodist Church, the Iglesia Pentecostal, the Tel Aviv Kosher Pizzeria, and fruit stands piled with mangoes, plantains, and sugar cane. From a radio somewhere the music of WTAQ, "La Mexicana," combines with the sunlight to create a festive, buoyant mood. For a moment, I am filled with wonder.

A police siren sounds in the distance, putting an end to this rapt orchestration. The carnivalesque moment has cast a spell, effacing the realities of social and economic inequality. My wife, a journalist, has documented the working conditions of those *helados* vendors, mostly undocumented immigrants who push their carts for miles under a hot sun for a few dollars a day. No discourse is truly free if not informed by this kind of knowledge. And yet the dialogue envisioned by Khatibi will only take place if inspired by the celebration of plurality, the conscious affirmation of the differences seen from my window. If there is an opening, then, its path leads through ambivalence, through an area of tension between the knowledge of inequality and the affirmation of difference, and in the vision of a world—really the dream of the present moment in history—in which the play of difference could range free of the structures of inequality.

BIBLIOGRAPHY

[Translations are mine except where otherwise noted.]

Abramson, Howard S. *National Geographic: Behind America's Lens on the World*. New York: Crown, 1987.

Achebe, Chinua. "An Image of Africa: Racism in Conrad's *Heart of Darkness*." *Massachusetts Review* 18 (1977): 782–794.

Agee, James, and Walker Evans. *Let Us Now Praise Famous Men*. Boston: Houghton Mifflin, 1941.

Allen, Charles. *Tales from the Dark Continent*. New York: St. Martin's Press, 1979.

Alloula, Malek. *The Colonial Harem*. Trans. Myrna Godzich and Wlad Godzich. Minneapolis: University of Minnesota Press, 1986.

Aristotle. *Politics*. Trans. Carnes Lord. Chicago: University of Chicago Press, 1984.

Attridge, Steve. "Dis-Oriented Fictions." *Encounter*. February 1986.

Baker, Samuel. *The Albert Nyanza*. London: Macmillan, 1898.

Balandier, Georges. *Sociologie Actuelle de l'Afrique Noire*. Paris: Presses Universitaires de France, 1963.

Barber, Karin. "Yoruba Oriki and Deconstructive Criticism." *Research in African Literatures* 15, no. 4 (Winter 1984): 497–518.

Barrows, David. *A Decade of American Rule in the Philippines*. New York: World Book, 1914.

Barthes, Roland. *The Eiffel Tower and Other Mythologies*. Trans. Richard Howard. New York: Hill and Wang, 1979.

———. *Essais Critiques*. Paris: Editions du Seuil, 1964.

———. *Mythologies*. Trans. Annette Lavers. New York: Hill and Wang, 1972.

Bataille, Georges. *Death and Sensuality: A Study of Eroticism and the Taboo*. New York: Walker, 1962.

Battestini, Simon P. X. "Deconstruction and Decolonization of the Self." *American Journal of Semiotics* 6, no. 1 (1988–89): 117–131.

Baudelaire, Charles. *Les Fleurs du Mal*. 1857. Reprint. Paris: Garnier, 1961.

Benjamin, Walter. *Illuminations*. Trans. Harry Zohn. New York: Schocken, 1969.

Bhabha, Homi. "Signs Taken for Wonders: Questions of Ambivalence and Authority Under a

Tree Outside Delhi, May 1817." In Henry Louis Gates, ed., *"Race," Writing, and Difference*. Chicago: University of Chicago Press, 1986.

Blixen, Karen (Isak Dinesen). *Out of Africa*. 1937. Reprint. New York: Modern Library, 1983.

Booth, Wayne. "The Company We Keep: Self-Making in Imaginative Art, Old and New." *Daedalus* (Fall 1982): 33–59.

Bourdieu, Pierre. *Distinction: A Social Critique of the Judgement of Taste*. Trans. Richard Nice. Cambridge, Mass.: Harvard University Press, 1984.

———. *Outline of a Theory of Practice*. Trans. Richard Nice. Cambridge, England: Cambridge University Press, 1977.

Brantlinger, Patrick. *Rule of Darkness: British Literature and Imperialism, 1830–1914*. Ithaca, N.Y.: Cornell University Press, 1988.

Brzezinski, Zbigniew. *Between Two Ages: America's Role in the Technetronic Era*. New York: Viking, 1970.

Buchan, John. *The African Colony: Studies in the Reconstruction*. Edinburgh: Blackwood, 1903.

———. *Prester John*. Boston: Houghton Mifflin, 1910.

Burton, Richard F. *Zanzibar: City, Island, and Coast*. London: Tinsley Brothers, 1872.

Cairns, H. Alan C. *Prelude to Imperialism: British Reactions to Central African Society, 1840–1890*. London: Routledge, 1965.

Carlyle, Thomas. *Occasional Discourse on the Nigger Question*. 1849. Reprint. Ed. Eugene R. August. New York: Meredith, 1971.

Churchill, Winston S. *Young Winston's Wars: The Original Despatches of Winston S. Churchill, War Correspondent, 1897–1900*. Ed. Fredrick Woods. London: Leo Cooper, 1972.

Clifford, James. *The Predicament of Culture: Twentieth-Century Ethnography, Literature, and Art*. Cambridge, Mass.: Harvard University Press, 1988.

Collingwood, R. G. *The Idea of Nature*. Oxford: Oxford University Press, 1944.

Conrad, Joseph. *"Heart of Darkness" and "The Secret Sharer"*. New York: New American Library, 1950.

Crane, Stephen. *Stephen Crane in the West and Mexico*. Ed. Joseph Katz. Kent, Ohio: Kent State University Press, 1970.

Culler, Jonathan. *Structuralist Poetics: Structuralism, Linguistics and the Study of Literature*. Ithaca, N.Y.: Cornell University Press, 1975.

Darwin, Charles. *Journal of Researches into the Geology and Natural History of the Various Countries Visited by the H.M.S. Beagle*. London: Henry Colburn, 1839.

———. *Origin of Species and the Descent of Man in Relation to Sex*. New York: Modern Library, 1936.

Davis, Richard Harding. *The Congo and Coasts of Africa*. New York: Scribner's, 1907.

———. *Three Gringos in Venezuela and Central America*. New York: Harper, 1896.

De Man, Paul. *Allegories of Reading*. New Haven: Yale University Press, 1979.

Dennery, Etienne. *Asia's Teeming Millions*. Trans. John Peile. 1931. Reprint. Port Washington, N.Y.: Kennikat Press, 1970.

Derrida, Jacques. *L'Autre Cap*. Paris: Minuit, 1991.

———. *Of Grammatology*. Trans. Gayatri Chakravorty Spivak. Baltimore: Johns Hopkins University Press, 1976.

———. *Writing and Difference*. Trans. Alan Bass. Chicago: University of Chicago Press, 1978.

Diamond, Stanley. *In Search of the Primitive: A Critique of Civilization*. New Brunswick, N.J.: Transaction Books, 1974.

Dickens, Charles. *Our Mutual Friend*. 1865. Reprint. New York: Dodd, Mead, 1951.

Diderot, Denis. *Supplément au Voyage de Bougainville*. Geneva: Droz, 1955.

Didion, Joan. *Salvador*. New York: Washington Square, 1983.

Douls, Camille. "Voyages dans le Sahara occidental et le Sud marocain." *Bulletin du Société normande de Géographie* 10 (1888): 1–36.

Eliot, T. S. *The Complete Poems and Plays, 1909–1950*. New York: Harcourt Brace & World, 1952.

———. *Selected Essays*. New York: Harcourt Brace & World, 1960.

Emerson, Ralph Waldo. *Complete Essays*. Boston: Houghton Mifflin, 1904.

Ewen, Stuart and Elizabeth. *Channels of Desire: Mass Images and the Shaping of American Consciousness*. New York: McGraw-Hill, 1982.

Fabian, Johannes. *Time and the Other: How Anthropology Makes Its Object*. New York: Columbia University Press, 1983.

Fanon, Frantz. *A Dying Colonialism*. Trans. Haakon Chevalier. New York: Grove, 1967.

———. *The Wretched of the Earth*. Trans. Constance Farrington. New York: Grove Press, 1966.

FitzGerald, Frances. *Fire in the Lake: The Vietnamese and the Americans in Vietnam*. New York: Vintage, 1972.

Flaubert, Gustave. *Flaubert in Egypt: A Sensibility on Tour*. Trans. and ed. Francis Steegmuller. Boston: Little, Brown, 1973.

———. *La Tentation de St. Antoine*. Paris: Garnier, 1954.

Forster, E. M. *A Passage to India*. New York: Harcourt Brace, 1924.

Foucault, Michel. *Discipline and Punish: The Birth of the Prison*. Trans. Alan Sheridan. New York: Vintage, 1977.

———. *The History of Sexuality*, vol. 1. Trans. Robert Hurley. New York: Vintage, 1980.

———. *Michel Foucault: Beyond Structuralism and Hermeneutics*. Ed. Hubert L. Dreyfus and Paul Rabinow. Chicago: University of Chicago Press, 1983.

———. *The Order of Things: An Archaeology of the Human Sciences*. New York: Vintage, 1970.

———. *L'Ordre du Discours*. Paris: Gallimard, 1971.

Freud, Sigmund. *Civilization and Its Discontents*. Trans. James Strachey. New York: Norton, 1961.

Geertz, Clifford. *The Interpretation of Cultures*. New York: Basic Books, 1973.

Gide, André. *Voyage au Congo*. Paris: Gallimard, 1948.

Gitlin, Todd. *The Whole World Is Watching: Mass Media in the Making and Unmaking of the New Left*. Berkeley: University of California Press, 1980.

Gobineau, Joseph-Arthur, Comte de. *Essai sur l'Inégalité des Races Humaines*. 1854. Reprint. 2 vols. Paris: Firmin-Didot, 1940.

Greene, Graham. *The Lawless Roads*. 1939. Reprint. Harmondsworth, England: Penguin Books, 1947.

———. *The Power and the Glory*. 1940. Reprint. Harmondsworth, England: Penguin Books, 1947.

Grosvenor, Gilbert. *The National Geographic Society and Its Magazine*. Washington, D.C.: National Geographic Society, 1957.

Halstead, Murat. *The Story of the Philippines and Our New Possessions*. Chicago: Our Possessions Publishing, 1898.

Hardy, Georges. *L'Art nègre: L'Art animiste des Noirs d'Afrique*. Paris: H. Lawrens, 1927.

———. *Histoire sociale de la Colonisation française*. Paris: Larose, 1953.

Headland, Isaac T. *China's New Day*. West Medford, Mass.: Central Committee on the United Study of Missions, 1912.

Hegel, G. W. F. *Lectures on the Philosophy of History*. 1830–1831. Trans. J. Sibree. Reprint. New York: Dover, 1956.

Heidegger, Martin. *The Question Concerning Technology*. Trans. William Lovitt. New York: Garland, 1977.

Hemingway, Ernest. *The Green Hills of Africa*. New York: Scribner's, 1935.

Huntington, Samuel P. *Political Order in Changing Societies*. New Haven: Yale University Press, 1968.

Jameson, Fredric. *The Political Unconscious: Narrative as a Socially Symbolic Act*. Ithaca, N.Y.: Cornell University Press, 1981.

Khatibi, Abdelkabir. *Figures de l'Etranger dans la Littérature française*. Paris: Denoël, 1987.

——— . *Maghreb Pluriel*. Paris: Denoël, 1983.

Kipling, Rudyard. *Collected Works*. New York: AMS Press, 1970.

——— . *Complete Verse*. New York: Doubleday, 1989.

Kirkpatrick, Jeane. "Dictatorships and Double Standards." *Commentary*, November 1979.

Kniebiehler, Yvonne, and Régine Goutalier. *La Femme au Temps des Colonies*. Paris: Stock, 1985.

Kristeva, Julia. *About Chinese Women*. Trans. Anita Barrows. London: Marion Boyars, 1977.

——— . *Powers of Horror: An Essay on Abjection*. New York: Columbia University Press, 1982.

——— . Interview in *All Area* 2 (Spring 1983): 36–44.

Lapierre, Dominique. *The City of Joy*. Trans. Kathryn Spink. New York: Warner Books, 1985.

Lawrence, T. E. *Seven Pillars of Wisdom: A Triumph*. 1926. Reprint. Harmondsworth, England: Penguin, 1962.

Leiris, Michel. "L'Ethnographe devant le Colonialisme." *Les Temps Modernes* 58 (August 1950): 357–374.

Lévi-Strauss, Claude. *Introduction to the Work of Marcel Mauss*. Trans. Felicity Baker. London: Routledge and Kegan Paul, 1987.

——— . *La Pensée Sauvage*. Paris: Plon, 1962.

——— . *Tristes Tropiques*. Trans. John Russell. New York: Athenaeum, 1971.

Livingstone, David. *Missionary Travels and Researches in South Africa*. London: 1865.

Lugard, Frederick. *The Dual Mandate in British Tropical Africa*. London: Frank Cass, 1922.

Lukács, Georg. *The Meaning of Contemporary Realism*. Trans. John and Doreen Weightman. New York: Washington Square, 1977.

Lyde, L. W. "White Colonisation of the Tropics." *United Empire* 1 (1910): 763–772.

McCarthy, Mary. *Vietnam*. New York: Harcourt Brace, 1967.

McLuhan, Marshall. *Understanding Media*. New York: New American Library, 1964.

Malraux, André. *La Tentation de l'Occident*. Paris: Grasset, 1926.

Marx, Karl. *Selected Writings*. Ed. David McClelland. New York: Oxford University Press, 1977.

Melville, Herman. *Typee*. 1846. Reprint. New York: Signet, 1964.

Mill, John Stuart. *The Negro Question*. 1850. Reprint. Ed. Eugene R. August. New York: Meredith, 1971.

——— . *Three Essays on Religion*. London: Longmans, 1874.

Miller, Christopher. *Blank Darkness: Africanist Discourse in French*. Chicago: University of Chicago Press, 1985.

——— . *Theories of Africans: Francophone Literature and Anthropology in Africa*. Chicago: University of Chicago Press, 1990.

Montaigne, Michel de. *Essays*. Trans. J. M. Cohen. Harmondsworth, England: Penguin, 1958.

Naipaul, Shiva. *North of South: An African Journey*. New York: Simon and Schuster, 1978.

Nandy, Ashis. *The Intimate Enemy: Loss and Recovery of Self under Colonialism*. Delhi: Oxford University Press, 1983.

Nerval, Gérard de. *Voyage en Orient*. Paris: Garnier, 1958.

Omang, Joanne. "How the Fourth Estate Invaded the Third World." *Washington Journalism Review*, June 1982.

Orwell, George. *A Collection of Essays*. New York: Harcourt Brace Jovanovich, 1954.

Parada, Esther. "C/Overt Ideology: Two Images of Revolution." *Afterimage* (March 1984): 7–16.

Parry, Benita. "Problems in Current Theories of Colonial Discourse." *Oxford Literary Review* 9, nos. 1–2 (1987): 27–58.

Peschel, Oscar. *The Races of Man and Their Geographical Distribution*. New York: Appleton, 1894.

Pratt, Mary Louise. *Imperial Eyes: Travel Writing and Transculturation*. New York: Routledge, 1992.

Proust, Marcel. *Pastiches et Mélanges*. Paris: Gallimard, 1949.

Real, Michael. *Mass-Mediated Culture*. Englewood Cliffs, N.J.: Prentice-Hall, 1977.

Ronaldshay, Lawrence Dundas, Lord. *India: A Bird's Eye View*. London: Constable, 1924.

Roosevelt, Theodore. *Through the Brazilian Wilderness*. London: John Murray, 1914.

Rousseau, Jean-Jacques. *A Discourse on Inequality*. Trans. Maurice Cranston. Harmondsworth, England: Penguin, 1958.

——— . *Essai sur l'Origine des Langues*. Bordeaux: Guy Ducros, 1968.

——— . *Political Writings*. Ed. C. E. Vaughan. New York: John Wiley, 1962.

Said, Edward. *Covering Islam: How the Media and the Experts Determine How We See the Rest of the World*. New York: Pantheon, 1981.

——— . *Orientalism*. New York: Vintage, 1978.

Sarraut, Albert. *Grandeur et Servitude Coloniales*. Paris: Sagittaire, 1931.

Schwab, Raymond. *Oriental Renaissance: Europe's Rediscovery of India and the East, 1680–1880*. Trans. Gene Patterson-Black and Victor Reinking. New York: Columbia University Press, 1984.

Shoumatoff, Alex. *African Madness*. New York: Knopf, 1988.

Sontag, Susan. *On Photography*. New York: Delta, 1973.

——— . *Trip to Hanoi*. New York: Farrar, Straus, 1968.

Spivak, Gayatri Chakravorty. *The Post-Colonial Critic: Interviews, Strategies, Dialogues*. Ed. Sarah Harasym. New York: Routledge, 1990.

Stafford, Barbara. *Voyage Into Substance: Art, Science, Nature, and the Illustrated Travel Account, 1760–1840*. Cambridge, Mass.: MIT Press, 1984.

Stanley, Henry Morton. *The Congo and the Founding of its Free State*. New York: Harper, 1885.

——— . *Coomassie and Magdala: The Story of Two British Campaigns in Africa*. 1874. Reprint. Freeport, N.Y.: Books for Libraries Press, 1971.

——— . *In Darkest Africa*. New York: Scribner's, 1891.

——— . *Stanley's Despatches to the New York Herald*. Ed. Norman R. Bennett. Boston: Boston University Press, 1970.

Stocking, George. *Victorian Anthropology*. New York: Free Press, 1987.

Suleri, Sara. *The Rhetoric of English India*. Chicago: University of Chicago Press, 1992.

Torgovnick, Marianna. *Gone Primitive: Savage Intellects, Modern Lives*. Chicago: University of Chicago Press, 1990.

Victoria, Queen of Britain. *The Letters of Queen Victoria*. 3 vols. Ed. George Earle Buckle. London: John Murray, 1932.

Vieuchange, Michel. *Smara: The Forbidden City*. Trans. Fletcher Allen. New York: Dutton, 1932.

Virgil. *Aeneid*. Trans. Frank O. Copley. Indianapolis: Bobbs-Merrill, 1965.

Waugh, Evelyn. *Remote People*. London: Duckworth, 1931.

White, Hayden. *Tropics of Discourse: Essays in Cultural Criticism*. Baltimore: Johns Hopkins University Press, 1978.

Wilson, Angus. *The Strange Ride of Rudyard Kipling: His Life and Works*. London: Secker and Warburg, 1977.

INDEX

David Spurr is Associate Professor of English at the University of Illinois at Chicago. He is the author of *Conflicts in Consciousness: T. S. Eliot's Poetry and Criticism* (1984) and of numerous articles on modern literature. He has also been a staff correspondent for United Press International in France and in Eastern Europe.

Library of Congress Cataloging-in-Publication Data
Spurr, David, 1949–
The rhetoric of empire : colonial discourse in journalism, travel writing, and imperial administration / David Spurr.
Includes bibliographical references and index.
ISBN 0-8223-1303-0. — ISBN 0-8223-1317-0 (paper)
1. English prose literature—History and criticism. 2. Developing countries in literature. 3. American prose literature—History and criticism. 4. French prose literature—History and criticism. 5. Imperialism in literature. 6. Colonies in literature. 7. Discourse analysis. 8. Rhetoric. I. Title.
PR129.D46S68 1993
809'.93358—dc20   92-23232 CIP